DAILY
AND PRAISE

VOLUME 1

DAILY PRAYER AND PRAISE

The BOOK of PSALMS
ARRANGED *for* PRIVATE
and FAMILY USE

Henry Law

VOLUME I
Psalms 1–75

THE BANNER OF TRUTH TRUST

THE BANNER OF TRUTH TRUST
3 Murrayfield Road, Edinburgh EH12 6EL, UK
P.O. Box 621, Carlisle, Pennsylvania 17013, USA

*

First published by James Nisbet & Co. 1878
First Banner of Truth edition 2000

ISBN 0 85151 789 7 for the
two-volume set

Volume 1: 0 85151 787 0

*

Printed in Finland by
WS Bookwell

PREFACE.

A BRIEF statement will show the simple purport of this work.

Christian households will surely be assembled on each day for domestic worship. Piety cannot allow the morning to open and the evening to close without united prayer for common blessings and united praise for common mercies. Religion will cease to be the pervading element in the house in which the inmates fail thus to present themselves together at the throne of grace.

It is impossible to over-estimate the blessings which may be expected from such family solemnities. They sweetly sanctify the home, and are a holy picture of celestial oneness. Love will then cement the hearts which together seek a heavenly Father's face—together vow obedience to His will—together consecrate their every faculty to His service—together bless Him

for their common hope—together adore Him for the
gift of Jesus, and all the preciousness of the Gospel-
revelation.

It is presumed, too, that a portion of Scripture will
have a place in these exercises, and that familiar com-
ments will enforce God's Word. The Book of Psalms
will doubtless not be excluded. Its central position
as the heart of Scripture—its devotional character as
part of the Jewish liturgy—its adaptation to every
circumstance of life, rather entitle it to especial con-
sideration.

Survey most superficially its contents. It traverses
every condition of man. It roams with the shepherd
in the meadows. It sits with the mighty monarch on
the throne. It flees with the fugitive on the hills, and
hides with him in the caves. It leads the conquering
host to victory. It walks with the busy in the crowded
haunts, and leaves not the lonely in their solitude. It
is a prop for the staggering steps—a guide for the wan-
derer—a counsellor when perplexities bewilder—a pillow for the weary head,—a sympathizing hand to wipe
the weeping eye,—a voice to whisper comfort to the
disconsolate. No words more cheer the dying saint.

The soul in extremest agony for sin finds here
a ready outlet for the bitterest streams of sorrow.
Words are here supplied to crave deliverance from

wrath. When interest in Christ is realized and joy is in the height of rapture, here are the wings to bear aloft to heaven.

But the main glory of this book is its identity with Christ. He brightly shines throughout its varied hymns. He is constantly the speaker, and in these breathings of His Spirit we receive convincing evidence that, without ceasing to be God, He was a perfect man, and pre-eminently a Man of Sorrows. We here are supplied with a vivid portrait of His character, His work, His love, His sufferings, His glory. It would be no difficult task to construct a Gospel from its prophetic language. It may be regarded as His manual during His career on earth. When, as the expiating God-man, He was uplifted on the accursed tree, and the iron entered into His soul, His misery goes forth in the moanings of a Psalm, " My God, My God, why hast Thou forsaken Me ? " He gives up the ghost uttering its confiding terms, " Into Thy hands I commend My spirit." He ascends amid the shouts, " Lift up your heads, O ye gates ! " He receives the welcome, " Sit Thou on My right hand."

In it the history of Israel's Church is shadowed out from its cradle in the iron furnace of Egypt, through its days of light and darkness, through its triumphs and reverses, through its rejection in unbelief, through its long and dreary desertion to its ultimate recovery and final glory. Prophets, apostles, ministering servants, have gathered flowers from this field. Whenever the Gospel is preached, weighty arguments, convincing proofs, telling exhortations, awful warnings, are extracted from its vast mine. Thus wide is the expanse of suggestions for prayer to which the Book of Psalms invites.

I thus reach the unpretending object of this work. It seeks to give some little aid, when in due course the Psalms are opened out. Divisions are made of appropriate length for such exercise, and devotional thoughts are adjoined tending to excite the spirit of prayer and praise. All attempt to elucidate by critical acumen is utterly eschewed. If it had been possible for the writer to introduce conclusions of learning, they would have been rejected as adverse to the plan. Time has not been employed to establish a connection between the speaker's feelings and historic events. When the reference is clear, no notice is needed. When it is obscure, it is more easy to increase than to remove uncertainty. It is enough to know that the Holy Spirit depicts real and not imaginary cases. It is the reader's profit to find identity in his individual experience. He will often be constrained to feel that He who indited these words knew accurately the secrets of each heart, and presents a mirror thoroughly divine.

It may interest the scholar to investigate the claims of diverse versions for acceptance. But the hour of prayer is not suitable for such research. Therefore the reasoning powers have never been thus summoned to give aid. To help devotion has been the one and only desire. Other works abound in which the gifts of mind have been nobly used to display the wonders of this Book. The one design here has been to make it a vehicle of piety. The object is attained whenever worship is made a real approach of the spirit unto God. It is hoped that the frequent appeals to the heart may exclude formality—that enemy to direct intercourse with God.

This observation finds excuse in the growing desire to multiply the objective and the picturesque in places of public worship. Surely attention directed to artistic decorations and mimicry of Rome's showy service tends to divert from close dealings with Heaven. Real prayer is not kindled by extraneous sights. It is the Spirit moving in the inner man.

May He, whose glory only has been sought, vouchsafe His blessing for the sake of Jesus Christ!

DEANERY, GLOUCESTER,
    April 1878.

THE PSALMS.

———◆———

I.

HERE two portraits are presented to our view. The godly man appears. His walk is holy, happy, fruitful, prosperous, heavenward. — The ungodly is entirely diverse. His course is worthless, and his end is woe. Spirit of God, grant now Thy light!

———————

1. "*Blessed is the man that walketh not in the counsel of the ungodly, nor standeth in the way of sinners, nor sitteth in the seat of the scornful.*"

All praise be to the grace of God that in this world of widespread sin some lovely spots are seen. There are the heirs of life. Born from above, to God they live. Abhorrence of all evil is their grand distinction. The godless have their schemes, their pleas, their plots, their evil counsels. In such vile course the blessed never walk. They resolutely eschew the hateful path. Sinners have their chosen way. How broad! how thronged! what multitudes move down the sad decline!

A

In this the blessed have no station. They hate the
filth. They keep their feet unsoiled. Wickedness has
its topstone. Scorn and derision proceed to mock
God's word, Christ's work, and all the lowly followers
of the Lamb. Too many love the sneering seat, and
impious jests find sympathizing smiles. Such company is counterpart of hell. The blessed man sits not
in such fellowship. We here are taught that in sin
there is gradation. Let us flee the first step. The
rolling stone descends with quickening speed.

2. " *But his delight is in the law of the Lord : and
in His law doth he meditate day and night.*"

The godly man has his delights. His cup is crowned
with joy. His board is spread with richest pleasures.
The Scriptures are his soul-refreshing feast. They
gladden him with views of God as his own God; Christ
as his own Saviour; the Spirit as his guide and sanctifying Comforter; heaven as his home for ever; and
all things ordered for his weal. The morning light
invites him to this sacred page. In the day his
thoughts cling closely to it. The evening's shadows
and night's wakeful hours call to rejoice in this trea-
sury of truth.

3. " *And he shall be like a tree planted by the rivers
of water, that bringeth forth his fruit in his season : his
leaf also shall not wither ; and whatsoever he doeth shall
prosper.*"

Behold the tree on the brook's verdant bank, whose
roots drink constantly the flowing stream ! The laden
branches bend with plenteous fruit. Unfading freshness decks the leaves. No lovelier object adorns
nature's field. It is a picture of the godly man. Deep

springs of grace supply his inner life. The fruits of righteousness, which are the Spirit's work, abound. He mocks not by deception's show. His fertility of holiness is rich, and large, and real. The Lord is with him of a truth; and where the Lord is, there is every good. Of Joseph it is sweetly said, " The Lord made all that he did to prosper in his hand." Of David we read, " He went on and grew great, and the Lord God of hosts was with him."

4. *" The ungodly are not so : but are like the chaff which the wind driveth away."*

The scene is changed. The ungodly widely differ. Nature shows, too, their picture. The fruitful tree gives place to chaff—light, barren, hollow, worthless— the refuse of the barn-floor. It yields no profit. It is cast out, the sport of winds. Driven away, it leaves no trace behind. Such are the godless. They minister no grace. They benefit no souls. None gain by converse with them. Unstable, they are tossed by every changing wind. Temptations drive them headlong. Terrible is their final doom. Jesus comes, " Whose fan is in His hand, and He will throughly purge His floor, and gather His wheat into the garner; but He will burn up the chaff with unquenchable fire."

5. *" Therefore the ungodly shall not stand in the judgment, nor sinners in the congregation of the righteous."*

Judgment is near. The Judge standeth at the door. The great white throne will soon be set. The dead shall be judged out of those things which are written in the books according to their works. They cannot flee the dread tribunal. There is no escape. No mask can hide their guilt. Their sins are all recorded. No blood blots out the stains. They plead no Saviour's merit. They have no interest in the saving cross. No solid ground sustains their feet. They cannot stand. Undefended, they receive the awful sentence, Depart! go, ye cursed. Thus they are cast far from the congregation of the righteous. May we live ever with this last scene before us, and never rest until clear evidence is ours that we have happy place in "the general assembly and church of the first-born, which are written in heaven."

6. *" For the Lord knoweth the way of the righteous: but the way of the ungodly shall perish."*

Amid all their trials, sorrows, pains, reproaches, let the righteous lift up rejoicing heads. The eye of God rests on their way. He called them to the narrow road. He upholds their feeble steps. He safely leads them to the glorious end. Unfailing watchfulness surrounds them. But the broad road, with its unrighteous throng, goes down assuredly to hell.

Holy Spirit, give us the portion of the blessed man! May we escape the doom of the ungodly!

II.

PSALM II. 1-6.

To oppose the kingdom of Christ is utterly vain, because it is established by the Father's power, and by the provisions of the eternal decree. Holy exhortation follows. May faith read reverently the prophetic hymn!

---

1. " *Why do the heathen rage, and the people imagine a vain thing ?* "

Pious anticipation might exclaim—Surely, when Jesus comes to bless this earth, adoring welcomes will receive Him. Surely each heart will call Him to its throne: each knee will bow: each tongue will shout His praise: thanksgivings will encircle Him. They who thus reason little know the devil's power and man's rebellious wickedness. The Spirit's eye foresees the black reality. Among the heathen rage shall be rampant. The favoured nation shall plot destruction. How base, how vain is this iniquity! It may well be asked, What prompts this hatred? Why does this frenzy madden?

2. " *The kings of the earth set themselves, and the rulers take counsel together, against the Lord, and against His anointed.*"

They who occupy earth's highest seats are fiercest to oppose. The Herods and Pilates take determined stand. The council of the priests and elders meet in dark conclave. In the beginning it was so. The same hatred has defiled succeeding thrones and courts. Against whom is this rage? Tremble, O earth, turn pale, ye heavens. This fury assails the Lord Jehovah and His beloved Son. The Father sends the Son anointed by the Spirit to be the promised Saviour, to execute the all-saving offices of Prophet, Priest, and King, to bless the Church with every blessing. And earth's chiefs combine to tread Him beneath insulting feet. Give ear: this is their frantic cry—

3. "*Let us break their bands asunder, and cast away their cords from us.*"

Self-will rejects restraint. Pride will not yield to rule. Licentiousness surmounts all barriers. Conceited reason lifts up defiant head. The gentle sceptre of Christ's kingdom, His sweet, His light, His easy, and His loving yoke, are hated as bands which curb and cords which fetter. When Jesus came, earth raised the cry, "We will not have this man to reign over us." It still resounds. When will man learn that widest liberty is true submission to the Gospel sway? He is a free man whom the Son makes free. He is a slave in whom unbridled lusts and passions rule. But can proud man prevail? Can he drive back the ocean's might with a feather? Can he lift up his puny hand, and bid the sun conceal its rays? Can he with straws bind the hurricane? Can he lay mountains low, exalt the vales, and change the laws of nature? Can he scale heaven and dethrone our God? Such, doubtless, is his frantic will. But give ear again:

4. "*He that sitteth in the heavens shall laugh: the Lord shall have them in derision.*"

Let us lift up our eyes to God. He sits upon His throne on high; while earth is all disquietude, wild in mad menace, He reigns in calm repose. The Spirit here takes images from human feeling to depict His unruffled contempt. Man laughs derisively, when puny efforts dash their feebleness against overpowering strength. Thus God shows undisturbed disdain of human fury.

5. "*Then shall He speak unto them in His wrath, and vex them in His sore displeasure.*"

God may be silent long; but patience is not impunity. Reprieve brings not release. When the appointed time is come, the sluice-gates open and wrath overflows. Who can conceive these terrors ? What must His displeasure be ? Who can endure when sore displeasure issues forth ? What weeping, what wailing, what anguish, what gnashing of teeth, when God arises to execute due judgment on His foes !

6. "*Yet have I set My King upon My holy hill of Zion.*"

In spite of earth's malignant rage, God manifests His King. He called His Son to be the heir of all things. Upon His shoulder supreme government is laid. His hand receives the sceptre of universal reign. He announces, " All power is given unto Me in heaven and in earth." Who can resist ? Who can withstand ? Our Jesus is God's King—by choice, appointment, will, and sovereign decree. Now He spiritually sits enthroned on Zion's holy hill. He reigns supreme in every true believer's heart. He is invited by rejoicing love. Lift up your heads, O ye gates, and be ye lift up, O portals of my soul, and the King

of glory shall come in. He enters, and all heaven
follows in His rear. He enters, and establishes the
kingdom of righteousness and peace and joy in the
Holy Ghost. This present session on Zion's holy hill
is now open to the eye of faith. But the day quickly
comes when Jesus' throne shall be universally conspicuous. The wicked cannot hinder. Their rage can
interpose no barrier. God hath spoken. It must be.
It must soon be. "Then the moon shall be confounded, and the sun ashamed, when the Lord of hosts
shall reign in Mount Zion and in Jerusalem, and
before His ancients gloriously."

III.

PSALM II. 7—12.

7. " I will declare the decree : the Lord hath said unto me, Thou art my Son ; this day have I begotten Thee."

Oh, wondrous thought ! Before the birth of time eternal councils willed the weal of man. A covenant of grace was firmly made. We live in hope of eternal life, which God, that cannot lie, promised before the world began. Jesus, in His love for souls, in tender zeal to fill our hearts with joy, and to cause streams of peace to flow, announces the decree. By His Spirit He unfolds it. In His Word He writes the record. Here He displays important articles. It was decreed that honour should await Him as God's co-eternal Son. For a brief period His deity was hid. In outward show He differed little from the sons of men. Occasionally heavenly rays brake forth ; but the sun's brightness was eclipsed. Thus, as man, He suffered and died. The resurrection-morn arrives. He strides forth the mighty conqueror of death and hell. The glorious rising has a glorious voice. With trumpet-tongue it tells the wondering world, Jesus is God's Son : this day removes all doubt : this day unveils Him. The Father hath begotten Him.—Another morn will brightly shine. Greater manifestations rapidly come on. Amid all glory Jesus will be shown again as God's co-equal, co-eternal Son. Who then can shake His kingdom's firm supports ?

8. " Ask of Me, and I shall give Thee the heathen for

Thine inheritance, and the uttermost parts of the earth for Thy possession."

Another article of the covenant is stated. Christ's kingdom shall exceed all bounds. The outcast heathen shall bend the knee. Earth's uttermost extent shall call Him Lord. But this shall be in answer to His prayer. In heaven the Son shall prosecute His suit. With supplication He shall urge His claims. His pleading shall recite His part performed—the ransom paid—the kingdom bought—all hindrances removed. He shall thus ask, and He shall thus obtain. Blessed Jesu, extend Thy wounded hands! Let not the Father rest until earth's length and breadth shall own Thy rule!

9. *"Thou shalt break them with a rod of iron: Thou shalt dash them in pieces like a potter's vessel."*

The covenant, moreover, states that all Christ's enemies shall lick the dust. Hate may continue. Opposition may oppose. But oh! how vain! Behold His might. A rod of iron is wielded by His hands. It breaks and cannot be withstood. Opposing strength is brittle as the potter's clay. He strikes, and it lies shivered atoms. Thus shall His kingdom trample down all foes.

10. *"Be wise now, therefore, O ye kings: be instructed, ye judges of the earth."*

But wrath yet lingers. Space is vouchsafed. Let it be duly used. A warning voice arrests earth's great ones in their mad career. It bids wisdom to awake, and sit submissively at Jesus' feet. The truest sage is a meek learner in the school of grace. To know Christ truly is the crown of knowledge.

1 1. "*Serve the Lord with fear, and rejoice with trembling.*"

Knowledge leads surely in the paths of service. Gospel-obedience is a blessed walk. It is the happy union of all grace. Strictest submission goes hand in hand with filial reverence. The cup of joy is mixed with tenderest dread of error. Love fears. Fear loves. Joy trembles, and trembling is glad.

1 2. "*Kiss the Son, lest He be angry, and ye perish from the way, when His wrath is kindled but a little. Blessed are all they that put their trust in Him.*"

Mercy still warns. It points to Jesus. It exhorts to give Him homage, because it is His due—to worship Him to whom all praise belongs—to love Him who has so loved us as in our stead to die. It forbids delay. Until our hearts be wholly His, we totter on destruction's brink. One spark of kindled wrath excludes for ever from salvation's way. What, then, will be their doom against whom wrath in full fury blazes?

Sweet melody concludes this hymn. It speaks of blessedness. It tells where true happiness now and for ever dwells. It is in faith. Faith is the saving and the happy grace. It tightly clings to Christ. It trusts Him at all seasons for all things. Oh! may this blessed state be ours. Truly blessed it is.

IV.

PSALM III.

Foes without number press upon the speaker.   Prayer
is his refuge.   Calmly he sleeps.   His fears are gone.
Speak, Lord, that thus our hearts may ever rest.

---

1. " *Lord, how are they increased that trouble me!
Many are they that rise up against me.*"

The first scene shows the monarch flying from his
heartless son.   Absalom advances with rebellious
hosts.   The outcast father looks upon the swelling
billows of foul treason.   Increasing numbers hunt his
life.   He sees, and he appeals to God.

Here, too, our Jesus may be heard.   The powers of
darkness are combined.   Hell and its legions terribly
assail.   Wicked men do their worst wickedly.   On all
sides troubles multiply.   Many voices cry " Crucify."
The servant follows in the suffering path.   The true
believer often will but moan.

2. " *Many there be which say of my soul, There is no
help for him in God.*"

Affliction has the aspect of desertion.   Many reason,
God's favour surely would disperse these clouds.—His
voice could quickly scatter all the ills.   David thus
persecuted seems to be cast off.   Here is the scoff of
Calvary.   " He trusted in God : let Him deliver Him
now, if He will have Him.   The thieves also, which
were crucified with Him, cast the same in His teeth."

3. "*But Thou, O Lord, art a shield for me; my glory and the lifter up of mine head.*"

In darkest days faith shines with brightest glow. In the wild storm it looks to God and sings. No weapon can succeed against it. God, even God Himself, surrounds His children as a shield. The shaft which touches them must pierce through God. Welcome, too, reproach and obloquy and scorn. No disgrace can soil their name. They are renowned among the sons of men. Their glory is their God. No billows can submerge them. God, even their own God, lifts up their heads. From deepest waters Jesus rose to God's right hand. Where the Head is, there too shall the members be.

4. "*I cried unto the Lord with my voice, and He heard me out of His holy hill.*"

The voice of the insulting foe may loudly cry; but faith outcries. It has direct admission to the courts above. The blood-bought way is ever open. The interceding Spirit prompts the appeal. The mediating Son presents it. The Father on His throne receives it. Heaven opens, streams of answering blessings flow down. No case is desperate to him whose call can bring almightiness to his aid. Here is our Jesus. In the days of His flesh, He offered up prayers and supplications, with strong crying and tears, unto Him that was able to save Him from death, and was heard in that He feared.

5. "*I laid me down and slept; I awaked; for the Lord sustained me.*"

The battle-field and the beleaguered fort present no downy couch. The alarms of war invite not to repose.

But God is a pillow to the head of faith. David lies down. His sleep is sweet. He arises with recruited strength. But deeper truth sounds in these words. Jesus calmly falls asleep. The new-made grave receives Him to its bed. On the third day He casts off sleep. He appears and testifies, God did not leave My soul in hell, nor suffer His Holy One to see corruption. So, too, believers fall asleep in Him. Short is the night of death. Soon shall they awake and shout, " O grave! where is thy victory? O death! where is thy sting?"

6. " *I will not be afraid of ten thousands of people, that have set themselves against me round about.*"

Faith is a fearless grace. It has quick ears to hear the voice of Heaven. It quickly catches the oft-repeated word, " Fear thou not, for I am with thee : be not dismayed, for I am thy God." Let man come on, boastful of numbers, and vain-glorious in the arm of flesh ; faith meets the hosts, strong in the Lord, making mention only of His name. The victory is sure. Jesus never lost a battle. No follower of His will ever fall.

7. " *Arise, O Lord ; save me, O my God : for Thou hast smitten all mine enemies upon the cheek-bone ; Thou hast broken the teeth of the ungodly.*"

Grace marvellously works. It begets intrepid confidence. And confidence begets increasing prayer. Trust knows no fear, and eschews presuming indolence. It waxes more importunate in prayer. It gives no rest to God. It knows its safety ; and therefore it cries, " Save me, O my God." Past experience supplies both arguments and hope. Thou hast brought shame and confusion on all vaunting foes: therefore, now arise and save.

8. "*Salvation belongeth unto the Lord: Thy blessing is upon Thy people.*"

Triumphant is the final chorus. It tells of God rich in salvation. Salvation is His property. He willed it. He provided it. He holds it. He gives it according to His sovereign purpose. It is deliverance from every peril. It is exaltation to the heights of heaven. His blessing ever rests upon His people. It gives them all things and never fails. Lord, save us, and we shall be saved. Bless us, and we shall be blessed! Amen.

V.

PSALM IV.

THIS psalm begins with prayer. Solemn expostulation and earnest entreaties follow. Then the believer's chief good appears in contrast to the lot of the ungodly. May that chief good be richly ours!

---

1. *" Hear me when I call, O God of my righteousness: Thou hast enlarged me when I was in distress; have mercy upon me, and hear my prayer."*

Acquaintedness with God brings mighty help to prayer. Strong arguments flow from experience. "Thou art my righteousness" is a prevailing motive. The believer stands pardoned through grace, and richly robed in Jesus' merits. One with Christ, he appears as free from guilt as God's own Son. He, too, can boldly point to past deliverances. Many had been his straits, but the bands were loosened, and God set him free. He thus gains courage for urgent prayers, and he learns the art of winning mercies. He plies it well. Prayer grows stronger by unwearied exercise.

2. *" O ye sons of men, how long will ye turn My glory into shame? how long will ye love vanity and seek after leasing?"*

True grace is pitiful of sin's mad ways, and seeks occasion to remonstrate. The service of God is glory. The wicked scorn it as contemptible. What folly can be worse! Their hearts delight in this world's empty bauble. They greedily pursue a mocking shadow. Wisdom expostulates, How long! When will such madness have an end!

3. "*But know that the Lord hath set apart him that is godly for Himself. The Lord will hear when I call unto Him.*"

There is a truth which annihilates such folly. God has a chosen seed. Eternal destination marks them as His own. They are godly because the Spirit seeks and calls and works most mightily within them. They are severed from the world as wheat from chaff, as gold from dross, as sheep from goats, as jewels from the quarry's dust. They are distinguished with most precious grace, especially with the gift of prayer. They often call, and never call in vain. Know this, ye sons of men, and cease your fruitless opposition.

4. "*Stand in awe, and sin not: commune with your own heart upon your bed, and be still.*"

Wise precepts here instruct. Ponder the greatness, the majesty, the power, the glory of Jehovah. Tremble in awe of His almightiness. Let holy dread repress each rebel thought. His arm is raised against all sin. Flee sin, then, as most sure destruction. Search the recesses of your treacherous hearts. Detect their secret whispers. Nip evil in its earliest bud. In still retirement, in night's tranquil hours, become acquainted with yourselves. Thus learn the happy art of checking wicked words. Become expert in silence.

5. "*Offer the sacrifices of righteousness, and put your trust in the Lord.*"

In worship let all formality be unknown. Outward service is vain show except the heart and all its powers wax warm. They who worship God must worship Him in spirit and in truth. But trust not in your holiest acts. Sin soils them all. Your best is nothing worth: nay, rather, it is before God's eyes a filthy rag. When all is done, your trust must be in tender mercy, in forbearing grace, in pardoning love, in the atoning blood. There is no hope for man but in the work of Christ.

6. *" There be many that say, Who will show us any good? Lord, lift Thou up the light of Thy countenance upon us."*

The restless worldling is ever craving and is ever void. Conscious of inward emptiness, he seeks contentment which he never finds. The flowers plucked soon wither in the hand. The sigh is frequent, Ah! that I knew where happiness resides! Believers know that all delights are in God's smile, in a sense of His reconciled love, in His abiding favour, in the sight of His glory in the face of Jesus Christ. This is the joy of joys, the heaven of heavens. For this incessant prayer should be made. Shine, gracious Lord! Cause darkness to flee far away! Let Thy bright beams bring light and floods of peace. May we ever revel in the rich joy of the Gospel's tidings!

7. *" Thou hast put gladness in my heart, more than in the time that their corn and their wine increased."*

Let the world scorn. Believers are the happy men. David's experience is their common lot. Their happiness is inward: the heart is its seat: it is implanted by God. It is real, substantial, and abiding. It laughs to scorn the transient merriment which earth's plenty gives. Excitement may follow the abundant harvest; revelry may exult in the luxuriant vintage; but the flare is momentary, and sinks in gloom. It is from earth, and earthly. The joy of the Lord is like the Giver—pure, perfect, and eternal.

8. " *I will both lay me down in peace and sleep : for Thou, Lord, only makest me dwell in safety.*"

How sweet is the peace resulting from God's smile ! No rage of earth or hell can ruffle it. In all disquietudes it is unmoved repose. What God bestows no power can disturb. His gift is safety. Safe then are His people. Such is the Spirit's teaching in this psalm. May our hearts be able to respond, Our glad experience attests these truths !

VI.

PSALM V.

FAITH prays, knowing that wrath will overwhelm God's foes, and mercies crown the righteous. May prayer be thus stirred up in us!

1, 2. *"Give ear to my words, O Lord; consider my meditation. Hearken unto the voice of my cry, my King and my God: for unto Thee will I pray."*

By varied terms the Spirit shows the varied exercise of prayer. Sometimes words flow in ready utterance. Sometimes deep feeling finds no vent: the spirit groans but cannot express. Sometimes the voice swells in agonizing cries. But prayer in every form ascends to heaven. May prayer in every form be our delight! Prayer, too, lays hold of God by all His gracious names. These names are all revealed to strengthen faith. Faith is well skilled to use them. Give ear, O Lord. Hearken, my King, my God!

3. *"My voice shalt Thou hear in the morning, O Lord; in the morning will I direct my prayer unto Thee, and will look up."*

Surely our earliest thoughts should rise to heaven, our earliest words should speak to God. Happy the life when every day begins with Him! The first should have our first employ. Let not the world intrude until our God be reverently worshipped. As arrows from the bow, let early prayers fly swift to heaven. Let, too, watchfulness follow, waiting to catch the accepting smile, and to acknowledge the returning blessings.

4, 5, 6. " *For Thou art not a God that hast pleasure in wickedness ; neither shall evil dwell with Thee. The foolish shall not stand in Thy sight : Thou hatest all workers of iniquity. Thou shalt destroy them that speak leasing : the Lord will abhor the bloody and deceitful man.*"

Let us remember that in prayer we draw near to the Holy, Holy, Holy Lord God of hosts. The court is holy ; the unclean may not enter. Ponder the holiness of Him whom praying lips address. Sin in its every form is hateful in His sight. The very angels have no worthiness before Him. Blessed Jesus ! we would draw near, cleansed in Thy blood, fair in Thy beauty, spotless in Thy merits, righteous in Thy righteousness.

Here, too, we have sin painted in diverse colours. The monster shows most hideous shapes. Words heaped on words describe its utter vileness. Are the ungodly wicked ? Sin is wickedness. Is evil to be abhorred ? It is evil. Is foolishness meet for contempt ? It is folly. Is iniquity most base ? It is iniquity. Is falsehood contemptible ? It is leasing. Is murder monstrous ? It is blood-stained. Is craft a vice ? It is deceit. This catalogue appals. This character is ours by nature. As such we could not rightly pray. Happy if we can add, " But we are washed, but we are sanctified, but we are justified in the name of the Lord Jesus, and by the Spirit of our God."

7. " *But as for me, I will come into Thy house in the multitude of Thy mercy ; and in Thy fear I will worship toward Thy holy temple.*"

True worship bends in lowliest humility. It comes crying for mercy to blot out misery, and it sees a multitude of mercies outnumbering the multitude of sins. To count our sins surpasses all our powers. But where sin abounds God's mercy far exceeds. True worship trembles at the majesty of God, but it is bold. Its eye is fixed on the appointed place where God has promised to come down and meet. This place is our most precious Jesus. We bless Thee, O our God, for our true mercy-seat, our real throne of grace.

8. " *Lead me, O Lord, in Thy righteousness, because of mine enemies : make Thy way straight before my face.*"

The believer knows that hostile eyes observe his walk, malignant to expose each erring step. His refuge is in prayer. He supplicates almighty guidance. He desires a heaven-high course. Lead me in Thy righteousness. Help me to see Thy way. He would walk on earth as in the courts above.

9. " *For there is no faithfulness in their mouth ; their inward part is very wickedness ; their throat is an open sepulchre ; they flatter with their tongue.*"

The picture shows the falseness of this hollow world. Intense iniquity pervades the heart. The mouth is opened to destroy. Their words are deathful darts. They bristle with destruction. The viper's poison lurks beneath their tongues. May we be followers of Him whose lips were grace !

10. " *Destroy Thou them, O God : let them fall by*

their own counsels; cast them out in the multitude of their transgressions; for they have rebelled against Thee."

These words are free from slightest tinge of vengeful malice. Their inmost breathing is divine. The believer sees the coming wrath. He knows God's vengeance will descend. God's honour must be vindicated : God's glory must shine forth in just perdition of rebellious foes. The believer rises into oneness with his God. He exults and triumphs in the final overthrow. Perfect love in heaven will sing, " Just and true are Thy ways, Thou King of saints."

11, 12. *" But let all those that put their trust in Thee rejoice : let them ever shout for joy, because Thou defendest them : let them also that love Thy name be joyful in Thee. For Thou, Lord, wilt bless the righteous; with favour wilt Thou compass him as with a shield."*

We turn from bitter anguish to joy in overflowing tide. The saints appear in triple phase. They trust, they love, they walk in righteousness. Triple mercy meets them. God is their defence : He makes them rich in blessing : His favour is their all-surrounding shield. A triple exhortation sounds, but all the notes combine in one. Rejoice : for ever shout for joy : be joyful in your God. May inward testimony prove our right to rejoice in the Lord alway, and again and again to rejoice !

VII.

PSALM VI.

HERE godly sorrow changes into godly joy. May we so mourn that we too may be comforted!

---

1. "*O Lord, rebuke me not in Thine anger, neither chasten me in Thy hot displeasure.*"

Seasons recur when sense of sin and bodily distress cast into lowest depths. God's anger threatens to descend in fury. The furnace of displeasure seems terribly to burn. If faith shall fail, despair must overwhelm the soul. But amid terrors faith survives: it knows its refuge and looks above. It doubts not that God still loves. When frowns most darken on His brow it pleads, Let not this chastening destroy; let not the flames devour.

2. "*Have mercy upon me, O Lord, for I am weak: O Lord, heal me, for my bones are vexed.*"

The fainting flesh shows sympathy. The anguish preys upon the total frame. Sickness of soul reduces every power. Prayer is redoubled. Incessant cries besiege the throne of grace. Misery calls mercy to arise. Disease implores the heavenly healer's aid. Blessed is the anguish which flees thus to God.

3. "*My soul is also sore vexed: but Thou, O Lord, how long?*"

Sorrow of soul is sorrow's fullest cup. All other bitterness is light beside it. The mourning days drag heavily; no dawn appears to chase away night's shade. The moan is heard, "How long, O Lord! how long?" He who would read the deepest lessons of these words must go with Jesus to the garden and the cross. By imputation He is made the sin of sin. Mountains on mountains of iniquity meet on Him. Unspeakably tremendous is the load; unspeakably tremendous is the wrath incurred. His own consent received the vicarious guilt. Just anger thickens round Him. He feels the horrors of His place. Prostrate in misery, He cries, "My soul is exceeding sorrowful, even unto death." Anguish cries, "My God, my God! why hast Thou forsaken Me?" The curse may not spare Him. Great is the mystery, but it is our salvation.

4. "*Return, O Lord, deliver my soul: Oh save me for Thy mercies' sake.*"

The sweetest joy is holy fellowship with God. It is heaven's foretaste to see His smile and hear the whispers of His love. To realize this oneness is faith's privilege. But when this presence is withdrawn, when mists obscure this sun, the soul can find no other comfort. There cannot be a substitute for God. There is no rest while sad desertion lasts. It is perdition's wretchedness. The sinking soul craves mercy. It agonizes: "Return, deliver, save!"

5. "*For in death there is no remembrance of Thee: in the grave who shall give Thee thanks?*"

There is fear lest sorrow's weight should snap the thread of life. Then means to tell of God's love, to speak of Christ, to sound His praise, to call poor sinners to His cross, to spread abroad His power to save, for ever cease. Let us prize and sedulously use con-

tinued health and length of days. They are a precious
talent. In bringing others to salvation's road, we rise
in heaven ourselves.

6, 7. "*I am weary with my groaning; all the night
make I my bed to swim; I water my couch with my
tears. Mine eye is consumed because of grief; it waxeth
old because of all mine enemies.*"

The picture of the sin-affrighted soul becomes more
dark. Outward expressions of deep woe abound: sighs
rack the heart: tears flow in copious streams: lustre
no longer sparkles in the eye: this bitter grief writes
old age on the brow. We see how terrible an enemy
is sin. When viewed apart from Christ, it is intolerable woe. What must it be in hell! Let us bless
Christ with every breath. He is the Lamb of God,
who takes it all away.

8, 9. "*Depart from me, all ye workers of iniquity;
for the Lord hath heard the voice of my weeping. The
Lord hath heard my supplication; the Lord will receive
my prayer.*"

The scene is changed. Light brightly shines; the
shades of night have vanished. Mercy descends with
healing on its wings. The groans are changed for
songs of joy. We see the all-prevailing power of
prayer. In darkest days let it take heaven by
storm. It grasps Jehovah's arm. It clings until all
blessings are vouchsafed. Renewed favours strengthen
the confidence that foes shall not prevail. Away,
depart,—you cannot lay me low. No commerce will
I have with you. Answers to prayer stir up resolves
to persevere. The suppliants who prosper are encouraged to pray more. Success begets continuance.

10. " *Let all mine enemies be ashamed and sore vexed :
let them return and be ashamed suddenly.*"

The Spirit here gives comfort to all harassed saints.
The language is prophetic. It runs through time ; it
shadows out the final scene. Shame and vexation are
treasured up for the ungodly. They sowed the seeds
of evil; they must reap the harvest of confusion. It is
hard to kick against the pricks.

The concluding words delightfully reveal our Lord.
We see manifestations of His power and triumphs.
Before His eye His enemies quail and fall backwards.
In His extremest anguish an angel flies to raise and
strengthen. Soon will the universe be witness to the
mandate, " Depart, ye cursed, into everlasting fire, prepared for the devil and his angels." May we so suffer
with Him, that we may reign together !

VIII.

PSALM VII. 1-8.

DAVID, stung by unjust reproach, appeals to God. He prays and foresees future judgment. The end is praise. When slanders fly around may we be similarly calm!

1, 2. "*O Lord my God, in Thee do I put my trust: save me from all them that persecute me, and deliver me; lest he tear my soul like a lion, rending it in pieces, while there is none to deliver.*"

David had felt the persecuting rage of man. In peril of life he often fled. Trembling, he had cried, "There is but a step between me and death." The enemy had pursued, athirst for blood, mad as the wildest beast of prey, with fangs extended to rend his limbs to atoms.

To this day malicious fury raves in sinful hearts. If no restraining barriers had interposed, all men of God would long since have been swept from earth. But when cruelty reviles, they know their stronghold. Their God is their high fortress of defence. They enter and are safe.

3, 4, 5. "*O Lord my God, if I have done this; if there be iniquity in my hands; if I have rewarded evil unto him that was at peace with me; (yea, I have delivered him that without cause is mine enemy;) let the enemy persecute my soul, and take it; yea, let him tread down my life upon the earth, and lay mine honour in the dust.*"

Pure conscience gives enlargement at the throne of grace. He can lift up the head who knows that every charge is false. David was pure of guilt towards Saul. He never sought to hurl him from his throne. He planned no traitorous plots; he sowed no seeds of insurrection. Far otherwise. When in the providence of God his cruel foe was helpless in his hands, when one blow would have crushed persecution, he would not strike. He cut off the mantle and bore off the spear to prove his power to slay—his generosity to spare. Thus conscious of innocence, he appeals to God.

Here Jesus shows Himself to faith's adoring eye. His walk on earth was perfect purity and perfect love. His one work was to scatter blessings and do good. But enmity could not be softened. Hate causeless was hate furious. He meekly testifies, " They hated Me without a cause; they laid to My charge things that I knew not of." The servant must not expect an easier lot. The more clearly he reflects his Lord, the more bitterly will hatred rage, and viler will be falsehood's accusation. Innocence stops not man's mouth, but it gives bold access to the ears of God.

6, 7. " *Arise, O Lord, in Thine anger, lift up Thyself because of the rage of mine enemies ; and awake for me to the judgment that Thou hast commanded. So shall the congregation of the people compass Thee about : for their sakes therefore return Thou on high.*"

Troubles last long that grace may more abound. The greater anguish kindles increased prayer. Importunity becomes more urgent. Heaven is assailed with cries that God would no longer seem indifferent, but awake, arise, and put on anger as a mantle. He is reminded of the known decree that judgment shall avenge His people and destroy rebellious foes. In all desires of execution of just wrath, faith's eye regards God's glory. When the Lord's wrathful arm is seen, His people will encircle Him with shouts of praise. Their sanctified joy will burn more brightly. Therefore, for their sake God is implored to show Himself on His high throne of power. These words cast light on this world's final scene. Judgment is indeed arranged. Irreversible decree demands it. Our Jesus will appear as Judge. A high tribunal will be His glorious seat. His ransomed flock will all be gathered round Him. He comes to be glorified in His saints and admired in all them that believe. Where, then, will persecutors stand? Oh! that the Spirit would arrest their course and bring them as lowly suppliants to the saving cross; for soon the day of mercy will be fled.

8. " *The Lord shall judge the people: judge me, O Lord, according to my righteousness, and according to mine integrity that is in me.*"

True religion is strictly personal. It looks inward; it diligently probes the heart. It deals rigidly with motives and with ways; it prays God to observe and judge. So David, conscious of righteous dealing towards Saul, prays that favour may regard him. This plea is quite consistent with deep sense of sin and consciousness of all shortcomings towards God. Low in deepest guilt before omniscient holiness, we may be free of injury towards man. May this sweet consciousness enable us to lift up the head, and boldly seek God's aid!

IX.

PSALM VII. 9–17.

9. " *Oh, let the wickedness of the wicked come to an
end ; but establish the just : for the righteous God trieth
the hearts and reins.*"

Sights and sounds of evil are anguish to a pious heart.
They pain him, because they are abhorrent to his new
nature. He turns from them as images of Satan; he
loathes them as rebellion against God. Hence he
burns with desire that they may be repressed. Hence
he wearies heaven with cries that God would drive iniquity into outer darkness. No faithful prayer ascends
in vain. Doubtless in answer to such cries much evil
is restrained. God's servants are maintained, and
grace is kept as a little taper in the world's deep gloom.
But evil will not die until our Lord returns. Then
shall the wickedness of the wicked reach its end. Faith
waits expectant of the blissful reign ; it visits in anti-
cipating thought the new heavens and the new earth.
Throughout there is no form of sin ; its hideous features are for ever gone ; the reign of righteousness is
come. Each heart is holy ; each look reflects God's
image ; every sound is pure. All is transcendent
happiness, for all is holiness. No evil will pollute the
glorious scene. God's discerning eye will then have
parted light from darkness. Without is sin and all
sin's slaves ; within is the Lamb's bride, all glorious
in her robes of white.

10. " *My defence is of God, which saveth the upright in heart.*"

How safe are they whom God's shield covers! No weapon wounds them. Satan's darts fall harmless at their feet. They live through all assaults, and they shall live for ever. But their own arm brings no defence. They are " kept by the power of God through faith unto salvation, ready to be revealed in the last time." Their character is as clear as their protection is secure. Through grace their hearts are wholly changed. Uprightness is their one delight; uprightness is their constant path.

11, 12, 13. " *God judgeth the righteous, and God is angry with the wicked every day. If he turn not, He will whet His sword ; He hath bent His bow, and made it ready. He hath also prepared for him the instruments of death ; He ordaineth His arrows against the persecutors.*"

Pledges are added unto pledges that the righteous have God to vindicate their cause. Faith treasures up these glad assurances, and gains strength and joy. There is no day nor hour in which God's anger against sin burns not. But there is respite. Forbearance checks the final blow. The wicked yet may turn ; he may abjure his vile rebellion. He may break Satan's yoke ; he may seek mercy. In penitence and shame he may flee humbly to the Saviour's cross. But if he will not turn, there is no hope. Destruction is then most sure. The Spirit gives a faithful picture of God ready to destroy. He stands in all the might of omnipotence. His arm uplifts His glittering sword; the edge is sharpened for resistless work. Other

weapons are prepared. He holds His bow bent for
execution. All instruments are ready, and all barbed
with death. His arrows are prepared for action. The
persecutors are the target to be pierced. Who can hear
this and fail to flee for covert to the wounds of Jesus !

14. "*Behold, he travaileth with iniquity, and hath
conceived mischief, and brought forth falsehood.*"

The faithful Word reveals the evil man. His inner
man is all iniquity; it is the offspring which he bears.
As noxious waters flow from noxious founts; as poison-
berries grow on upas trees; so sin in all shapes flows
from him. Plots of mischief are conceived; plans of
falsehood are nurtured. They come to birth, they
start to life, to fill the world with misery, and to blacken
earth with crime. They are of their father the devil,
and all their words and works savour of hellish origin.

15, 16. "*He made a pit, and digged it, and is fallen
into the ditch which he made. His mischief shall return
upon his own head, and his violent dealing shall come
down upon his own pate.*"

The evil labour hard to work their own destruction.
Their feet are caught in their own net. Into their own
pits they fall. They sharpen weapons mainly to wound
themselves. Their arrows shot on high fall back on their
own heads. Goliath's sword severs his head. Haman
hangs on his own gibbet. Adonibezek laments, "As I
have done to others, so God hath requited me." Dogs
lick the blood of Jezebel in the place where she had
slain Naboth. Eliphaz records a common experience,
" I have seen they that plough iniquity and sow wickedness reap the same." The man who rends the oak
may be destroyed by the rebound.

17. "*I will praise the Lord according to His right-eousness; and will sing praise to the name of the Lord most high.*"

The end comes on. It is all joy to the redeemed. They sing; they sing aloud; they sing for ever. The praises of the Lord are their incessant and unwearied song. They laud Him according to His righteousness. Now they give praises from their inmost souls; but oh, how dull their hearts! how weak their voice! how poor, how meagre, their most lively efforts! Their harps are tuneless; their best melody lacks life. They turn with shame from their best attempts. They reach not the very outskirts of their theme. But when they reach their home, their songs are commensurate with Jehovah's glorious name. They praise the Lord according to His righteousness. May this delight be ever ours!

X.

PSALM VIII.

GOD'S name is excellent in all His works, but especially in Christ. O God! reveal Thy name to us. The
Spirit, who gave these words, gives their interpretation
by the lips of Jesus and an Apostle.

1. " *O Lord, our Lord, how excellent is Thy name
in all the earth! who hast set Thy glory above the
heavens.*"

How precious is the right of faith to claim an
interest in God! It would be vain to say that the
Lord is Lord unless we could annex, "O Lord our Lord."
But in His own Son God gives Himself to us. Each
true believer may exult, " This God is our God for ever
and ever."

What thought can grasp God's glory! Its dazzling
brightness defies the sight of mortal eye. Its breadth
and length, its depth and height, exceed all space.
It more than fills the universe and soars above the
heaven of heavens. None less than God can grasp this
knowledge. But earth is chosen as the favoured spot
of wondrous revelation. His name is here made
manifest in the face of Jesus Christ. Throughout
earth's wide expanse His name is gloriously sounded.
All other knowledge fades in comparison. We stand
amazed at the surpassing excellence.

2. " *Out of the mouth of babes and sucklings hast Thou*

ordained strength because of Thine enemies, that Thou mightest still the enemy and the avenger."

We know not what circumstance in David's life prompted these words, but our minds revert to a most interesting scene. In Jerusalem young children throng our blessed Lord. Tender voices raise the shout, "Hosanna to the Son of David." Jesus reminds the angry priests that the cry was prefigured in their Scriptures. "Have ye never read, Out of the mouths of babes and sucklings Thou hast perfected praise?" We see, too, this word inscribed on the Gospel's mighty course. How poor, how weak, how feeble in themselves are the messengers of grace! They go forth as infants against hosts of giants, as David against Goliath. Against them the wit, the learning of the world combine in strong array. The Gospel's voice seems tiny to compete, but it prevails. The idols of the world succumb. The cleverest arguments of vain philosophy, the mightiest efforts of conceited reason, the Dagons of skill and learning lick the dust. The enemy is stilled. Opposing lips are mute. There is a power in God's own truth, proclaimed by feeblest lips, before which Satan and his legion and all the disputants of earth must ever quail. Let no true minister of Christ complain that He is weak. He is strong in speech whom God instructs. He will prevail by whose mouth the Spirit deigns to utter truth.

3, 4. *"When I consider Thy heavens, the work of Thy fingers, the moon and the stars, which Thou hast ordained; what is man, that Thou art mindful of him, and the son of man, that Thou visitest him?"*

When we uplift our eyes to the sparkling canopy of

a clear night, what wonders excite admiration! The
moon revolves in brilliant majesty. Countless orbs,
each perhaps the centre of its own system, stud the
expanse with lustre. What must their great Creator
be! How far that power must surpass conception
which willed them into being! But, marvel of
marvels! that great power looks with tender care
on man! Low as he is, and vile and base, and stained
with all iniquity, yet God loves him, ever tends
him with most watchful eye, and visits him with all
the blessings of salvation. But Jesus is here. He
is pre-eminently the Son of man. He is born one
of our family, bone of our bone, flesh of our flesh. As
such, He condescends to our low level. He is made in
all points like unto us, sin only excepted. As such,
He needed heavenly aid. As such, He was upheld and
succoured during His earthly course, and borne victorious through all His trials.

5, 6, 7, 8. "*For Thou hast made him a little lower
than the angels, and hast crowned him with glory and
honour. Thou madest him to have dominion over the
works of Thy hands; Thou hast put all things under his
feet; all sheep and oxen, yea, and the beasts of the field;
the fowl of the air and the fish of the sea, and whatsoever
passeth through the paths of the seas.*"

The decree names Jesus as the heir of all things.
When He arose from deepest depths of degradation,
He proclaimed, "All power is given unto Me in heaven
and in earth." And yet a little while and His glorious
kingdom will be established here, and earth, with all
who breathe life's breath, the total universe, with all
that it contains, shall own His sway. In the name of

Jesus every knee shall bow; every tongue shall confess that He is Lord, to the glory of God the Father.
In this our present tabernacle we groan, being bur-
dened, looking for the glorious appearing of our great
God and Saviour.   May we by faith and prayer and
every holy grace hasten His coming!   Then will the
chorus swell with rapturous praise through all the
redeemed earth:

9. *" O Lord, our Lord, how excellent is Thy name in
all the earth."*

Even so, come, Lord Jesus.

XI.

PSALM IX. 1–10.

FERVENT praise acknowledges God's help and righteous judgments. Prayer follows for continued favours. May we thus praise! May we thus pray!

1, 2. "*I will praise Thee, O Lord, with my whole heart; I will show forth all Thy marvellous works. I will be glad and rejoice in Thee: I will sing praise to Thy name, O Thou most high.*"

The Lord is worthy to be praised with all our energies, with all our powers, in every pulse of our affections, in every movement of our minds, in all places, and at all times. Heaven is unwearied praise. Earth would be heaven begun, if our whole hearts were wholly tuned to praise. It is our duty, and it should be our chiefest joy, to tell aloud God's wondrous works. But ah! how weak are our best efforts! Where shall we find beginning? Where shall we find an end? Love joyed in us before the worlds were framed. Goodness and mercy have followed us from the cradle to this hour. Christ died for us. Christ lives for us. Christ soon will come again to receive us unto Himself, that where He is there we may be also. Let us praise with our whole hearts. Let us be glad and rejoice in Him.

3, 4, 5. "*When mine enemies are turned back, they shall fall and perish at Thy presence. For Thou hast maintained my right and my cause ; Thou satest in the throne judging right. Thou hast rebuked the heathen, Thou hast destroyed the wicked, Thou hast put out their name for ever and ever."*

Have not believers every cause for joy ? They have foes around and they have foes within. Against these foes their own strength is as nothing ; but God is their victory. He arises to their help. His presence crushes opposition. He does all for us, and we bless His name. Present deliverance is earnest of the coming triumph. A day draws near when on His glorious throne our blessed Lord shall sit. This throne is based on righteousness. From it all righteous judgment will go forth. On it the rightful cause of believers will be maintained. Their cause is good. It cannot be gain-sayed. They claim their pardon on the plea that all their debt is cancelled in Christ's blood—that all de-mands of justice are satisfied in Him : they ask for heaven on the ground that they are clothed in right-eousness divine, and meetened in Christ for the mar-riage supper of the Lamb.

6. *" O thou enemy, destructions are come to a perpetual end ; and thou hast destroyed cities ; their memorial is perished with them."*

The redeemed anticipate the devil's final fall. They fear not to confront him. They bid him mark, that as he destroyed, so now he is destroyed. They foresee his hateful work concluded, his destroying power broken, and his sceptre for ever shivered. Doubtless he wrought terrible destructions in the earth. He laid waste populous cities. He so utterly demolished them that no vestige could be found. As they were swept into oblivion, so the devil's empire shall for ever perish.

7, 8. "*But the Lord shall endure for ever; He hath prepared His throne for judgment; and He shall judge the world in righteousness, He shall minister judgment to the people in uprightness.*"

What a glorious kingdom now succeeds! All rule, all authority and power, are now put down. God is enthroned the only Lord. His sceptre is uprightness. Thus He shall reign for ever and ever. Sin is for ever annihilated. It no more can disturb, or vex, or soil. The righteous God rules over a righteous world. His people shall be all holy. Holiness and love shall be on each brow. Holiness alone is the atmosphere of the new earth.

9. "*The Lord also will be a refuge for the oppressed, a refuge in times of trouble.*"

But until the restitution of all things shall arrive, oppression will not cease, and times of trouble will continue. The irreconcilable enemy will use each opportunity to malign, to vex, and to destroy. The prince of this world will hate the godly. His fiery darts will thickly fall. But a ready refuge is at hand. That refuge is the Lord, and His covert is impregnable. All acts of Satan are weak against it. He cannot force its barrier gates; he cannot scale its walls. Salvation is its ramparts; omnipotence is its strength.

10. "*And they that know Thy name will put their trust in Thee: for Thou, Lord, hast not forsaken them that seek Thee.*"

The knowledge of the Lord begets all confidence. It is ignorance which trembles. The name which manifests His glorious perfections annihilates distrust. We may, indeed, trust fully; for the Lord hates putting away. Those whom He loves He loves unto the end. In Him there is no variableness nor shadow of turning. The mother may forsake her sucking child: the father may forget his first-born son: friend may abandon friend; but the word stands for ever sure, " I will never leave thee nor forsake thee." Holy Spirit! show us more of this unchanging love!

XII.

PSALM IX. 11–20.

11. "*Sing praises to the Lord which dwelleth in Zion; declare among the people His doings.*"

To the elder church the Lord revealed Himself as seated between the cherubim on the mercy-seat. Christ is this seat to us. In Him we have constant access to our God, and always find a ready welcome. In Him we draw near to God, and He draws near to us. But the fulness of this truth will not be known until the glorious manifestation of the incarnate God; until He shall take His seat on the throne of David, and sit royally on Zion's hill. In knowledge of His present mercy, in forethought of His coming kingdom, let praise be ever on our lips. Let our constant utterance magnify His doings past, His doings present, and His doings in the coming age.

12. "*When He maketh inquisition for blood, He remembereth them: He forgetteth not the cry of the humble.*"

This earth has drunk the blood of martyrs. Jesus bled on Calvary's tree. An apostate church is drunk with the blood of the saints. But will such wickedness escape unpunished? A disclosing day draws near. Then murderous hands will find that they were slaughterers of their own souls. Then shall the crown of martyrdom be found to be exceeding glory; then will it be fully seen that every mournful cry and every humble prayer of the afflicted saints made impress on the heart of God—were written there indelibly, fully to be answered in the appointed time. Faithful prayer can never be in vain.

13, 14. *"Have mercy upon me, O Lord ; consider my trouble which I suffer of them that hate me, Thou that liftest me up from the gates of death ; that I may show forth all Thy praise in the gates of the daughter of Zion : I will rejoice in Thy salvation."*

How sweet it is in the full confidence of faith to place all troubles in the hand of God ! Such prayer is very humble. Mercy is ever sought in deepest consciousness of unworthiness. There is confession that the gates of death endanger, unless deliverance is marvellously wrought. Why do believers thus seek aid ? Their ruling motive is, that with their renewed lives they may praise Him who thus delivers, and may by lip and life exalt His praise. Renewed mercies deepen joy. It is the constant song, " I will rejoice in Thy salvation." The theme demands our loudest adoration. Let us go forth in spirit and anticipate the day when we shall join the countless multitude, and cry, "Salvation to our God, which sitteth upon the throne, and unto the Lamb."

15, 16, 17. *" The heathen are sunk down in the pit that they made : in the net which they hid is their own foot taken. The Lord is known by the judgment which He executeth. The wicked is snared in the work of his own hands. The wicked shall be turned into hell, and all the nations that forget God."*

The final veil is here again withdrawn. The Spirit calls us to behold the wretched sinners' doom. They plotted ruin to the saints : in ruin they are overwhelmed. They craftily spread snares : they now are caught, and all escape is hopeless. Into a pit of deep and endless woe they sink. Their multitude is great : their numbers exceed calculation. But num-

bers vanish before God's might. They cast God from
their minds: they would not think of His authority
and power; but now they cannot fail to recognise His
hand. The final execution proclaims His work.
Over their prison-house there is inscribed, A God forgotten is a God avenged. A God unknown in time
must fearfully be known throughout eternity. Would
that poor sinners, ere it be too late, would cease to
kick against the pricks! Sin will recoil on sinful self.

18. "*For the needy shall not alway be forgotten: the
expectation of the poor shall not perish for ever.*"

Times of trouble seem to have long course. Sighs
oft inquire, When will this darkness cease—when will
these sorrows end? But a bright morn will surely
dawn. The help expected will exceed all thought.
No word will fail on which faith hopefully relied.

19, 20. "*Arise, O Lord; let not man prevail: let the
heathen be judged in Thy sight. Put them in fear, O Lord;
that the nations may know themselves to be but men.*"

The cry is earnest. Fear seems to tremble lest
God's cause should sink, and puny man stand conqueror. God tarries that the saints may stir Him up.
Their supplications will be heard. The ungodly shall
be taught that at their best they are weak flesh and
blood. Their strength is nothingness before Jehovah's
arm. It is mad folly for potsherds of the earth to
strive against their Maker.

May we be ever found one with our blessed Lord!
May His cause be our cause! His victories our victories! His heaven our heaven! His throne our throne
for ever!

XIII.

PSALM X.

THE main feature in this psalm is the foul portraiture of evil. Prayer follows in full confidence that God will arise and judge. May the Spirit raise hatred of evil in our hearts!

1. " *Why standest Thou afar off, O Lord? why hidest Thou Thyself in times of trouble?* "

There is much weakness in the strongest faith. It is prone to sink when billows swell and storms descend. Trials assume desertion's form. Darkness seems to imply that God cannot be near. The sun eclipsed seems gone for ever. But faith in weakest hours still prays, and meekly questions, Wherefore is it so?

2. " *The wicked in his pride doth persecute the poor; let them be taken in the devices that they have imagined.*"

The Spirit proceeds to draw a full-blown portrait of sin. The mask is withdrawn. The monster is dragged forth to light. The hideous features are revealed. The Spirit's pen cannot exaggerate. The dark colours are not too dark. The deep ingredient of the wicked heart is pride. This scorns the humble followers of the Lamb, and seeks to trample them beneath insulting feet. But often do oppressive schemes recoil, and plots involve self-ruin.

3. " *For the wicked boasteth of his heart's desire, and blesseth the covetous, whom the Lord abhorreth.*"

In arrogance the wicked boasts that his desires shall prosper. And who can hinder him ? He loves the hoarders of poor pelf. In spite of God's abhorrence they are his delight.

4. *" The wicked, through the pride of his countenance, will not seek after God; God is not in all his thoughts."*

His haughty carriage vaunts independence. He stoops not to study God's will. He is no suppliant at wisdom's gate. God is not the substance of each thought, but rather rashness says, " There is no God."

5. *" His ways are always grievous; Thy judgments are far above out of his sight: as for all his enemies, he puffeth at them."*

His every step insults both God and man. His dim eye grovels on the ground. It has no power to pierce the heavens and read God's will. His insolence contemns his foes.

6, 7. *" He hath said in his heart, I shall not be moved, for I shall never be in adversity. His mouth is full of cursing and deceit and fraud: under his tongue is mischief and vanity."*

In self-complacency he thinks prosperity must ever last, and evil days can never come. He cannot speak but floods of evil issue forth. His words are open curses and insidious falsehoods.

8. *" He sitteth in the lurking-places of the villages; in the secret places he doth murder the innocent; his eyes are privily set against the poor."*

Evil words lead on to evil deeds. He craftily devises murderous acts. He narrowly observes the poor and feeble, thirsting for their blood.

9, 10. *" He lieth in wait secretly as a lion in his den ;*

he lieth in wait to catch the poor; he doth catch the poor
when he draweth him into his net. He croucheth and
humbleth himself, that the poor may fall by his strong
ones."

Sometimes as a beast of prey he croucheth for a
desperate spring: sometimes as a crafty huntsman he
spreads entangling nets. By every art he seeks to
execute his hateful plots.

11. "*He hath said in his heart, God hath forgotten:*
He hideth His face: He will never see it."

False thoughts of God deceive him. Impunity
persuades him that God disregards. He flatters himself that omniscience marks him not.

12. "*Arise, O Lord: O God, lift up Thine hand; for-*
get not the humble."

These sights of sin impel believers to the mercy-
seat. They turn away. They look above. They
seek their God. They tell out their fears. They ask
His succour. They commit the persecuted to His
care. They stir Him up to have them in remembrance.

13, 14, 15. "*Wherefore doth the wicked contemn God?*
He hath said in his heart, Thou wilt not require it.
Thou hast seen it; for Thou beholdest mischief and spite,
to requite it with Thy hand: the poor committeth himself
unto Thee: Thou art the helper of the fatherless. Break
Thou the arm of the wicked and the evil man: seek out
his wickedness, till Thou find none."

How vain the atheistic thought that God sits still
in unconcern! From His high throne He ponders all
the ways of men. In right time He will avenge His
honour. The helpless shall indeed be holpen; the

boastful arm of wickedness shall be shivered. All evil shall be dragged to light; no sin shall go un-punished.

16. "*The Lord is King for ever and ever: the heathen are perished out of his land.*".

Glorious light shines forth. The throne of God is set. He rules, He reigns, in majesty supreme for ever. His enemies are all destroyed. Throughout the blissful realm no trace of evil can be found. His happy subjects now lift up the head. One shout is heard, Glory, glory to our God!

17, 18. "*Lord, Thou hast heard the desire of the humble: Thou wilt prepare their heart, Thou wilt cause Thine ear to hear; to judge the fatherless and the oppressed, that the man of the earth may no more oppress.*"

Good Lord, increase our faith in the power and prevalence of prayer! The eternal world will show that supplication never craved in vain. Grace prompts the desire, inspires the words, prepares the heart, and gives the full reply. When God comes forth to answer and to help, what can feeble flesh avail! It perishest for ever. From this view of the wickedness of the wicked, their righteous doom, the glories of the coming kingdom, let us bless Him who has delivered us from the wrath to come, and called us to His kingdom and glory.

XIV.

PSALM XI.

CONFIDENCE relies on God when storms of trouble
threaten. The terribleness of final judgment is revealed. May perfect shelter be our happy lot!

---

1. "*In the Lord put I my trust: how say ye to my
soul, Flee as a bird to your mountain?*"

Happy the soul which calmly rests on God! He is
a rock so firmly based and so exceeding high, that
swelling billows dash in vain, and raging storms in-
nocuously beat. Feet planted on it are safe as God is
safe. His power is omnipotence. Who can upset it?
His love can never change. His wisdom knows no
bounds. His truth can never fail. Let us then trust
Him, at all times, in all places, under all trials. Let
us trust Him with our souls and bodies, for time and
for eternity. Let us trust Him with all our matters and
with all our friends. Safe in His arms we may defy
all foes.—But they will taunt with sneering malice.
They will exclaim, Make haste to flee. There is no
safety but in flight. As the affrighted bird seeks
refuge in the high and distant hills, so fly with rapid
wing. To tarry is destruction. Tarry not.

2. "*For, lo! the wicked bend their bow, they make
ready their arrow upon the string, that they may privily
shoot at the upright in heart.*"

Peril may be near. The wicked hate and plot:

their bow is strong: their arrows ready: their eyes are watchful. If opportunity be given, their venomed shafts will inflict deadly wounds. Thus Jesus walked amid incessant snares. At every turn some ambush was concealed. What crafty questions spread entangling nets! So too it is each day with us. The enemy is ever near. Let us look up. Let our daily cry be heard, "In the Lord put I my trust."

3. "*If the foundations be destroyed, what can the righteous do?*"

The foundations of our trust are firm, and never can be moved. We have received a kingdom that cannot be shaken. What is the strong foundation of our trust? It is Christ. It is His glorious person, His deity and manhood indissolubly joined, His everlasting love, His finished work, His precious blood, His expiating death, His all-atoning cross, His resurrection-might, His session at the right hand, His never-ceasing intercession, His well-ordered providence, His coming kingdom, His eternal reign. How blessed, how encouraging, are these truths! Not one can be gainsayed, not one can disappoint. We may rest all our weight on them. They cannot sink. If any flaw could be discerned, if any weak part showed insecurity, we might indeed despond. But building on this solid base, we may indeed reject all taunts. We have a strong city. Salvation hath God appointed for walls and bulwarks.

4. "*The Lord is in His holy temple; the Lord's throne is in heaven: His eyes behold, His eyelids try, the children of men.*"

Ours is no visionary trust. Of old our God was

present in the sanctuary. True worshippers might there approach and find that He drew nigh to them. Christ is our mercy-seat. In Him we meet our God; in Him our God meets us. What then shall be our fear? But more; our God sits high enthroned in heaven. He rules arrayed in power omnipotent. How safe are they who are protected by His arm! His eye sees every outward act and searches every inward thought. His people never are unseen. No darkness can conceal His foes. We may then confidently trust.

5. "*The Lord trieth the righteous; but the wicked, and him that loveth violence, His soul hateth.*"

Many are indeed our trials, but all are ordered for our good. Thus faith is tested: leaks in the vessel are discovered: sincerity is discerned: weak parts are strengthened: the walk becomes more close, more wary, and more strict. These probings are among our blessings. "Blessed is the man that endureth temptation, for when he is tried he shall receive the crown of life, which the Lord hath promised to them that love Him." But all iniquity is hateful in His sight. His holy nature abhors sin.

6. "*Upon the wicked He shall rain snares, fire, and brimstone, and an horrible tempest: this shall be the portion of their cup.*"

They cannot escape just wrath. Their frightful doom is here portrayed. Mercy warns of this destruction, that men forewarned may flee to Christ. Images of agony are here combined. What Sodom and her plains foreshowed is coming reality. A fiery deluge overwhelms its victim. A flaming lake engulphs. There is a cup which they must drink. The cup is hot to overflowing with all extremity and intensity of torment. Wrath is not yet gone forth. Let all who hear fly speedily to Christ.

7. *" For the righteous Lord loveth righteousness : His countenance doth behold the upright."*

Righteousness will execute what righteousness denounces. Justice maintains for ever that rebels are thus punished. But saving smiles beam sweetly over the redeemed flock. God now beholds them in all love. They soon shall see Him in all glory. Holy Spirit ! keep us ever in the light of His countenance !

XV.

PSALM XII.

FEARING that the godly cease and the ungodly vaunt, prayer is made and confidence is professed in God's pure Word. Supported by such comfort, may we never fear!

1. "*Help, Lord; for the godly man ceaseth; for the faithful fail from among the children of men.*"

Amid the trials of this sinful world there is sweet solace in the company of holy men. Their counsel strengthens; their example cheers; their fellowship delights; their meek endurance teaches patience; their zeal excites to work. We joy in their joy; we gain grace from their grace. But they are not always near. We oft shed tears beside their graves. It may be that adverse circumstances fix our dwellings where evil is most prevalent. Many have mourned this desolation. Lot's heart is vexed in Sodom. Elijah wails his lonely state. Jeremiah weeps in friendless solitude. Paul sadly writes, "Only Luke is with me." But comfort is not linked to man. Faith can fly straight to heaven. Prayer can bring down the joy of joys, the presence of our God. The fervent cry, "Help, Lord," can turn earth's desert into smiling paradise. The saint feels that he is not alone when God is by his side. The heart is glad when Jesus holds communion.

2. "*They speak vanity every one with his neighbour:*"

with flattering lips and with a double heart do they speak."

Where grace is absent insincerity prevails. Ungodly converse has taint of unreality. The unconverted heart—the birthplace of all speech—is double. From feigning source there must flow feigning words. Dissimulation within dissimulates without. Hatred and mischief, injury and wrong, fraud and oppression, are deeply plotted, while the look blandly smiles, and flattery conceals the base intent. Ah, world! ah, treacherous world! thou art a truthless cheat.

3, 4. *" The Lord shall cut off all flattering lips, and the tongue that speaketh proud things: who have said, With our tongue will we prevail; our lips are our own: who is lord over us ?"*

Sad is the blinding power of sin. Proud reason dreams that independence is its heritage. It bows not to God's sovereign rule. It claims a seat above the throne of God. It owns no power superior to itself. The true believer widely differs. He feels, I am not my own. I am bought by the precious blood of Christ. I gladly give myself, my all, my every word, my every work, to my Redeemer's cause. My highest honour is to be the servant of my glorious Lord. My noblest work is to act out His will. My happiest life is to serve Him. But these deceivers mainly deceive themselves. Flattering others, they are self-injuring. Their lips prepare their own destruction. The Lord hears, records, and will most surely punish. Wisdom proclaims, " By thy words thou shalt be justified, and by thy words thou shalt be condemned."

5. *" For the oppression of the poor, for the sighing of*

the needy, now will I arise, saith the Lord ; I will set him
in safety from him that puffeth at him."

The prayer ascends, "Help, Lord." The answer
comes, "Now will I arise." Prayer speedily brings
heaven to aid. God's eye never fails to mark the
cruel treatment of His suffering saints. His ear
receives each feeble breathing of His persecuted
children. It was so when Israel groaned in the
Egyptian furnace. "I have surely seen the affliction
of My people which are in Egypt, and have heard
their cry by reason of their taskmasters; for I know
their sorrows." In every age it has been so. It
will be so until the reign of peace be sweetly settled.
Until that day the world will see oppression working
and deliverance checking.

6. "*The words of the Lord are pure words: as silver*
tried in a furnace of earth, purified seven times."

While falsehood, deceit, and wrong abound in evil
men, the faithful Word is near to comfort. No insincerity pollutes it. It is pure from all alloy, as silver
perfectly refined. It has been the staff of many suffering pilgrims, and it never fails. It will sustain when
other props are gone.

7. "*Thou shalt keep them, O Lord ; Thou shalt pre-*
serve them from this generation for ever."

The Church has lived through every age, and still
it lives. There have been times when signs of life
were very feeble. The quivering spark has seemed
almost extinct. The daughter of Zion has been left
as a cottage in a vineyard, as a lodge in a garden of
cucumbers. But God's power has not deserted them.
They have been kept by His mighty power through

faith unto eternal life. And safely they will be preserved, until they stand together a countless multitude in Emmanuel's land.

8. " *The wicked walk on every side, when the vilest men are exalted.*"

It may be that earth's highest seats are occupied by men most reprobate. A Pharaoh, a Herod, a Nero, may wield the tyrant's sceptre : then vice and villainy will show unblushing front. On all sides wickedness will riot. Let us in such distress pour out the cry, " Help, Lord," and the Lord will speedily arise. With such assurance, let us not despond !

XVI.

PSALM XIII.

THE soul long troubled here at last finds peace. Lord, may our faith never fail! Joy is at hand.

1, 2. "*How long wilt Thou forget me, O Lord? for ever? how long wilt Thou hide Thy face from me? How long shall I take counsel in my soul, having sorrow in my heart daily? how long shall mine enemy be exalted over me?*"

Discipline is needed in the school of grace, and therefore it is not withheld. A loving Father orders it—a loving hand applies it. The purport and the issue are increase of grace. Lurking sins are thus detected. Weakness in faith's fabric is repaired. Secret foes are dragged to light and slain. Prayer and dependence and matured experience gain power. Fruits of righteousness are ripened. A shaken tree takes deeper root. To effect this, tokens of God's presence are withdrawn. The much-loved smile smiles not. The tender whispers are no longer heard. Precious communion fails to cheer. The sighing spirit mourns desertion. It is as a forsaken dwelling. No ray of love illumines the surrounding darkness. Fears whisper, God is for ever gone. Dreary days drag on their dreary length. In the morning there is the wail, "How long?" In the evening it is still, "How long?" The soul is much perplexed. Harassing doubts intrude.

Questions arise. What is the purport? When will be the end? Thus daily sorrow is the daily bread. Thus grief and heaviness pervade the day. The cry is oft-repeated, "How long? how long?" Affliction deepens because the enemy appears to triumph. It is his joy when saints are sad. He rears his head when they lie low; his cause is crowned when adversity fills their cup. This knowledge aggravates their misery. The cry continues, "How long! how long?" David is here. This is a path which his feet often trod. Each child of God is here. In this darkness they often walk. But above all, the Man of Sorrows is here too. There is no cup of anguish which His lips tasted not. These words anticipate the bitter cry, "My God, my God! why hast Thou forsaken Me?"

3. "*Consider and hear me, O Lord my God: lighten mine eyes, lest I sleep the sleep of death.*"

In every state faith has its sure employ. In darkest night, amid the howling storm, in dreariest solitude, in racking pains, from the whale's belly, in the battlefield, when the foes rush with overwhelming might, when hope seems hopeless, when all remedy is fled, when heaven seems closed, in agonies of death, in jaws of hell, it prays. There is no state which excludes prayer. There is no place without an access to the mercy-seat. Faith never forgets, The Lord is my God. I have a property in Him. Thus it can ever cry, " Consider and hear me, O Lord my God." Relief and comfort are implored. The present gloom seems as an instant death. A ray of love is sought to give reviving light. The smile of God's countenance is desired to keep the eyes from closing in dark death.

4. "*Lest mine enemy say, I have prevailed against him; and those that trouble me rejoice when I am moved.*"

There is fear lest the enemy shall triumph, and the tottering cause of truth should fill the wicked with malicious joy. Thus David trembled; but his fears were visionary. Opposing foes could not detain him from the throne. Thus Satan seemed about to triumph when Jesus was dragged to trial and uplifted on the cross. Truth seemed about to fall and victory to crown hell's efforts. But how short the hope! The conquering Saviour bursts detaining bonds. He rises omnipotent to vanquish all hell's arts and might. In Him His people live. In Him they will prevail. In Him they soon will sit on thrones of glory. In Him they soon will place victorious feet on Satan's neck. Therefore we will trust and not be afraid.

5. "*But I have trusted in Thy mercy; my heart shall rejoice in Thy salvation.*"

God's mercy is sure ground of trust. It cannot fail. It is higher than the highest heavens. It extends throughout all space. Its one delight is to alleviate misery. Under its sheltering wings may we delightedly repose! Joy is ever ready to refresh the soul. But true joy grows not in the field of earthly things. This fruit hangs not on carnal trees. It is not quaffed from goblets of wealth, and luxury, and worldly pleasures. It lives in heavenly clime. It feeds and feasts on God's salvation. Is it not joy to clasp this boon to the heart, and to know assuredly, By grace am I saved, through faith, and that not of myself; it is the gift of God! By grace am I saved, through the sprinkling of the blood of Jesus, and the covering of His glorious righteousness. By grace am I saved, through the in-dwelling of the Holy Ghost.

6. *" I will sing unto the Lord, because He hath dealt bountifully with me."*

Joy is not silent. It lifts up the voice. It sends forth the incense of praise. It has a boundless theme. It tells of all God's dealings. They are infinite, even as God Himself. He gives till He can give no more. He spares not His only-begotten Son. He adds His Holy Spirit. Shall He not also freely give us all things? Let us now commence our endless song. Let us now strike the harp which never shall grow tuneless. Let us sing unto the Lord, who hath dealt bountifully with us. Help us, O God, the Holy Ghost!

XVII.

PSALM XIV.

THE inhabitants of the world are represented as lying
in wickedness. But the year of the redeemed is foreshadowed. May we tremble at this sight of sin, and
joy in prospect of deliverance!

———

1. " *The fool hath said in his heart, There is no God.
They are corrupt, they have done abominable works,
there is none that doeth good.*"

The heart is the index of the man. Its language
reveals the real character. If we could hear the secret
whispers of the graceless heart, the sound would be but
one. The godless think there is no being greater than
themselves. Their conceit rejects divine supremacy.
It scorns to yield to any yoke. Such men exist in
fearful numbers. The faithful Word declares it, and
moreover adds that they are fools. They pride themselves in higher wisdom; but their real place is
maddest among the mad. Their light is utter darkness, their boasted wisdom is extremest folly. Atheism
in heart is wickedness on the lip. The spring is impure; what can flow from it but poisonous waters!
The tree is dead at core; the branches must be rotten.
Their works, the offspring of their thoughts, are
streams of abomination. They pollute the earth in
which they are enacted. Hateful to God, they injure
man. Are there not some bright exceptions? Not

one by nature. There is no good but what the Spirit prompts. Where He is absent only evil dwells ; and He is far from unregenerate men.

2. " *The Lord looked down from heaven upon the children of men, to see if there were any that did understand, and seek God.*"

We are directed to Jehovah on His heavenly throne. His piercing eye surveys the universe. It reads the secrets of every heart—of every man. No thought escapes omniscient view. What is the purport of the all-pervading search? To ascertain whether all thoughts are turned to God—whether His knowledge is the prime pursuit—whether prayer asks for revelation of His will—whether His mind is sought in the clear pages of His Word—whether His works are studied as emblems of His character. Thus to seek God is proof of wisdom. Let no man boast of understanding whose mind rejects this wise employ. God looks for this. What is His verdict ?

3. " *They are all gone aside, they are altogether become filthy : there is none that doeth good, no, not one.*"

We read how things were before the Flood. The heart of graceless man is still the same. Every imagination of the thoughts of his heart is only evil continually. They wander far from paths of righteousness and truth ; their feet are set in error's broad decline ; their garments are sin-soiled. In God's sight their words are filth, and pollution in extreme defilement. Let us bless God that the blood of Jesus can cleanse from all such stains, and make us whiter than the whitest snow.

4. " *Have all the workers of iniquity no knowledge ?*

who eat up My people as they eat bread, and call not upon the Lord."

Jehovah sees this universal evil, and now He speaks. The voice is strong expostulation. It traces sin to the true source—ignorance. If truth were sought and seen, and loved and followed, how different would be man's walk! Men work iniquity because their minds are blinded. Evil breaks forth in persecution; but who are the persecuted? "My people," saith the Lord. We hear the tender voice, "Saul, Saul, why persecutest thou Me?" The issue is the absence of all prayer. They call not upon the Lord. Here four foul marks of unregenerate man are shown— ignorance, iniquity, persecution, prayerlessness.

5. "*There were they in great fear: for God is in the generation of the righteous.*"

But to the wicked there is no calm peace. Their minds are ill at ease. Clear tokens show that God is mighty in His people's midst. His presence is their sure defence. God must lose His throne ere they can be subdued. Nebuchadnezzar saw this and was astonished. He looked into the flaming furnace and exclaimed, "Lo, I see four men loose walking in the midst of the fire, and they have no hurt; and the form of the fourth is like the Son of God." Well may they fear whose weapons are thus directed against God.

6. "*Ye have shamed the counsel of the poor, because the Lord is his refuge.*"

The godly make the Lord their refuge. He is the high tower to which they always fly. Beneath the covert of His wings they seek protection. The perse-

cutors sneer: they ridicule such trust. What! look
for help to an unseen arm! Thus Jesus was reproached.
But experience shows, in countless instances, that none
seek God in vain.

7. " *Oh that the salvation of Israel were come out
of Zion! when the Lord bringeth back the captivity of
His people, Jacob shall rejoice, and Israel shall be
glad.*"

This frightful sight brings in a glorious dawn.
Israel's long night shall cease. She shall arise and
shine. Her light shall come: her tedious years of
cruel thraldom shall reach a blessed close: her sons
from distant lands shall return: her every promise shall
have exact fulfilment. From Jerusalem the blessed
tidings of salvation shall go forth. If the casting
away of them has been the reconciling of the world,
what shall the receiving of them be but life from the
dead! Then indeed shall joy and gladness be the
portion of Israel's sons. Then shall praise and
thanksgiving ring throughout earth's length and
breadth. Let us trust, and pray, and hope. Bright
days shall come. Hasten it, O Lord, in Thine own
time!

XVIII.

PSALM XV.

HERE is a beauteous picture of the holy man.   Holy
Spirit, mould us into this blessed form!

———————

1. *" Lord, who shall abide in Thy tabernacle? who
shall dwell in Thy holy hill?"*

Profession is not always real.   Many may cry,
" Lord, Lord," who shall at last be outcasts.   Hence
it is all-momentous to escape deception, and to know
assuredly our state.   Here is the question put.   Here is
the answer given.   He who alone reads well the heart,
He who discerns the wheat from chaff, hears the appeal
and gives reply.   Who then maintains communion
with the Lord, who talks with God upon His mercy-
seat, who shall for ever dwell with Him in the new
heavens and the new earth, who shall receive the welcome, " Come, ye blessed children of my Father, inherit
the kingdom prepared for you from the foundation of
the world?"   Who will be Zion's inmates when the
tabernacle of God is with men, and He shall dwell
with them, and they shall be His people, and God
Himself shall be with them, and shall be their God?
The reply forbids mistake.   God's people are all
righteous.   Holiness is written on their brow.   Holiness pervades their heart.   Holiness directs their
steps, supplies their words, and is the very essence
of their being.   They are new-born by the Spirit's

power. The divine nature is implanted. Let not,
however, this decisive test mislead. Our holiness presents no title at God's bar; it blots out no sin; it
pays no debt; it arrests not condemnation; it weaves
no justifying robe; it presents no shadow of a claim.
Christ, and Christ only, justifies; His blood alone can
cleanse from sin; His death alone appeases wrath.
His pure obedience, placed to our account, is the only
robe for heaven. Holiness is not our title, but it is
assuredly our character. It is the evidence before
God and man that we are really Christ's. It is the
test of union with the Lord; it is the proof that we
are one with Him. By faith we have an interest in
Christ and all Christ's work. By works we prove
that the gift of faith has been received. With earnest
prayer that godliness may be our element of life and
meetness for the new Jerusalem, let us now ponder
the beauteous portrait drawn by the Spirit's hand.

2. " *He that walketh uprightly, and worketh righteousness, and speaketh the truth in his heart.*"

His walk is rectitude. His ear drinks in the
mighty mandate, " Walk before Me, and be thou perfect." A constant effort restrains from devious ways.
His delight is in the study of God's holy law, and his
whole life evinces effort to obey. His heart is guileless, and his lips give proof. Pure is the inward
fountain, and pure the flowing stream.

3. " *He that backbiteth not with his tongue, nor doeth
evil to his neighbour, nor taketh up a reproach against
his neighbour.*"

His tongue is strictly bridled. He hates the vile
defaming which bespatters his neighbour's name. No

injury to person or to credit proceeds from him. If evil whispers are addressed to him, they find a check. He propagates no scandal. His charity will cover sins however many.

4. "*In whose eyes a vile person is contemned; but he honoureth them that fear the Lord. He that sweareth to his own hurt, and changeth not.*"

His estimate of men rests not on outward show. Where he sees signs of gracelessness he withholds respect, although riches and honour and the world's applause exalt the man. But true respect is given where God is feared. He holds that godliness is honour. His conscience swerves not from a pledge because performance may give trouble. Truthfulness, not self-interest, is his rule.

5. "*He that putteth not out his money to usury, nor taketh reward against the innocent. He that doeth these things shall never be moved.*"

He knows that the love of money is the fruitful source of all evil. Therefore he never strives to gain by others' need. He shuns extortion. No bribe can tempt him to overreaching acts. Such are the principles which sway his heart. Such prove that he is Christ's, ruled by His law, moved by His love, treading in His paths, seeking His glory. And he shall not be moved. Amid the wreck of worlds, he is secure in Christ his ark. He will stand when the white throne is set. His dwelling will be firm in realms of everlasting day. But who can try himself by this strict rule, and not be conscious of shortcoming? Who will not smite upon the breast and cry, "God be merciful to me a sinner"? Again, we bear in mind this righteousness is not our plea. If it were so we fail. It is our evidence, and though imperfect, it is true. Its imperfection drives us more to cling to Christ. He and He only is the essence of righteousness. All righteousness He fully wrought. He casts His glorious covering over all our failings. In Him we are completely justified. In Him we joy with joy unspeakable and full of glory. O God, we thank Thee for Christ Jesus !

XIX.

PSALM XVI.

To the believer there is much joy in present state. There is, too, bright hope of rising to eternal life. May this joy and hope be our abiding portion!

---

1. *"Preserve me, O God: for in Thee do I put my trust."*

The Spirit draws aside the veil, and shows that Jesus is mainly present in this psalm. May we peruse it walking by His side, listening for His voice!

He who was emphatically a Man of Sorrows was emphatically a man of faith. As such He was, too, a man of prayer. In all the trials of His low estate, the mind of Jesus rested on His God. When perils came as a devouring flood, He looked upward for preserving aid. Happy the members who trust and pray in the meek spirit of their Head!

2, 3. *"O my soul, thou hast said unto the Lord, Thou art my Lord: my goodness extendeth not to Thee; but to the saints that are in the earth, and to the excellent, in whom is all my delight."*

Jesus professes that His inmost soul claims God as His God. Happy are our souls when they respond, O God, Thou art our God. The blessed state of God is perfect; it is infinite: the heaven-high pyramid cannot receive a higher stone. Redemption's work, which manifests His glory, cannot augment His bliss.

Let not the foolish thought be ours that we can enlarge infinitude. We read the wondrous word, that from everlasting Wisdom's delights were with the sons of men. In the days of Christ's flesh, the calm retreat of Bethany, the converse with His chosen followers, reflect this truth. Blessed be God, there still are saints on earth! Blessed are they who hold communion with them.

4. " *Their sorrows shall be multiplied that hasten after another god: their drink-offerings of blood will I not offer, nor take up their names into my lips.*"

How prone is man to cast away the true and living God, and with deluded mind to rush to idol-worship! To multiply gods is to multiply sorrows. They are all devils, and their work is to torment. The godly man abhors their offerings, and spurns their very names. There was an offering of blood which Jesus offered: may we delight in it as all salvation!

5, 6. " *The Lord is the portion of mine inheritance and of my cup: Thou maintainest my lot. The lines are fallen unto me in pleasant places; yea, I have a goodly heritage.*"

Our blessed Jesus more than walked patiently in all His path below. There was joy set before Him which gladdened His every step. In Christ God is our God for ever. Can we desire more? How rich is this portion! How reviving is our cup! How can we bless His grace enough who has called us to this ennobling state? Angels are ours to guard. Providences are ours to secure our bliss. The God-Man's blood is ours to wash out every sin. A righteousness is prepared to robe us for the courts above. Heaven is promised as our endless home. We have a goodly heritage.

7. "*I will bless the Lord, who hath given me counsel: my reins also instruct me in the night seasons.*"

Jesus bears the sweet name of Counsellor, and sweetly does He execute His office. He sends His Spirit to admonish and gently to direct. This is His gracious work. To Him be all the praise. He adds instruction in times of silence and of solitude, when the world is far away. He visits the deep recesses of the heart. He communes with the secrets of the soul, and deeply writes His lessons of pure wisdom. Let us again say, "Bless the Lord."

8, 9. "*I have set the Lord always before me: because He is at my right hand, I shall not be moved. Therefore my heart is glad, and my glory rejoiceth: my flesh also shall rest in hope.*"

The mind of Jesus ever rested on God's will. He came to earth, He lived, He worked, He died to glorify His Father. He knew that God was ever by His side. He feared not the assaults of men or devils. His cause could never totter. He surely marched to triumph. Therefore in all His trials His heart was tranquil and His lips sang praise. He knew indeed that He must hang a dead man on the Cross; He must exhaust death's bitter cup. But His tomb was bright in prospect that the dark bed would soon be left. All His members share this trust. May this faith be largely ours! The eye that ever looks for God may ever see Him. He is ever near, and near to help. Can he be moved on whose right hand God stands!

10. "*For Thou wilt not leave My soul in hell; neither wilt Thou suffer Thine Holy One to see corruption.*"

The Spirit here foreshows the glorious truth that death could not detain our Lord. Christ breaks the icy shackles; He leaves the short imprisonment. No corruption taints the sacred body. He stands again alive on earth. Infallible proofs demonstrate that He who was dead is now alive. Except the Lord's near coming should prevent, we too must sleep the sleep of death. From corruption we are not screened. Decay will riot on these frames. But short will be death's triumph. The trump will sound. Corruption shall put on incorruption.

11. "*Thou wilt show Me the path of life: in Thy presence is fulness of joy; at Thy right hand there are pleasures for evermore.*"

The heart of Jesus was sustained by joys before Him: joys in His Heavenly Father's throne—joys which should have no end. Shall not we too lift up expectant heads? The voice of truth assures us, "The glory which Thou gavest Me, I have given them." Thought staggers. Minds are narrow to embrace the bliss; but faith entirely believes. Hope bounds toward the fulfilment. Happy the hours which flow in meditation on fulness of joy and pleasures with God for evermore! To gaze on the prospect is heaven begun. What will the reality bestow? Lord grant that we may quickly know!

XX.

PSALM XVII. 1–7.

ABUNDANT prayers are made. The end is confirmation of confidence. May we thus pray, and thus be comforted !

———————

1, 2. *" Hear the right, O Lord, attend unto my cry, give ear unto my prayer, that goeth not out of feigned lips. Let my sentence come forth from Thy presence ; let Thine eyes behold the things that are equal."*

Let us scan narrowly the character of true prayer. It wears no mask of truthless insincerity. It speaks not feignedly with hypocritical pretence. It utters deep-felt truth from honest heart. Thus it wrestles like agonizing Jacob, and prevails. This boldness gains much strength from inward consciousness of rectitude. He who secretly loves evil may dissemble, but he fails to pray. In strict exactness, no lips but those of Jesus could adopt these words. On earth He was as pure from sin as God in heaven. Truth was constrained to say, I find in Him no evil. But a great day comes, when all believers shall thus plead before the judgment-seat. We shall crave justice, because in Jesus we have fulfilled each tittle of the law, because in Him we have endured each penalty. " Hear the right " will be a conquering cry. God will be just, and justify Christ-pleading sinners.

3, 4. *" Thou hast proved mine heart ; Thou hast visited me in the night ; Thou hast tried me, and shalt find*

nothing ; I am purposed that my mouth shall not trans-
gress. Concerning the works of men, by the Word of Thy
lips I have kept me from the paths of the destroyer."

No man but the God-man could court omniscient
scrutiny. We know this, and we adore Him ; for His
pure righteousness was wrought for us, and is imputed
to us.

But though sin is mixed with all we do, our every
nerve should strive for righteousness without one flaw.
Here the heart, the mainspring of the man, is uncovered
unto God. In times of darkness, when no mortal eye
can see, and interruption cannot distract, close intercourse is held with God. He is invited to visit and
to search. There is resolve that erring words shall
not offend. A godly bridle shall restrain the lips.
Grace from the tongue shall answer grace in the heart.
The walk, too, shall be far from Satan's devious paths.
His broad road is a downward path. He is the fell
destroyer. All who are led by him go headlong into
destruction's pit. The Spirit has supplied a perfect
chart. His Book gives guidance for every word, for
every work, at every moment, in all circumstances.
Feet planted on this rock can never fall. The Bible
students will ever shine as lights. They will reach
heaven's haven.

5, 6. " *Hold up my goings in Thy paths, that my foot-*
steps slip not. I have called upon Thee, for Thou wilt
hear me, O God : incline Thine ear unto me, and hear my
speech."

Purposes may be sincere and strong; but our own
strength is utter weakness. The firmest staff of human
growth is but a feeble reed. Grace must support us

or we fall. The Spirit must enable or we fail. Hence prayer increases in intensity. The more we grow in grace, the more we feel our need. The more we climb the heavenward hill, the more we dread backsliding. Each advance makes us more fearful of decline. Hence the ripest saint is most intent in prayer.

7. "*Shew Thy marvellous loving-kindness, O Thou that savest by Thy right hand them which put their trust in Thee from those that rise up against them.*"

Many rose up against our blessed Lord. From all He was delivered. He trusted and was not confounded. The same foes are ours. But let no fears depress us. We shall laugh all to scorn. But in the conflict, nothing so cheers as sense of God's love. Moses prayed, "Show me Thy glory." The reply was, "I will make all My goodness pass before thee." His goodness is His glory. The sun at mid-day is a wondrous sight. How glittering are the countless rays! But the sun is darkness beside the effulgence of God's love. When it encircles and inspirits us, we are waived to victory's high ground. Let us often pray, "Shew Thy marvellous loving-kindness."

XXI.

PSALM XVII. 8–15.

8, 9. *" Keep me as the apple of the eye, hide me under the shadow of Thy wings, from the wicked that oppress me, from my deadly enemies, who compass me about."*

The pupil of the eye is the body's tenderest part. The slightest touch—a particle of dust—inflicts keen pain. Hence skill and care elaborately screen it. Safeguards are multiplied around. Similar is the care which saints implore. A promise is dispensed which tells that this care is ever near. The Lord in tender mercy cries, " He that toucheth you toucheth the apple of Mine eye." Nature's most tender proof of anxious love is shown in the parent bird. When the storm threatens, or danger from some enemy appears, the little brood is quickly gathered, and extending wings are spread around them. They are so covered that no eye can see them; they nestle in warm shelter and are safe. This is fit emblem of God's guardian care. Hear the sweet voice of Jesus, " O Jerusalem, Jerusalem ! how often would I have gathered thy children together, even as a hen gathereth her chickens under her wings, and ye would not." This prayer involves a promise of all help. Let faith oft shoot these darts to heaven. Full answers will come down.

10. *" They are enclosed in their own fat: with their mouth they speak proudly."*

The faithful often plead the character of their foes. They are sensuous and carnal; they trench themselves in pleasures, indulgences, parade.   Pride dwells within, and arrogance makes boast.

11, 12. " *They have now compassed us in our steps : they have set their eyes bowing down to the earth ; like as a lion that is greedy of his prey, and as it were a young lion lurking in secret places.*"

Intent to catch, they spread their nets around. Their stratagems and snares beset.   With look demure, they seem to be innocuous ; but they are cruel as the ravenous lion, and crafty as the lion's whelp which springs from secret ambush.   Such are the features of the persecutor.

13, 14. " *Arise, O Lord; disappoint him, cast him down : deliver my soul from the wicked, which is Thy sword : from the men which are Thy hand, O Lord, from men of the world, which have their portion in this life, and whose belly Thou fillest with Thy hid treasure : they are full of children, and leave the rest of their substance to their babes.*"

Adopting this version, our minds receive a weighty lesson.   We are taught that the wicked are God's sword ; that the men of the world are His hand.   The Spirit in other Scriptures has revealed the same.   Of the Assyrian it is said that he is the rod of God's anger and the staff of His indignation.   It is the Lord's voice, " Thou art my battle-axe and weapons of war ; for with thee will I break in pieces the nations, and with thee will I destroy kingdoms."   Thus evil passions are employed to chasten, to reprove, to keep us low, to do us good.   Thus Satan raging in man's heart is only instrumental to subserve God's ends. Man's violence and spite are overruled.   They will accomplish destined work ; they little know their true design; they are real blessings, though disguised to God's own people. But while they are employed to harass, the saints must pray; they must be suppliants for speedy help. "Arise, O Lord, disappoint him and cast him down." And we may plead the vile condition of our foes. They are of the earth and earthly; they seek no portion beyond this sin-soiled world; they glean abundance of its worthless husks; they feast on its unsubstantial pleasures; they amass its gilded baubles, and transmit their hoarded treasures to their babes.

15. "*As for me, I will behold Thy face in righteousness: I shall be satisfied, when I awake, with Thy likeness.*"

Contrast the true believer's lot. He loves to gaze on God's unclouded face. Clad in pure righteousness, enrobed in beauty compared with which the sun is pale, decked in perfection fit for the palace of the King, he will be welcomed to the heaven of heavens. Though for a little time his flesh may slumber in the grave, yet he will surely wake. The hour is coming in the which all that are in the grave shall hear His voice and shall come forth. Then He will change our vile body, that it may be fashioned like unto His glorious body. We shall be like Him, for we shall see Him as He is. Then indeed we shall be satisfied. What more could be desired? What more could be conceived? What more could Heaven bestow? The glorified spirit reinhabits a glorious frame; the resurrection robes are now put on, and they must shine for ever. No lapse of age can change their hue. This wedding-garment is ever new. Gazing on this prospect, we may care little for those short-lived troubles. They need not fear the face of man who soon will see the face of God.

XXII.

PSALM XVIII. 1–18.

MIGHTY deliverance is realized, and utter discomfiture of every foe. May we intelligently swell the note of praise !

———————

1, 2. "*I will love Thee, O Lord, my strength.   The Lord is my rock, and my fortress, and my deliverer ; my God, my strength, in whom I will trust ; my buckler, and the horn of my salvation, and my high tower.*"

These fervent words show David's glowing heart. When seated on the throne of victory he saw his foes all low in dust, and felt that God had done it.   He exhausts all warlike terms to show that God was his stronghold, God his armour, and God his power. God kept him safe ; God gave him conquest.   What can he render in return ?   He gives his heart.   He gratefully exclaims, " I will love Thee, O Lord." David soon disappears.   Jesus Himself strides forth. David's typical career suggests this noble song; but in its fulness it is Messianic.   Faith hears it flowing fresh from Jesus' heart.   It reads here redemption's conflict, redemption's triumphs, and it is exceeding glad. How feelingly would Jesus' lips exclaim, O my Father, I will love Thee.   Thou hast been my fortress !

3. "*I will call upon the Lord, who is worthy to be praised : so shall I be saved from mine enemies.*"

It is a precious gift to know that faithful prayer is sure deliverance, and that our God is worthy of all praise. He is more worthy than thought can think or words express.

4, 5, 6. " *The sorrows of death compassed me, and the floods of the ungodly made me afraid. The sorrows of hell compassed me about; the snares of death prevented me. In my distress I called upon the Lord, and cried unto my God: He heard my voice out of His temple, and my cry came before Him, even into His ears.*"

The Man of sorrows is before us. When bearing the penalty of our sins to the uttermost, His soul was exceeding sorrowful, even unto death. In prayer He sought relief; by prayer He gained support.

7, 8, 9, 10, 11, 12, 13, 14, 15. " *Then the earth shook and trembled; the foundations also of the hills moved and were shaken, because He was wroth. There went up a smoke out of His nostrils, and fire out of His mouth devoured: coals were kindled by it. He bowed the heavens also, and came down: and darkness was under His feet. And he rode upon a cherub, and did fly; yea, He did fly upon the wings of the wind. He made darkness His secret place; His pavilion round about Him were dark waters and thick clouds of the skies. At the brightness that was before Him His thick clouds passed; hailstones and coals of fire. The Lord also thundered in the heavens, and the Highest gave His voice; hailstones and coals of fire. Yea, He sent out His arrows and scattered them, and He shot out lightnings and discomfited them. Then the channels of waters were seen, and the foundations of the world were discovered at Thy rebuke, O Lord, at the blast of the breath of Thy nostrils.*"

We may not pause to marvel at the dazzling splendour of this brilliant picture. It is a poetic fervour in

F

full blaze. Image succeeds image, revealing almighty vengeance arrayed in terribleness, and flying in awful majesty to sustain His chosen. David, thus speaking, felt that prodigies had helped his cause; that God Himself had fought in his behalf. If all the hidden wonders of his wondrous career were open to our view, if we had witnessed all the marvels which amazingly delivered him, we should not wonder that such fervid language burst from his lips. But in the Antitype the picture's colours are not overlaid. During the garden-agony, during the horrors of the Cross, we conclude that an awful conflict was enacted unseen by mortal eye. We read indeed of nature's throes. In spirit we see darkness unparalleled: we feel the tremblings of the quaking earth; but we see not the hidden battle: we see not all hell in fury to secure the victory: we see not Jehovah arising in His strength, and rousing His instruments of wrath to crush the desperate foe and to sustain His suffering Son. We follow the guidance of this picture, and we ponder a deep mystery.

16, 17, 18. "*He sent from above, He took me, He drew me out of many waters. He delivered me from my strong enemy, and from them which hated me; for they were too strong for me. They prevented me in the day of my calamity; but the Lord was my stay.*"

We learn how real, how agonizing, was the anguish of our Lord. To pay sin's penalty was to endure hell. But He prevailed, for God was with Him. His trials were thus foreseen, but He encountered them. He waded conqueror through the many waters, for God was by His side. Let us bless Him who suffered, and by suffering saved us: let grateful love adore Him.

XXIII.

PSALM XVIII. 19–36.

19. " *He brought me forth also into a large place: He delivered me, because He delighted in me.*"

The conflict ended in most glorious life. Our Jesus was exalted to supremest glory, and received all power in heaven and earth, because God loved Him as His Son, who had fulfilled His total will.

20, 21, 22, 23, 24. " *The Lord rewarded me according to my righteousness; according to the cleanness of my hands hath He recompensed me. For I have kept the ways of the Lord, and have not wickedly departed from my God. For all His judgments were before me, and I did not put away His statutes from me. I was also upright before Him, and I kept myself from mine iniquity. Therefore hath the Lord recompensed me according to my righteousness, according to the cleanness of my hands in His eye-sight.*"

One zeal burned steadily in Jesus' heart. He came to earth to do His Father's will. To this polestar His course was always pointed. He came to do redemption-work, to save lost sinners, to atone for sin, to bring in perfect righteousness, to satisfy the law's demand, to keep its beauteous code, to honour all God's attributes, to bring glory to His name. He ceased not till He cried, " It is finished," and received the welcome, " Sit Thou on My right hand."

25, 26, 27. "*With the merciful Thou wilt show Thyself merciful; with an upright man Thou wilt show*

Thyself upright; with the pure Thou wilt show Thyself pure; and with the froward Thou wilt show Thyself froward. For Thou wilt save the afflicted people; but wilt bring down high looks."

God's dealings with His incarnate Son all flowed in the channel of truth and justice. Pure godliness had claims. These claims were duly satisfied. So, too, no grace in the believer's heart is overlooked. God meets and cheers with blessings all who by the Spirit's help strive to walk closely with Him. Each grace sows seeds of favour. Especial pity marks the sufferers in oppression's furnace. Bruised Israelites are comforted. Haughty Pharaohs are cast down.

28, 29. *" For Thou wilt light my candle: the Lord my God will enlighten my darkness. For by Thee I have run through a troop; and by my God I have leaped over a wall."*

In darkest moments of desertion Jesus well knew that a bright dawn was near. The sun eclipsed is not the sun extinguished. The shadow will soon pass, and the returning rays will be more joyous. Thick troops may seem to choke the way, strong batteries may impede. But when God helps, no obstacles can check. A way is opened through opposing ranks. Strength is supplied to overleap all hindrance.

30, 31. *" As for God, His way is perfect: the Word of the Lord is tried: He is a buckler to all those that trust in Him. For who is God save the Lord? or who is a rock save our God ? "*

Knowledge of God is comfort in all times. It was so to our Head on earth. It has been so to every saint. It will be so till Jesus shall return. His

dealings with His Church are perfection. No flaw
therein was ever found. There is one testimony, " He
hath done all things well." His truth is often tested ;
but each trial proves that it is firm and pure. Who
ever stood behind His armour and received wound ?
He is well shielded whose shield is the Lord. Vain
is all other help. Beside Jehovah there is no God.
All other confidences mock and deceive. He only
stands a rock immovable. All earthly props and
stays are shifting sand ; when the storm comes they
shake and fall.

32, 33, 34, 35, 36. " *It is God that girdeth me with
strength, and maketh my way perfect. He maketh my
feet like hinds' feet, and setteth me upon my high
places. He teacheth my hands to war, so that a bow of
steel is broken by mine arms. Thou hast also given me
the shield of Thy salvation; and Thy right hand hath
holden me up, and Thy gentleness hath made me great.
Thou hast enlarged my steps under me, that my feet did
not slip.*"

Christ waged a ceaseless warfare. Cruel assaults
gave Him no rest. But He could sing that no help
was withheld, and that God's arm wrought glorious
triumphs for Him. We now advance to a terrific fight.
But let no fears unnerve. Our foes are doubtless
many, strong, untiring, raging, infuriate ; but armour
and ability are prepared. The armour is spiritual and
wrought by God, because the enemy is bitter and
satanic. Let us gird ourselves with every portion.
It will be found sufficient. Let us look upwards to
our great Captain. He will infuse courage and might ;
He will gird up our weak loins ; He will instruct us

to use well our weapons. All His dealings will be
tenderness and love. Sweet whispers will encourage;
gentle smiles will animate. Happy experience will at
last clap the hand, and sing, " Thy gentleness hath
made me great." Harshness is not in Him whom our
souls love and our feet follow.

XXIV.

PSALM XVIII. 37–50.

37, 38, 39, 40. " *I have pursued mine enemies, and
overtaken them; neither did I turn again until they
were consumed. I have wounded them that they were
not able to rise: they are fallen under my feet. For
Thou hast girded me with strength unto the battle: Thou
hast subdued under me those that rose up against me.
Thou hast also given me the necks of mine enemies, that
I might destroy them that hate me.*"

David's experience here speaks. When calm in
peace, high in supreme dominion, undisturbed by wars
and hostile menace, he cast his eyes back on his
eventful course. Many indeed had been his fights;
perils frequently had been extreme; but conquest
followed conquest, until he rested on a peaceful
throne. But he knew well that conquering strength
was not his own; he saw the source of his supremacy:
he trampled on the necks of foes because God laid them
low before him. Here is a picture of the aged pilgrim
pondering his bygone trials. He has passed through
outward troubles leaning on his God. The deep waters
overwhelmed not because the heavenly hand sustained.
The lusts, the passions, the corruptions of the inner
man failed to destroy the inner life, because grace was
infused to fan the threatened embers. Faith testifies,
I live because Christ lived within me. Mine is the
joy: the victory is the Lord's. But here the prominent figure is the blessed Jesus. The day fast

comes when He shall reign supreme. Satan and
hell's legion must lick the dust. The wretched multitude who have joined his ranks and fought against
the Gospel-truth must gnash the teeth, all crushed
beneath His chariot-wheels. A kingdom shall be set
up in which pure righteousness shall reign. No foe
shall interrupt the universal peace. No jarring note
shall mar the melody of Hallelujah.

41, 42, 43, 44, 45. *" They cried, but there was none
to save them ; even unto the Lord, but He answered them
not. Then did I beat them small as the dust before the
wind ; I did cast them out as the dirt in the streets. Thou
hast delivered me from the strivings of the people, and
Thou hast made me the head of the heathen : a people
whom I have not known shall serve me. As soon as
they hear of me they shall obey me : the strangers shall
submit themselves unto me. The strangers shall fade
away, and be afraid out of their close places."*

It seems the Spirit's joy to lengthen out the note
of triumph. We see the enemies of Christ at last
convinced of their lost state. They call, they seek,
they bow the knee. But all submission is in vain.
The Word is fulfilled, " I will laugh at your calamity,
I will mock when your fear cometh." How terrible
is that word, " Too late !" Here, too, the Gospel's
triumphs in the heathen world are shadowed forth.
The heathen are His inheritance. The chosen seed
will hear the good Shepherd's voice, and gladly hasten
to salvation's fold.

46, 47, 48. *" The Lord liveth, and blessed be my
rock ; and let the God of my salvation be exalted. It is
God that avengeth me, and subdueth my people under me.*

*He delivereth me from mine enemies ; yea, Thou liftest
me up above those that rise up against me : Thou hast
delivered me from the violent man."*

Praise should never cease. It is a joyful exercise ;
it is the due acknowledgment of countless mercies.
Throughout eternity remembrance will record God's
marvellous aid in days of trouble, and at each remembrance harps will again be struck. The song will
swell anew, " Blessed be our rock ; let the God of our
salvation be exalted."

49. *" Therefore will I give thanks unto Thee, O
Lord, among the heathen, and sing praises unto Thy
name."*

Again we are told of the triumphant song. Let it
be no new song to us ; let its sweet notes be now
familiar to our lips ; let us pray for grace to .realize
the wondrous mercies which encompass us ; let our
thoughts seldom wander from the Cross. Oh ! what
a sight of wonder ! How precious is that expiating
blood ! Let us ponder its worth, and the marvels it
has wrought, till our hearts become one blaze of love,
our lips one note of praise.

50. *" Great deliverance giveth He to His King, and
showeth mercy to His anointed, to David, and to his seed
for evermore."*

Faith gladly answers, Yea, how true ! how true !
Jesus was greatly delivered from all the hate of hell,
from all the bands of death, from every opposing foe.
The typical David lived a long life of constant deliverances. It shall be so to all the promised seed.
Great deliverances are their portion ; constant mercy
is their attendant. May the thought deepen in each

believing heart that they are on the conquering side: that no weapon formed against them shall succeed: that soon the warfare will be all accomplished, and that they shall magnify the conquering Lamb with conquering song! May we sing with them!

XXV.

PSALM XIX.

Two witnesses proclaim God's glory. His Works and Word harmoniously respond. May the joint testimony teach us!

1, 2. *" The heavens declare the glory of God ; and the firmament showeth His handy-work. Day unto day uttereth speech, and night unto night showeth knowledge."*

Debased and senseless is the mind which creation's wonders fail to touch. Survey the canopy above our heads. It is magnificent in all which constitutes beauty and splendour in perfection. From morn to night light strides along its azure path, illumining the world. When evening's shades prevail, the stars hang out their countless lamps, and stud with spangles the brilliant concave. We marvel ; we admire. We trace the great Creator's skill and reverently adore. It must be mighty mind which planned this exquisite machinery. It must be mighty power which framed these glowing orbs, and gave them their appointed courses. They could not will their own formation. They could not deck themselves with brightness. It must, too, be gracious benevolence which arranged such lovely helps and solace for us. On all the heavens God's glory is inscribed. The skies in all their parts show what His hands have wrought. The record never ceases. Day

follows day, repeating the instruction.   Night succeeds
to night, telling the great Creator's praise.

3, 4, 5, 6. *" There is no speech nor language where their
voice is not heard.   Their line is gone out through all the
earth, and their words to the end of the world.   In them
hath He set a tabernacle for the sun ; which is as a bridegroom coming out of his chamber, and rejoiceth as a strong
man to run a race.   His going forth is from the end of
the heaven, and his circuit unto the ends of it : and there
is nothing hid from the heat thereof."*

The lessons of the firmament are universal.   Where-
ever man breathes, in torrid or in frigid zones, the
canopy of day and night speaks the same voice.
Throughout earth's length and breadth the heavens
teach plainly the invisible things of God, even His
eternal power and Godhead.   Let the sun's voice
especially be heard.   The heavens are his splendid
tent.   In the dawn he breaks forth arrayed in gladness, as a joyous bridegroom.   He strides along stately
in giant-strength.   He girds all heaven in his path,
and with his all-penetrating rays searches earth in all
its parts.   In all his course, in all his might, one is
his witness.   God is my Maker.   Worship him.   So
then they are without excuse who read not God in
creation's volume.   The Spirit by the mouth of Paul
declares their guilt, and passes just sentence, and seals
their reprobation.   The Spirit, too, adopts these terms
to show the Gospel's progress through all lands.   Let
this inspirit missionary zeal !

7, 8, 9, 10, 11. *" The law of the Lord is perfect, converting the soul : the testimony of the Lord is sure, making
wise the simple : the statutes of the Lord are right, rejoic-*

*ing the heart : the commandment of the Lord is pure,
enlightening the eyes : the fear of the Lord is clean, enduring for ever : the judgments of the Lord are true, and
righteous altogether.   More to be desired are they than
gold, yea, than much fine gold ; sweeter also than honey,
and the honey-comb.   Moreover, by them is Thy servant
warned : and in keeping of them there is great reward."*

From the witness of God's Works there is an easy
transit to the witness of His Word.   Both spring from
the same source ; both spread abroad the same truth—
God's glory.   Six distinct titles here designate the
Word.   Each bears a separate character, and each
describes a separate effect.   How worthy is this glorious Word of constant study ! Let it be read on
bended knee till all its efficacy moulds our hearts.
None are so wise and happy as the Bible-taught.   This
study is the richest feast.   It regales the soul far
more than sweetest dainties can please the palate.   It
gives wise warning for our every hour.   Obedience is
wise blessedness.

12, 13. *" Who can understand his errors ? cleanse Thou
me from secret faults.   Keep back Thy servant also from
presumptuous sins ; let them not have dominion over me :
then shall I be upright, and I shall be innocent from the
great transgression."*

Every step which strays from the strict path of
perfect love is error.   Who can count up these countless deviations ! They far exceed the ocean's sands.
They may be hidden from man's eye, but all are patent
to omniscient scrutiny.   Let the thought drive us to
the all-atoning blood, and prompt the earnest prayer,
Cleanse me, O Jesu, cleanse.   Especially let us seek

grace to keep us from bold sins of mad presumption against God's rule. Indulged, they soon establish habits which rule with tyrant's force; and may lead to sin against the Spirit, for which no pardon can be found.

14. "*Let the words of my mouth, and the meditation of my heart, be acceptable in Thy sight, O Lord, my strength, and my Redeemer.*"

Precious, indeed, will be this psalm if it thus leads to wrestling hold of Christ, who is all strength and all redemption to us.

XXVI.

PSALM XX.

INTERCESSION is our duty and our privilege. Trust in
God secures success. May we be encouraged to pray
and not to faint !

1, 2. " *The Lord hear thee in the day of trouble; the
name of the God of Jacob defend thee. Send thee help
from the sanctuary, and strengthen thee out of Zion.*"

David desires entreaties for himself, and suggests
petitions for his praying people. He was tossed on
the waves of ever-swelling trouble. At home, abroad,
there was incessant din of war. He knew the only
source of true success. He excites others to besiege
heaven for him. In his kingly office he was a clear
type of Christ. In this type David's great Lord and
Son stoops to solicit prayer. He stands before us as
one in need; troubles grow thick around Him; the
whole artillery of hell assails; He looked to heaven,
and asks others to crave audience for Him. We can
look back and see how answers came. All the perfections of God which constitute His name came forth
in His behalf. The God of Jacob was His shield.
The heavens opened. A ministering angel hastened
to uphold the prostrate God-man.

3. " *Remember all Thy offerings, and accept thy burnt-
sacrifice.*"

In this petition faith looks onward to the great

Redeemer. Jesus indeed made offering to God. He offered Himself the victim upon the altar: He laid down His life a whole burnt-sacrifice: He fulfilled all which every blazing altar and every bleeding victim had prefigured: He was not spared. Avenging wrath descended, and fullest penalty was inflicted. Justice presented scales, and they received their whole demands. It is our joy to know that the shed blood prevailed. Each faithful suppliant can remind our God that full atonement has been made for every sin; that all due wrath has been expended on our surety; that His death is our death; His sufferings are our sufferings; His payment is our payment; the curse inflicted upon Him is our redemption. We may kneel joyfully before the throne, and with assurance cry, Remember the offering of the dying Jesus; accept the burnt-sacrifice of the atoning Lamb.

4. " *Grant Thee according to Thine own heart, and fulfil all Thy counsel.*"

The heart of Christ is fixed on God's glory. He cries, " Thy law is within My heart." His burning desire was that all God's attributes should receive honour from His work. This glory is secured when mercy and truth meet together, righteousness and peace kiss each other. All His desire shall be accomplished. He shall see of the travail of His soul and shall be satisfied. Success shall gloriously crown His work. The Gospel-scheme shall triumph.

5. " *We will rejoice in thy salvation, and in the name of our God we will set up our banners: the Lord fulfil all thy petitions.*"

The Church beholds salvation won and all desires

of Christ fulfilled. It is a wondrous, precious, glorious sight. God is honoured; Christ is magnified; sinners are saved. What is the feeling which breaks forth? It is joy—joy unspeakable and full of glory. Let every heart be glad, let every lip sing praise. In knowledge of this manifested glory let us unfold the banner; let us press to the ranks of the redeemed; let us march in happy fellowship to Immanuel's land.

6. " *Now know I that the Lord saveth His anointed: He will hear him from His holy heaven with the saving strength of His right hand.*"

The life in the believer's soul, his clear perception of redemption's truth, his realizing views of deep interest in Christ, leave no doubt that Christ was heard in all His prayers, and that God put forth all the strength of His right hand to bring Him through His work. Oh! blessed knowledge of all precious truth!

7, 8. " *Some trust in chariots, and some in horses; but we will remember the name of the Lord our God. They are brought down and fallen; but we are risen, and stand upright.*"

The folly of carnal confidence is next portrayed. Except the Lord be on our side, the multitude of war-like equipage are as the chaff before the wind. The Lord speaks, and Pharaoh and his hosts fall an easy prey to the unsparing sea, while Israel, relying on their God, stand conquerors on the shore, and sing the song of triumph. Holy Spirit! open our eyes to see our nothingness in ourselves! Our best is worthless. May we eschew all fancied righteousness, and fix adoring thoughts on the great name and saving work of Jesus!

9. "*Save, Lord: let the King hear us when we call.*"

Salvation should be the first and foremost, the sum and substance, of our every desire. What will all earth, and all earth's treasures, and all earth's pleasures profit, except our souls be saved! For salvation let our cry besiege heaven's gates. Happy the thought that on the throne a King is seated who never casts out prayer! Let us come boldly, and importune assiduously. Calling in Christ's name, we cannot fail. We have a motto for this day and evermore—"Save, Lord: let the King hear us when we call."

XXVII.

PSALM XXI.

THIS ode of triumph celebrates our exalted Head. May we thus sing on earth by faith, and lengthen out the strain through endless days!

1, 2. *" The king shall joy in Thy strength, O Lord; and in Thy salvation how greatly shall he rejoice! Thou hast given him his heart's desire, and hast not withholden the request of his lips."*

We fall far short of this psalm's precious teaching if we restrict our musings to the type. Let David first be seen rejoicing in his royal crown, but let him soon fade before the rising of the King of kings. Here we may bathe our souls in the deep waters of Christ's truth. For the joy set before Him, He endured the cross, despising the shame. But the joy then in prospect is joy now fully realized. He sits rejoicing on the Father's right hand. The conflict is past; the battle is fought; the victory is won; every peril is escaped; every foe is vanquished. He has been strong to conquer, and He ascribes the strength to God's empowering hand. Salvation is achieved; it is salvation through the will and help of God, and in it greatly He exults. The utmost desires of His heart are granted. He could not wish nor ask for more. The cup of gladness overflows.

3. *" For Thou preventest him with the blessings of*

goodness : Thou settest a crown of pure gold on his head."

During the struggle and the deep abasement, God ever went before Him, strewing blessings in His path ; God's goodness ever paved His way.   And now He is crowned—crowned as Conqueror, crowned as King. High is the throne on which He sits ; omnipotent is the sceptre which He wields.   The government is placed upon His shoulders.   All power is given Him in heaven and in earth.   Happy the subjects of this triumphant Lord !

4. *" He asked life of Thee, and Thou gavest it him, even length of days for ever and ever."*

In deepest agony He cried unto God, who was able to save Him from death, and His prayer was heard. The word is fulfilled, " With long life will I satisfy Him, and show Him my salvation."   Our High Priest appears, and His happy testimony is, " I am He that liveth and was dead ; and behold I am alive for evermore, Amen, and have the keys of hell and of death."   He is the resurrection and the life.   He is our life.   All who are one with Him have for their portion the everlasting life of glory.

5, 6, 7. *" His glory is great in Thy salvation : honour and majesty hast Thou laid upon him.   For Thou hast made him most blessed for ever : Thou hast made him exceeding glad with Thy countenance.   For the king trusteth in the Lord ; and through the mercy of the Most High he shall not be moved."*

The Spirit multiplies to show Christ's present blessedness.   Great is His glory through God's saving hand.   He is heir of all the majesty which heaven can give. He is God over all, blessed for evermore. Blessed Himself, He holds all blessings for His people. We, too, are blessed with all spiritual blessings in heavenly places in Him. But what is His all-surpassing joy ? It is to bask for ever in His heavenly Father's smile. If He has sympathy with us, should not we, too, have sympathy with Him ? If our sorrows are His sorrows, should not His joy be ours ? It is added that His joy is the fruit of faith. He trusted and is thus exalted. Let us believe and we shall similarly triumph.

8, 9, 10, 11, 12. "*Thine hand shall find out all Thine enemies; Thy right hand shall find out those that hate Thee. Thou shalt make them as a fiery oven in the time of Thine anger: the Lord shall swallow them up in His wrath, and the fire shall devour them. Their fruit shalt Thou destroy from the earth, and their seed from among the children of men. For they intended evil against thee; they imagined a mischievous device, which they are not able to perform: therefore shalt Thou make them turn their back, when Thou shalt make ready thine arrows upon thy strings against the face of them.*"

Jesus arises from His throne to consummate His final victory. Then screening refuges shall fail. They shall call upon rocks and mountains to conceal. They shall flee into every hiding-place which terror can devise. But wrath shall drag them forth. Fearful images portray their hopeless ruin. They shall agonize as in the flames of burning ovens. Fire shall seize them as its prey. Immitigable anguish shall devour them. How vain will be their flight when the arrows of the Most High pursue them! When that day shall come, may we be on the Conqueror's side!

13. *" Be Thou exalted, Lord, in Thine own strength : so will we sing and praise Thy power."*

Such is the fitting chorus to this song of triumph. Let every believer's voice call Jesus to His final exaltation. When that great day shall come, may we lift up the voice and celebrate His glorious power! Let us exalt Him now in heart, by life, in lip, by every faculty, and at each moment. Let the eternal song be no new song to us!

XXVIII.

PSALM XXII. 1–10.

THE deepest anguish of our suffering Lord is here portrayed. The story of the Cross is told in minute detail. Light breaks forth at last. May we gaze and adore !

———————

1, 2. "*My God, my God, why hast Thou forsaken me? why art Thou so far from helping me, and from the words of my roaring? O my God, I cry in the day-time, but Thou hearest not; and in the night-season, and am not silent.*"

We take our stand at Calvary. The Cross is erected. Jesus, the God-man, our proxy, our Redeemer, hangs thereon. We look, and we receive assurance that verily He is bearing our curse, and drinking to the dregs our cup of wrath, and receiving into His inmost soul the sword of justice, and suffering the extremities of penal anguish. For three hours the grossest darkness veils the world. We may not pierce the mystery. What mind could bear to realize the tremendous transaction ? We learn all that we need to know from the shrill cry which burst from the sufferer's heart. He testifies that God, His God, was no more present. His countenance was wholly hid. Utter desertion overwhelmed Him. He cried for help, but no help came. He roared through extremest anguish, and was not

silent; but no answer came. It was the hour and
power of darkness. Hell could not do more to terrify
and excruciate. He was abandoned to its fury: He
was surrendered to its worst. Here we have fullest
proof that our Lord's sufferings were real; but they
were not for Himself. They were all really substitutional. We have a real curse-bearer, and we really
suffer in Him. But against all feeling, when all things
were most adverse, faith still survived and retained
hold of God. From desertion's lowest depth faith
cried, " My God, my God.'

3, 4, 5. " *But Thou art holy, O Thou that inhabitest*
the praises of Israel. Our fathers trusted in Thee: they
trusted, and Thou didst deliver them. They cried unto
Thee, and were delivered: they trusted in Thee, and were
not confounded."

It is faith's happy province, when outward comforts
utterly depart, still to justify God. Faith cannot
blame, disparage, or cast doubt on Him. Against all
outward sense it knows and witnesses that God is
holy; it knows that God is entitled to all praise.
Praise is His due desert: His people's praises are His
home. In darkest times faith gathers strength from
ages of experience: it looks to the elders of God's
house: they all were partakers of confiding grace.
It is thrice repeated that they trusted. To trust
they added prayer. The end was sure. Deliverance came, and they were not ashamed. Though
He slay us, yet let us trust Him. Light is sown for
the righteous. We read a wondrous word as falling
from the lips of Jesus—" Our fathers." He states
that He is thoroughly one with us. He is born very

man, a member of our family : our fathers are His fathers, and His Father is our Father.

6. " *But I am a worm, and no man ; a reproach of men, and despised of the people.*"

Jesus foresaw His deep humiliation. He takes the place of a scorned reptile. He is deemed scarcely worthy to be ranked on a level with the human race. In after days the prophet sounded a like note of degradation. He is despised and rejected of men, a man of sorrows and acquainted with grief, and we hid, as it were, our faces from Him. Let us gratefully remember that His low estate is our exaltation. He thus sinks that we may be uplifted.

7, 8. " *All they that see me laugh me to scorn : they shoot out the lip, they shake the head, saying, He trusted on the Lord that He would deliver Him : let Him deliver Him, seeing He delighted in Him.*"

We return to Calvary. The whole scene here appears in predictive light. As the prophet wrote, so literally it was transacted. Hear the inspired historian : " They that passed by reviled Him, wagging their heads.—Likewise also the chief priests, mocking Him, with the scribes and elders, said, He trusted in God ; let Him deliver Him now, if He will have Him." The sight of extremest misery moved not their cruel hearts. They revelled in their victim's pain : their sneers and taunts wound deeper than the nails. His grief surpassed all grief, even as His love exceeded love. By these His stripes we are healed.

9, 10. " *But Thou art He that took me out of the womb ; Thou didst make me hope when I was upon my*

*mother's breasts. I was cast upon Thee from the womb:
Thou art my God from my mother's belly."*

Faith draws support from recollection of the earliest
mercies. The goodness which watched over infancy
and childhood are too often overlooked as common
dealings. But the enlightened eye in all this watchful
care discerns God's gracious hand. It is our wisdom
to trace each providence to special love. They dwell
in regions of delight who see God everywhere, and
in all concerns. In all things Christ is our bright
example! May He who is the giver of all faith give
unto us faith strong as His own! As He trusted, so
may we trust!

XXIX.

PSALM XXII. 11–21.

11. "*Be not far from me, for trouble is near; for there is none to help.*"

Faith quickly flies to God. Its feet frequent the well-known path of prayer. In nearness of trouble it finds nearness to the mercy-seat. Absence of human help is not a loss if it secures the help of heaven. Welcome all earthly destitution, if God supply the void.

12, 13. "*Many bulls have compassed me: strong bulls of Bashan have beset me round. They gaped upon me with their mouths, as a ravening and a roaring lion.*"

We return in spirit to the cross. The dying Jesus looks around; multitudes beset Him; with open mouth ferociously they gape. Throughout the mass there is no sign of pity; all hearts seem dead to common feelings of humanity; they show the properties of the wildest beasts; they are savage as the untamed bull; they thirst for blood as the devouring lion. This is the saddest picture of man's malignity. What frightful fury raged against Jesus, the perfect model of holiness and love! His only offence was that He trod this earth as God. We see what man is when no grace restrains. If we love Jesus, whom the world thus hated, let us give praise to grace, which causes us to differ.

14, 15. "*I am poured out like water, and all my bones are out of joint: my heart is like wax; it is melted in the midst of my bowels. My strength is dried up like a potsherd; and my tongue cleaveth to my jaws; and Thou hast brought me into the dust of death."*

The suffering Jesus thus described His miserable state. In graphic terms He tells of His extremity of agony and His extremity of weakness. The pain · of the cross was bitterest pain ; the weight of the body, suspended by the nailed hands and feet, violently strained the whole frame. It was almost dislocation of each bone ; every joint was wrenched. But still no bone may suffer fracture. A clear type announced their soundness, and wondrously was the type fulfilled. The picture shows the whole frame dissolving ; it retains no firmness, no consistency ; it utterly yields and flows away in weakness, as resistless water yields to touch. Strength of spirit, too, collapses. As wax melts, softens, and offers no resistance to subduing heat, so the heart lay prostrate beneath subduing misery. What is so weak and brittle as the clay of the potter baked and dried up by fire ? So the fire of God's wrath brought down to nothingness the sufferer's strength. The clammy mouth showed that the vital juices were dried up, and death usurped undisturbed dominion. In all this anguish Jesus realizes His heavenly Father's hand. This is Thy doing. I sink into the dust of death. But Thy hand thus lays Me low.—Jesus thus dies, because His people were thus sentenced ; and He thus mounts the cross to die their death, that He might bear to the uttermost their curse. He mercifully selects a term to show how exactly He bore their penalty. The sentence said, " Unto dust thou shalt return." Jesus calls God to witness, "Thou hast brought Me into the dust of death."

16, 17, 18. "*For dogs have compassed me ; the assembly of the wicked have enclosed me : they pierced my hands and my feet. I may tell all my bones: they look and stare upon me. They part my garments among them, and cast lots upon my vesture.*"

This wondrous passage establishes beyond all controversy that none but Jesus is the subject of this Psalm. To none other can these terms apply. In Him they receive entire and exact fulfilment. Another prophet writes, "They shall look upon Me whom they have pierced." The history relates the very fact. No ground is left on which unbelief can place its foot. Let us give thanks, knowing that by these wounds we are saved, by these stripes we are healed. The very garments of our suffering Lord are here foretold ; the seamless texture of His upper vest ; the mode in which they are distributed ; the Roman soldiers utterly without knowledge of this Scripture, devoid of all intention to accomplish, worked them out to the very letter. It is a wondrous word, "These things also the soldiers did."

19, 20, 21. "*But be not Thou far from me, O Lord : O my strength, haste Thee to help me. Deliver my soul from the sword ; my darling from the power of the dog. Save me from the lion's mouth : for Thou hast heard me from the horns of the unicorns.*"

Here new images appear to show the bloodthirsty rage of the unrelenting murderers. We have seen their fury as bulls and lions ; we now see their fierceness as dogs and unicorns. Fierce fury could not be more

fierce.   Again, we see that no trials can quench the
flame of faith, or check its rapid flight to God.   It
ever realizes, When I am weak in myself, I have God
for my strength.   In the lowest depths of misery, it
clings to deliverance as a sure anchor.   Jesus testifies
on the cross, " Thou hast heard Me."   He was not saved
from dying : but He was saved from death.   He died,
for He must endure our death.   But death could not
detain. He lives again ; He was fully heard.   Glorious
victory !   He dies for us, and by His death, He has
abolished death.

XXX.

PSALM XXII. 22–31.

22. " *I will declare Thy name unto my brethren : in the midst of the congregation will I praise Thee.*"

The horrors of the cross give place to joy. From this deepest misery we hear a jubilant note. Jesus now speaks as risen from the dust of death, as going forth arrayed in power, and crowned with majesty and honour. He states His mission to reveal to the Church all the perfections of His heavenly Father, and ever present by His Spirit in the assemblies of His people, to fill their mouths with Jehovah's praise. He will make their hearts a flood of gratitude, and cause the streams of thanksgiving to overflow. How great is His mercy and condescension in thus uniting us to Himself as brethren! He who is Jehovah's fellow, one in essence with the Father, God over all, blessed for evermore, looks with intensest love on us poor miserable worms and vilest sinners, and is not ashamed to call us brethren. In the days of His abode on earth we hear His voice, " Go unto my brethren : " again, " Go, tell my brethren." We adore Him as Firstborn among many brethren. Let us with all boldness ever draw near, and tell Him our every sorrow and our every need. He has a loving brother's loving heart towards us.

23, 24. " *Ye that fear the Lord, praise Him: all ye the seed of Jacob, glorify Him ; and fear Him, all ye the seed of Israel. For He hath not despised nor abhorred*

*the affliction of the afflicted; neither hath He hid His
face from him; but when he cried unto Him, He
heard."*

From the cross the voice of Jesus stirs up His
people to laud and glorify His Father's name. They
are described as they who fear. Their filial love is
ever tremulous of giving offence. Their love is mingled
with revering awe. Mercy to Jesus on the cross is a
rich topic of thanksgiving. He was, indeed, the despised and rejected of men. He drank the bitterest
dregs of affliction's cup. But though for a while forsaken of the Father, He was ever His dearly beloved,
and His every prayer was heard and answered. Warmed
by this thought, let us obey our Lord, and sing God's
praises, ardent with love, lowly in fear.

25. *" My praise shall be of Thee in the great congregation: I will pay my vows before them that fear Him."*

The heart of Jesus is ever intent to bring glory to
the Father. It is His joy to awaken the notes of
praise wherever His congregations meet. He remembers, too, the work which He is pledged to execute.
Never will He cease, never will He remit His efforts,
until the whole company, given by the Father's love,
are sought and found, are melted and renewed, and
brought by faith to welcome His complete salvation.

26, 27, 28. *" The meek shall eat and be satisfied; they
shall praise the Lord that seek Him: your heart shall live
for ever. All the ends of the world shall remember, and
turn unto the Lord; and all the kindreds of the nations
shall worship before Thee. For the kingdom is the Lord's;
and He is the Governor among the nations."*

Another distinctive mark of Christ's little flock is

meekness. They are true followers of Him who sweetly said, "I am meek and lowly in heart." Abundance of refreshing feast is provided for them. Christ is their bread of life. Christ is their daily manna. Christ is their feast of fat things. They hear His welcome, "Eat, O friends, drink, yea, drink abundantly, O beloved." They are fully satisfied, and they return abundant praise. Jesus, though dying, knew that He should live for ever, and living would be the life of all who trusted in Him. Surely their life is far from harm who know that "their life is hid with Christ in God." At present the world is full of all disquietude and evil. But this confusion and iniquity will soon give place to the reign of righteousness. Christ is heir of all things. His righteous throne will soon be set, and then from the rising of the sun to its decline pure worship will be given to Him.

29, 30, 31. "*All they that be fat upon earth shall eat and worship : all they that go down to the dust shall bow before Him ; and none can keep alive his own soul. A seed shall serve Him ; it shall be accounted to the Lord for a generation. They shall come, and shall declare His righteousness unto a people that shall be born, that He hath done this.*"

The sorrows of the cross end in glorious triumph. What marvels of extensive blessedness spring from these seeds of agony and blood! The Word shall receive full accomplishment, "Wherefore God also hath highly exalted Him, and given Him a name which is above every name, that at the name of Jesus every knee should bow, of things in heaven, and things in earth, and things under the earth." Until the bright

H

day of His return, a constant succession called by His grace, quickened by His Spirit, adopted into His family, shall spring up to call Him Lord, and render devout service. They shall flow on in uninterrupted streams, proclaiming from age to age His glorious righteousness, as their robe to justify, as their ornament for heaven. Rejoicing in full salvation, they shall ascribe all to His finished work. Deep in self-abasement, they shall magnify His grace. One shall be their song. This glory is all His work. He hath done this. May we thus sing !

XXXI.

PSALM XXIII.

JESUS leads His flock like a shepherd.   May we rejoice in the delights of His fold !

———————

1. " *The Lord is my Shepherd, I shall not want.*"

Happy the soul that, looking to Jesus as the great, the good, the one Shepherd, can add in truth, And He is mine.   I have heard His calling voice; I have seen His inviting smile; I have fled to Him; I have entered into His fold; I have committed myself to His guardian care; He has received me; He has given me most gracious welcome; " I am my Beloved's, and my Beloved is mine."   With what joyous rapture may the inmate of the fold continue, " I shall not want !"   How can need be mine ?   He who is pledged to my support has all resources in His hand; He has all power in heaven and earth.   He who has promised to give me eternal life will not suffer me to perish by the way.   The end secured is security along the road. We sometimes err in our desires.   In blindness we crave injurious pastures.   It is our wisdom to leave all to Him.   He is all wisdom and all love.   He will tend wisely and most kindly.   All good things will assuredly abound.   Perhaps we err if we claim this psalm as our exclusive portion.   Jesus Himself once knew the need of the poor sheep; but He found a

Shepherd in His heavenly Father, and He lacked nothing.

2. "*He maketh me to lie down in green pastures: He leadeth me beside the still waters.*"

A picture of rural beauty expands before us. We see a happy flock resting in calm quietness in fields rich in luxuriant plenty; we see them guided to meadows through which refreshing streams glide tranquilly. The scene is perfect. Here is repose amid abundance. Nothing disturbs the calm enjoyment. The antitype is the believer's soul secure from all alarms, peaceful in knowledge of the Lord's protection, feasting on the rich provision of His Word, regaled with sustaining promises, nurtured by the Spirit's rich supplies, reposing under the shadow of the cross, drinking the cooling streams of scriptural teaching, delighting in the sacramental feast. How ample is this sweet provision! Who will not thankfully exclaim, "I have all, and abound?" — This picture also exhibits Jesus. Amid His many troubles His soul could calmly rest on the assurance of His Father's love, and feed rejoicingly on covenant engagement.

3. "*He restoreth my soul: He leadeth me in the paths of righteousness for His name's sake.*"

There are times when grace appears to fade, when trials trouble and depress, when lively vigour faints and deadness chills the soul. Sad indeed would be the issue unless the watchful Shepherd rendered succour; but He assists the downcast; He shows reviving smiles; He brings the cordial of some precious promise. The withering leaf renews its

freshness; the tottering limbs again are strong; the
heavenward path in ways of righteousness is again
stoutly trod. Jesus often drank depression's weakening
cup. His soul was troubled; but help from above
restored unwavering strength.

4. " *Yea, though I walk through the valley of the
shadow of death, I will fear no evil: for Thou art with
me; Thy rod and Thy staff they comfort me.*"

Our sorest trial is when, with feeble step, we traverse
the cheerless vale of death. The clime is chilly.
Nature fails. We shrink from the icy hand; but
still there is no fear. The tender Shepherd is by
our side: His gentle guidance removes apprehension.
The waters fail to overwhelm. Sweet texts bring
light, and the Spirit applies comfort. Thy rod, Thy
staff, the emblems of the Shepherd's care, drive back
the threatening foes, and give sustaining strength.
To lean on Jesus in the darkest hour is light and joy
and peace. The Good Shepherd knows the chilly hand
of death. He has passed this darksome vale; but His
God was with Him. Ministering angels brought
support. He found no evil, and no evil shall destroy
His sheep.

5. " *Thou preparest a table before me in the presence of
mine enemies: Thou anointest my head with oil; my cup
runneth over.*"

Our enemies stand round in vast array, but they
cannot destroy enjoyments. In their sight God spread
a banquet of delights. His inward unction causes
the heart to show all kinds of radiant joy, as the
countenance refreshed with unguents. We hold a
cup: God's hand supplies it: He pours in pleasures

to the extent of capacity to receive. The overjoyed believer feels, " Stay, stay ; it is enough ; " but still the goblet overflows. Who can measure the delights of God's presence, smile, and word ?

6. " *Surely goodness and mercy shall follow me all the days of my life ; and I will dwell in the house of the Lord for ever.*"

Such is faith's sweet assurance. While days below continue, goodness and mercy, close as closest shadow, shall bring up the rear. What good thing can be absent if the Lord be present, and Jesus confirms the pledge, " Lo, I am with you all the days, even to the end of the world ? " Failure there can never be. No sheep will perish or be left behind. All will be safely gathered in the many-mansioned house. There will the Great Shepherd ever dwell amid His ransomed flock. Great Shepherd, Thou art our all ; we lovingly adore Thee !

XXXII.

PSALM XXIV.

JESUS ascends in triumph to His throne in heaven. May we in spirit thither ascend, and with Him continually dwell!

1, 2. "*The earth is the Lord's, and the fulness thereof; the world, and they that dwell therein: for He hath founded it upon the seas, and established it upon the floods.*"

A noble chorus ushers in this ode of triumph. Loud acclamations tell that God is the great Creator, the sovereign owner of the universe. Language contains not a grander sentence than the words first seen upon the Bible-page, "In the beginning God created the heavens and the earth." He bade the dry land to appear, and to rest on subsiding waters as its supporting column. All nations who throng its surface, all animal and vegetable life, all its rich treasures, all its lovely beauty, receive their being from His word. He spake and they were made. His rightful lordship is indisputable. We are His, and He made us. With what lowly reverence should we bow before Him! How meekly should we yield to His supremacy! How constant should our efforts be to glorify Him with body, soul, and spirit, which are His!

3. "*Who shall ascend into the hill of the Lord? or who shall stand in His holy place?*"

He who pervades all space, whose centre is everywhere
and circumference nowhere, is represented to our minds
as reigning in an especial palace. An earthly city was
the type of this heavenly abode. The hill of Zion
which received the Ark was symbol of His presence.
Hence the inquiry, Who shall live and reign for ever
with the Lord ? is aptly symbolized by asking, Who
shall mount the hill of Zion, and have firm footing in
the holy place. How studiously should we examine
our claim to such felicity !

4, 5, 6. " *He that hath clean hands, and a pure heart ;
who hath not lifted up his soul unto vanity, nor sworn
deceitfully. He shall receive the blessing from the Lord,
and righteousness from the God of His salvation. This
is the generation of them that seek Him, that seek Thy
face, O Jacob.*"

It is a grand and everlasting truth, " Without holiness no man shall see the Lord." His dwelling is
essential purity. No speck of sin can enter where He
dwells. Hence no one who ever breathed life's breath
or trod this earth, save Jesus, can enter by His own
right and in His own name. His hands alone were
never stained by sin : His heart alone was one home
of unsullied purity. No vain things had attraction for
His mind. No guile defiled His spirit. He had full
claims to all the blessings of the New Jerusalem.
Justly He receives His due. But this blessedness belongs not only to the Head ; His members share with
Him. All who by faith are one with Him, all who
constitute His body, are clean, and pure, and righteous,
even as He is. His all-cleansing blood for ever washes
out their many sins. His glorious righteousness is

reckoned as their very own. His indwelling Spirit wholly sanctifies their inner man. Hence through grace they shall ascend the holy hill; hence they shall stand within the holy place. This is the chosen generation, the royal priesthood, the holy nation, the peculiar people. The Spirit helping, they seek the Lord with all the heart, even the face of the great God of Jacob.

7. "*Lift up your heads, O ye gates; and be ye lift up, ye everlasting doors; and the King of glory shall come in.*"

The Spirit here exhibits a wondrous picture of our Lord's triumphal ascent. We are taught to see Him drawing near attended by multitudes of the heavenly host. He reaches the gates of the eternal citadel. Admittance is demanded; the portals are summoned to fly open. The gates so barred against rebellious man are now commanded to uplift their heads. It is announced that the King of glory stands without.

8. "*Who is this King of glory? The Lord strong and mighty, the Lord mighty in battle.*"

The guardians of the portals are represented as responding. They must be certified of the claim of Him who thus draws near. They ask, Proclaim His name, His purport, and His right. Why is He free to enter? A ready answer cries, "The Lord strong and mighty, the Lord mighty in battle." Jesus is returned; He went forth strong in the might of His omnipotence to do battle against Satan and hell, and death and the grave. The fight is fought, the victory is won. All enemies are dashed to pieces. He is here, dragging the captives fast bound to His victorious wheels; He comes crowned with all conquest. Admit Him. The crown is His by right of Satan's empire demolished. The exulting challenge is repeated.

9. " *Lift up your heads, O ye gates ; even lift them up, ye everlasting doors ; and the King of glory shall come in.*"

The inquiry, the response, are still the same.

10. " *Who is this King of glory ?　The Lord of hosts, He is the King of glory.*"

Lo, He is enthroned on the right hand of the Majesty on high. May our poor hearts lift up their heads ! May He there sit and rule, and reign for ever !

XXXIII.

PSALM XXV. I–II.

REPENTANCE and contrition find vent in confession and prayer. May these holy exercises be the home of our souls !

---

1. *" Unto Thee, O Lord, do I lift up my soul."*

Sweet are the hours of intercourse with God. At every moment we may draw near. The way stands widely open through the rent veil. Christ's body broken and His streaming blood procure immediate access. But true prayer is not formality. It is soul-work. In it the world and all its cares and vanities are left behind. Faith spreads rejoicing wings and soars above the heaven of heavens. The man of prayer lifts up his soul.

2, 3. *" O my God, I trust in Thee: let me not be ashamed; let not mine enemies triumph over me. Yea, let none that wait on Thee be ashamed : let them be ashamed which transgress without cause."*

It is faith's holy privilege to deal unreservedly with God : to open out its real condition : to call Him to witness that all vain confidences are renounced, and that all trust rests on Him. Such may fearlessly supplicate that no disappointments may cause shame ; and that no foes may humble them. They who lift up the soul to God will lift up the head above all the fears of men. Faith, too, is an expansive grace. Its arms embrace all true believers. It strives that others should share its blessedness. But it well knows that shame must be the sinner's doom. For sin there cannot be excuse. No cause provokes it. The sinner sins because it is his nature and his will.

4, 5, 6. "*Show me Thy ways, O Lord; teach me Thy paths. Lead me in Thy truth, and teach me: for Thou art the God of my salvation; on Thee do I wait all the day. Remember, O Lord, Thy tender mercies and Thy loving-kindnesses; for they have been ever of old.*"

Faith is emboldened to ask great things from knowledge of the character and works of God. It can appeal, Thou art the God who willed and wrought salvation for me: it is Thy purpose and decree to save me to the uttermost. Hence Thou hast given Jesus for me, and me to Jesus. It can look back to a long train of tender mercies from the earliest days. It joys to count them out before the Lord. It plies the argument, Thou hast been very gracious. Thou art the same. Oh! be Thou gracious now; and on these cogent grounds it bases the prayer, " Show me Thy ways; lead me, teach me." I am blind, and prone to err. Open my eyes clearly at each moment to discern Thy will. Take my outstretched hand and guide me safely in salvation's path. All the day I need Thy help, and seek it; all the day be Thou my ready guide.

7. "*Remember not the sins of my youth, nor my transgressions: according to Thy mercy remember Thou me for Thy goodness' sake, O Lord.*"

In the case of the ungodly, sins forgotten by him are not sins forgiven. In the case of the believer, sins forgiven by God are not obliterated from memory. The believer ofttimes reviews his course from earliest years; he reads and re-reads the annals of the past. They are dark, and stained with countless sins and countless aggravations. He is humbled to the dust. But he remembers Jesus, and God's boundless love in Him. He flees from the court of justice to the throne of grace. He pleads, nor pleads in vain, that God would deal with him in accordance with the covenant of grace.

8, 9. " *Good and upright is the Lord; therefore will He teach sinners in the way. The meek will He guide in judgment; and the meek will He teach His way.*"

When prayer pauses, faith gathers strength in meditation. It reflects that God is love, and faithfulness, and truth. It refreshes itself at this deep well of consolation. God's goodness calls; His promises assure. Therefore no sinner, coming in penitence and faith, may fear repulse. A ready welcome will be granted. The teaching Spirit will guide wisely. All who are truly humbled and thus wear the livery of the chosen flock will tread assuredly salvation's road.

10. " *All the paths of the Lord are mercy and truth unto such as keep His covenant and His testimonies.*"

May grace be ever ours to adhere closely to the everlasting covenant; to base all our hopes on Christ, its surety, in whom all its terms are fully satisfied, and who, by His Spirit, reveals its purport to us. May the like grace enable us to study diligently His holy precepts, and to keep our feet most steadily in their path. Then how blessed will be our earthly course! All God's dealings with us, though sometimes dark to sense, will issue from unfailing love, and prove that His Word is immovable as the everlasting hills.

11. *" For Thy name's sake, O Lord, pardon mine ini-quity ; for it is great."*

Prayer cannot long be silent. The burden of sin will press again. It will again appear in aggravated colours. Its magnitude deepens the sense of need of pardon. It proves that there is no remedy but in free grace. It clearly sees that God's glory is His forgive-ness of all sin through the blood and righteousness of Christ. It therefore descends more lowlily in contri-tion's vale, and importunes more loudly that God would gain glory in the way of pardon. Great, indeed, is our iniquity. May we confess our miserable state, and not remit our cries, that God's glory may be great in blotting all out !

XXXIV.

PSALM XXV. 12—22.

12, 13. " *What man is he that feareth the Lord ?   Him shall He teach in the way that He shall choose.   His soul shall dwell at ease ; and His seed shall inherit the earth.*"

We do not err when we discern Christ Jesus as the high and full response.   In Him each grace was perfect.   In His earthly course His holy reverence was supreme.   He ever knew by heavenly light His appointed path.   His calm serenity was never ruffled. And He looked onward to the blissful time when His seed in countless multitudes should reign undoubted heirs of earth.   All His children are conformed to His image.   With lowly awe they reverence their God. His fear restrains the movement of their minds. His Spirit guides their steps.   Their souls are kept in perfect peace.   And yet a little while the full delights of the millennial reign shall cause their cup to overflow.

14. " *The secret of the Lord is with them that fear Him ; and He will show them His covenant.*"

There are heights and depths of truth in the everlasting covenant which unaided man can neither reach nor fathom.   The Gospel-scheme is a wondrous volume. No eye without God's light can rightly read its pages. But to all who tremble at the Word, the enlightening Spirit comes.   He opens out the hidden mysteries. He draws aside the veil and shows the secret transactions in the courts of heaven : and all the wondrous

achievements of Christ's life and death. The enrap-
tured soul sees truths which angels ponder with amaze.
Who can describe the ecstasies of this knowledge?
But all the pupils in this school of light have one
mark; they fear the Lord.

15, 16. " *Mine eyes are ever toward the Lord; for He
shall pluck my feet out of the net. Turn Thee unto
me, and have mercy upon me; for I am desolate and
afflicted.*"

When we can realize possession of the true principles
of faith, we may claim all its privileges. Faith's eye
is fixed on God. It swerves not from its polar star,
therefore it reaps the rich abundance of the promises.
Deliverance from every snare is pledged. Therefore
with eye never turning from God, the believer walks
securely through a path beset with snares. As it
moves onward it is constant in petition. It often feels
that loneliness and trouble depress, that friends are
few, and sorrows many; but it faints not. It has
firm trust that God will tenderly regard; that mercy
will never fail; that no billows will overwhelm true
faith.

17, 18. " *The troubles of my heart are enlarged: O
bring Thou me out of my distresses. Look upon mine
affliction and my pain, and forgive all my sins.*"

The believer's day varies, as the surface of the sea.
There are periods of lulling calm, then the billows
swell and raise gigantic heads. There is always knowledge that self can give no help. There is the immediate cry to God, who alone can rescue. But while
attention is implored to pains of mind and body, the
deepest misery is especially remembered. There is no

anguish like the sense of sin. Hence the constant prayer, Forgive all my sin. We may urge this with all boldness and all hope, for the precious blood cleanseth from all sin.

19, 20. *" Consider mine enemies, for they are many; and they hate me with cruel hatred. O keep my soul, and deliver me : for I put my trust in Thee."*

The believer might indeed tremble, if he went forth alone to his daily conflict; for many are his foes, and bitter their cruel hate. Nothing can soothe their vengeful hostility. No pity melts within their breasts. But the believer has omnipotent aid beside him. If foes are many, the help is infinite. The humble plea, " I trust in Thee," will bring all heaven to the rescue. The trusting soul will verily be kept. " O Lord, increase our faith."

21. *" Let integrity and uprightness preserve me ; for I wait on Thee."*

No grace was ever perfect but in the holy, harmless Son of God. Integrity was indeed the girdle of His loins, and uprightness the sandals of His feet. But hatred of sin, and honesty of purpose, must be the inmates of our hearts. These graces prompt and strengthen prayer; but they are no valid grounds, claiming acceptance. For faith instantly looks from them to God, and adds, " I wait on Thee, from Thee only comes my help."

22. *" Redeem Israel, O God, out of all his troubles."*

We may boldly ply this heaven-taught prayer with our eyes fixed on Jesus. He of God is made unto us redemption from every trouble and from every sin. He has bought us as His own, with His most precious

I

blood. He will keep us, He will bless us, as His purchased flock. Soon shall we know the full blessedness of this redemption. He will claim the purchased kingdom for His purchased flock, and they shall live and reign for ever on redeemed ground, beneath the banners of redemption. Blessed Lord, hasten the time! Fully redeem Thine Israel!

XXXV.

PSALM XXVI.

PRAYERS, professions, and resolves are here interlinked.
May the Holy Spirit deduce holy lessons for us!

---

1. "*Judge me, O Lord; for I have walked in mine
integrity: I have trusted also in the Lord; therefore I
shall not slide.*"

The voice of Jesus should be here first heard. He
appeals from all injustice of the courts of men to
Heaven's tribunal. He could claim vindication of His
cause on the firm ground that all His ways were perfect holiness. Every one that is born of Him will
strive to be pure and holy, even as He is pure and
holy. May our faith be strengthened by incessant
effort and incessant prayer; for when our trust is
firm, we shall move firmly along the slippery paths of
life.

2, 3. "*Examine me, O Lord, and prove me; try my
reins and my heart. For thy loving-kindness is before
mine eyes; and I have walked in Thy truth.*"

The heart is deceitful above all things. Who can
know it? Who can have full acquaintance with its
intricate and devious windings? Hence the sincere
man will often pray God to come with the light of His
Spirit, and the torch of His Word, to search each deep
and hidden corner, that no Achan may lurk undetected.

Happy the prayer which is supported by the plea,—
Mine eyes are ever gazing on Thy wondrous love, and
all my steps are set in the holy way of Thy revealed
truth.

4, 5. *" I have not sat with vain persons, neither will I
go in with dissemblers. I have hated the congregation of
evil-doers; and will not sit with the wicked."*

There is no communion of light with darkness.
There is no fellowship between righteousness and
unrighteousness. The believer must come out and be
separate. He must not touch the unclean thing.
How rich his gain! The Lord will receive all who
thus withdraw and dwell in them, and walk in them.
He will be their God : they shall be His people.

6. *" I will wash mine hands in innocency: so will I
compass Thine altar, O Lord."*

The Temple and all its rites and all its furniture
was one clear Gospel - lesson. The laver was the
cleansing blood of Jesus. Constant ablutions typified
the washing out of guilt. The altar, with its dying
victims, streaming blood, and curling smoke, proclaimed
the all-atoning sacrifice. Jesus oft tarried in these
courts. His eyes would rest on symbols significant of
His work. The believer, in spirit, will frequent this holy
ground. Abhorring sin he seeks the laver that no
stain may soil him. His happy walk is round the
altar ; gazing on it at each step, delighting by faith to
see his dying Lord, clasping to his heart the truth,—
for me He died, for me His blood was shed, in Him I
am completely saved.

7. *" That I may publish with the voice of thanksgiving, and tell of all Thy wondrous works."*

Views of redemption lead to grateful love, and prompt the voice of praise. They warm the heart; they cause the lips to sing; they fill the inner cistern; and the waters overflow. There is no theme so joyous as the Lord's wondrous works. Faith strives to speak, but due utterance fails. It is far easier to tell ocean's drops than to portray the Saviour's love, His worth, His righteousness, and the glories which He has purchased. But still, the more we speak, the more we feel; the more we feel, the more we speak.

8, 9, 10. " *Lord, I have loved the habitation of Thy house, and the place where Thine honour dwelleth. Gather not my soul with sinners, nor my life with bloody men; in whose hands is mischief, and their right hand is full of bribes.*"

The sanctuary displayed God's glory. Bright rays shone forth from many symbols. The blessed Jesus loved to frequent this mystic spot. The ordinances of God were His delight. It became Him to fulfil all righteousness. This mark distinguishes His · children. In public worship they joy to lift up the voice of praise. They haste with happy step to join the assemblies in which united prayer is made. There is an awful contrast. There is a bundle of tares that shall be burned. There is an assemblage in which every form is sin, and every sight is unmasked ungodliness. Hell is no fiction. The very thought is horror. What must be the dread reality! Let the thought give power to the prayer,—Oh, gather not my soul with such!

11. " *But as for me, I will walk in mine integrity: redeem me, and be merciful unto me.*"

The thought of the second death gives energy to the resolve to walk with God now, that we may dwell with Him for ever. The resolve is scarcely formed, but life returns. The truth appears that our best is only evil. The affrighted believer flies to redeeming blood; he cries for mercy; he avows that his only hope is in the cleansing blood. His constant prayer must be, God be merciful to me a sinner!

12. "*My foot standeth in an even place: in the congregations will I bless the Lord.*"

Hope revives. Faith realizes that it firmly rests on ground immovable. It receives a kingdom which cannot be shaken. It looks beyond the earthly courts and congresses of pious men to the innumerable throng. It forgets the present praise in forethought of the never-ending song. Their one ecstatic chorus will for ever swell,—Blessings to our God, and to the Lamb. Lord, meeten us to bear our part!

XXXVI.

PSALM XXVII. 1–7.

FAITH makes strong professions, and utters earnest prayers. May such be the exercise of our hearts unto life eternal!

———————

1. "*The Lord is my light and my salvation; whom shall I fear? the Lord is the strength of my life; of whom shall I be afraid?*"

This ode commences with a noble outbreak of triumphant confidence. Faith is in loftiest exercise. Foes indeed surround; they are distinctly seen. Their presence and their might is not ignored. But no fear troubles; no dismay appals. Why? The believer knows that he is united to his Lord, and one with Him in the closest bonds; and that he has full interest in all the Lord's perfections. No darkness can bewilder, for the Lord is his light. No destruction can overtake, for the Lord is his salvation. His life can never perish, for the Lord is its strength. May we never rest until our lips can sing thus happily!

2. "*When the wicked, even mine enemies and my foes, came upon me to eat up my flesh, they stumbled and fell.*"

Here is the character of the adversaries of the Lord. They are the wicked. They are Cain-like, who was of that wicked one, and slew his brother. And wherefore

slew he him? Because his own works were evil, and
his brother's righteous. We see striking fulfilment in
the garden of Gethsemane. The traitor enters with his
evil band. Jesus meets them calm in the majesty
of deity. His eye, His voice shiver their hardihood.
They cannot stand before Him. They go backward
and fall to the ground. Such the sure downfall of all
the foes of Jesus.

3. "*Though an host should encamp against me, my
heart shall not fear; though war should rise against me,
in this will I be confident.*"

Hosts of men are less than nothing compared with
heavenly guards. When the trembling servant cried,
"Alas! my master, how shall we do?" the prophet
answered, "Fear not, for they that be with us are more
than they that be with them." Elisha prayed, "Open
his eyes that he may see." He saw, and behold the
mountain was full of horses and chariots of fire round
about Elisha. Even so, let us only believe and we
are safe.

4. "*One thing have I desired of the Lord, that will I
seek after; that I may dwell in the house of the Lord all
the days of my life, to behold the beauty of the Lord, and
to enquire in His temple.*"

One supreme desire occupies the believing heart.
He longs for close communion with the Lord. He
diligently uses all appointed means. He seeks the
ordinances which God's presence sanctifies. Such is the
constant habit of his soul. It is no transient impulse.
He pursues this hallowed intercourse all the days of
his life. His eyes would see the beauty of the Lord:
the lovely charm of His transcendent grace, displayed

in redemption's wondrous work. His soul thirsts after fuller knowledge. His ardent cry is, " Show me Thy glory."

5. " *For in the time of trouble He shall hide me in His pavilion : in the secret of His tabernacle shall He hide me ; He shall set me up upon a rock.*"

The result of faithful obedience is assurance of security. When troubles come like a flood, they cannot reach the tranquil worshipper. He is calm in the recesses of his Lord's presence. The curtains of His pavilion are spread around him. He stands high upon a rock. That rock is Christ. They who are thus uplifted are far above the reach of hostile shafts. From his high stronghold he can look down and smile on all the rage of those who would destroy him. This rock is near. We are invited to its refuge. Let our steps hasten ; then we are safe indeed.

6. " *And now shall mine head be lifted up above mine enemies round about me : therefore will I offer in His tabernacle sacrifices of joy ; I will sing, yea, I will sing praises unto the Lord.*"

Assurance should be ever sought, and it may be scripturally won. The head no longer will hang down. It will put on the helmet of salvation. It will look down in triumph on foes now impotent to hurt. This assurance brings offerings to the Lord's altar. They are the sacrifices of thanksgiving. It has, too, a joyful voice. It ever sings, and the song is praises to the Lord. Here is a test to prove our state. We, surely, are loiterers in the plain, and have not reached the height of scriptural delight, unless our hearts continually send up the incense of abounding thanks.

7. " *Hear, O Lord, when I cry with my voice : have
mercy also upon me, and answer me.*"

Assurance is far from presumption.   While earth is
the home, need will be present.   Grace must be sought,
and, therefore, with all praise, prayer will be intermixed.
The sinner, with all knowledge of salvation, still has
knowledge of his sinful state.   Therefore he never
ceases to seek mercy.   Knowing that God will hear
and answer, he still will importune, Let answers come :
give sweet tokens that my prayers prevail.

XXXVII.

PSALM XXVII. 8–14.

8. " *When thou saidst, Seek ye My face; my heart said unto thee, Thy face, Lord, will I seek.*"

Faith hears the voice of God sweetly speaking in the Scripture page. It calls, it invites, it allures. It warns to arise and flee the vanities of earth. It tells of their emptiness. It promises peace and delight in the reconciled smile of God. The enlightened soul simply obeys. It flies away, and basks beneath the rays of heaven.

9, 10. "*Hide not Thy face far from me; put not Thy servant away in anger: thou hast been my help; leave me not, neither forsake me, O God of my salvation. When my father and my mother forsake me, then the Lord will take me up.*"

The brightest sun may soon be overcast. Clouds may arise, and storms threaten, and darkness and chilliness interpose. Thus sense of sin, and consciousness of deep corruption, may stir up misgivings. Prayer wrestlingly beseeches that the smile so gladly sought may not become averted, and that no just wrath may close the door of conscious acceptance. Former supports are urged in plea. God is addressed as pledged by covenant to save, and bound by strongest ties never to desert or fail. Earthly bonds are easily dissolved. Affection may decay. Fickleness begets estrangement. Distance may part. Death comes, and desolation sits where happy fellowship once reigned. But God's love in Christ is strong, immutable, eternal. He has the Father's heart, which beats with tenderness, incapable of diminution or of change. O Father, ever be a Father unto us!

11. *" Teach me Thy way, O Lord, and lead me in a plain path, because of mine enemies."*

We again see how warily assurance walks. The firm belief that God cannot forsake increases diligence to desire for constant guidance. The holy fears awaken lest ignorance should lead into unrighteous ways, and cause the watchful enemy to exult. Teach me, lead me, are wise prayers. They bring the Spirit's light to shine upon the path, the Spirit's hand to give sustaining aid.

12. *" Deliver me not over unto the will of mine enemies: for false witnesses are risen up against me, and such as breathe out cruelty."*

We tread no path of trial or of suffering which is not hallowed by our Lord's preceding step. We taste no bitter cup which His lips have not drained. No misery afflicts us which He has not previously endured. The stings of calumny are keen. It is anguish when false tongues persist in charging falsely. Jesus felt this. No scrutiny could find fault in Him; but still His judges must have show of evidence; therefore, false witnesses were bribed to fabricate malicious tales. There is great mercy in these foreshadowing views of Jesus. They imprint the stamp of inspiration on the blessed Word. David not only stands a conspicuous type, but words are placed upon His lips which find fulfilment in the varied trials of our Lord. We thankfully adore the mercy. We feel in our grateful hearts, The Scriptures are eternal truth: we may firmly trust them. They cannot be broken.

13. "*I had fainted, unless I had believed to see the goodness of the Lord in the land of the living.*"

The original sentence is strikingly incomplete. The words, I had fainted, are adapted as implying the soul's forlorn and sinking state, if faith and hope had not sustained it. But amid all sorrows and fears a joyful expectation cheered our Lord. He looked onward to the final display of God's goodness in the land of the living. He knew that death could not detain Him. He foresaw the glorious land, where He should reign the living head of a living family. Let our hearts confidently look onward. Soon the shadows will have passed away,—the day will dawn, goodness will be the one atmosphere, and living souls will ever live.

14. "*Wait on the Lord; be of good courage, and he shall strengthen thine heart: wait, I say, on the Lord.*"

The wonderful Counsellor exhorts His followers to be strong in Him. He bids them trust as He had trusted, and they would find as He had found. May the Spirit help us to act out this precious lesson! May He so nerve our spirits that no despondency may ever weaken! And may our eyes be ever raised to heaven, waiting until mercies issue forth. If they tarry, still let us wait. In due time surely they will come.

XXXVIII.

PSALM XXVIII.

EARNEST prayer is followed by exulting praise. May prayer lead us to glad thanksgivings !

---

1. " *Unto Thee will I cry, O Lord my rock: be not silent to me: lest, if thou be silent to me, I become like them that go down into the pit.*"

Strong resolves are the girdle of the faithful man. Among these none is more prominent than fixed intention that prayer shall never cease.   It is prayer's wont to single out some gracious revelation of our God, and earnestly to plead it.   Here God is reminded that He is His people's Rock.   As such He is immovable, and they who rest on Him cannot be shaken.   Billows of trouble may lash.   Storms of persecution may arise. But they remain secure.   Sure replies flow as a gladdening stream.   Sometimes they may seem to be delayed. These times are chilling.   If they continue long, life would grow faint, and death would hasten to extend its hand.

2. " *Hear the voice of my supplications when I cry unto Thee, when I lift up my hands toward thy holy oracle.*"

The mercy-seat was a sweet symbol of the blessed Jesus.   To Him the eye should look, the voice be raised, the hands uplifted in each exercise of prayer.

His merits perfume each address; His worth gives
value, and His intercession gains acceptance. Prayer
without Christ is empty sound. It is vain sound.
The lips may mutter, but no blessings are obtained.

3, 4. " *Draw me not away with the wicked, and with
the workers of iniquity, which speak peace to their neighbours, but mischief is in their hearts. Give them according to their deeds, and according to the wickedness of their
endeavours: give them after the work of their hands;
render to them their desert.*"

The most exalted believer is still a miserable sinner.
Sin is a malady under which he daily groans. It is a
foe with which he daily struggles. He hates it in its
every form. Especially he loathes deceit, and craft,
and fraud. Hence earnest cries that he may be severed
from its contact now, and from its doom for ever. He
knows that justice will erect its throne : that rigid
scrutiny will weigh each word and work : that final
reckoning will assign true judgment. He looks onward to the great white throne and its award. He
humbly acquiesces in the sentence which will there be
given. Even so, Lord. The Judge of all the earth is
righteousness and truth.

5. " *Because they regard not the works of the Lord,
nor the operation of His hands, He shall destroy them,
and not build them up.*"

Our God hides not Himself. Man's ignorance of God
is wilful and self-chosen. His power and Godhead are
written in letters of light throughout creation's page.
His constant interposition in the world's course, in
favour of His people and His truth, always speaks
loudly. This witness disregarded seals the sad doom.

If eyes and ears refuse to learn, sentence is most just.

6. " *Blessed be the Lord, because He hath heard the voice of my supplications.*"

The answer comes. Promises to prayer are all fulfilled. Then what joy abounds! The voice is still upraised, but now the note is changed. Clouds of grateful incense rise to the courts above.

7. " *The Lord is my strength and my shield; my heart trusted in Him, and I am helped: therefore my heart greatly rejoiceth; and with my song will I praise Him.*"

A season of rapturous joy succeeds. God is gratefully acknowledged as supplying inward power to resist evil and to exhibit faith. How strong is he who has Jehovah for his strength! But the Lord is more. He wards off all foes, and presents Himself as His people's shield. We see, too, the power of faith. It brings sure help. He who can say, I trust, will surely add, All succour is supplied. Then joy overflows—joy of heart—joy to unlimited extent. The lips sing sweetly, and God is the happy theme.

8. " *The Lord is their strength, and He is the saving strength of His anointed.*"

The believer is one of a large company. Each one is feeble without God; but each partakes of heavenly strength in Him. Each as one with Christ is anointed with unction from above; and each rejoices in that strength which brings salvation.

9. " *Save Thy people and bless Thine inheritance: feed them also and lift them up for ever.*"

The gift of prayer is for the common weal of God's

chosen. They are dear to Him; and it is joy to Him to hear petitions in their behalf. They are dear as His people, heirs of His kingdom, sheep of His fold. Lord, hear our cry. Save them to the uttermost with Thy salvation. Bless them with all Thy blessings; feed them in Thy wholesome pastures; lift them up above the reach of harm; and from the dust of death, to the highest glories of Thy kingdom.

XXXIX.

PSALM XXIX.

JEHOVAH'S voice is mighty.   It sounds in the storms of nature, in the outgoings of grace, in the terrors of the dissolving world.   May our listening ears be ever open !

1, 2. " *Give unto the Lord, O ye mighty, give unto the Lord glory and strength.   Give unto the Lord the glory due unto His name ; worship the Lord in the beauty of holiness.*"

The high ones of the earth are called to wisdom. They are counselled to estimate rightly their real state ; to lie in lowliness before Jehovah's majesty; to acknowledge His high supremacy; to see in Him the source of all their earthly greatness ; to ascribe due glory to His all-glorious name.   Especially they are called to Gospel-worship, adoring Christ in the sanctuary, where all is beauty, and all the beauty is pure holiness. Would that each crown were placed at Jesus' feet !

3. " *The voice of the Lord is upon the waters: the God of glory thundereth ; the Lord is upon many waters.*"

The rising of a storm is vividly portrayed.   The eye of the spectator rests upon the sea.   From its waters a distant rumbling is heard.   The sound becomes exceeding loud.   The thunder roars.   The God of glory speaks in awful tone.   The God of glory still speaks terribly when the roar of thunder proclaims the Gospel-truth. The terrified conscience hears and quakes. It was so on the day of Pentecost. It is so still in the recesses of many hearts. The full consummation draws near. Then, in the Prophet's words, " The Lord shall roar out of Zion, and utter His voice from Jerusalem; and the heavens and the earth shall shake."

4. " *The voice of the Lord is powerful; the voice of the Lord is full of majesty.*"

As the storm thickens, the majestic power of the Lord is more appalling. When the Gospel-voice goes forth to subdue the heart, the might is irresistible. It rides forth terrible in majesty. They who now yield will calmly smile when this voice shakes terribly the earth.

5, 6. " *The voice of the Lord breaketh the cedars; yea, the Lord breaketh the cedars of Lebanon. He maketh them also to skip like a calf; Lebanon and Sirion like a young unicorn.*"

The storm moves onward towards the north. It thickens over the vast forests of Lebanon. It shivers the strong cedars of those hills. The mountains seem to tremble in affrighted agitation. The nimble boundings of the calf and buffalo are figures of their trembling motion. Thus the Gospel, working with power, lays low all lofty thoughts. Then the heart trembles, and the conscience quakes. These emblems are weak to show the terrors of the great day, when the earth shall reel to and fro, and its deep foundations tremble in affright.

7. " *The voice of the Lord divideth the flames of fire.*"

The forked lightning now flares. Divided flashes

dart fire on the earth. It is the voice of the Lord
which sends them forth.   Let Jehovah's power be
adored.   Here the wonders of the day of Pentecost are
clearly seen.   The Spirit comes in tongues of fire, and
rests on the Apostles' heads.   Thus His rays penetrate
the heart, give light, and purify.   May the Spirit
enlighten all our darkness !   May we be kept watching,
for the day of the Lord will come as a thief in the
night, in which the heavens shall pass away with a
great noise, and the elements shall melt with fervent
heat ; the earth, also, and the works therein shall be
burned up.

8. " *The voice of the Lord shaketh the wilderness; the
Lord shaketh the wilderness of Kadesh.*"

The storm envelops the whole heavens from north to
south.   It rages through the wilderness below Judea.
There are no limits to its fury.   The voice of the
Gospel has no boundaries.   It is gone forth into all the
earth.   By the Spirit's power it will gather in converts
from all lands.   Universal, too, will be the wonders of
the great and terrible day of the Lord.

9. " *The voice of the Lord maketh the hinds to calve,
and discovereth the forests ; and in His temple doth every
one speak of His glory.*"

The effects of the storm are mighty.   The affrighted
hinds produce their young.   The leaves fall thick, and
show the stripped branches.   These, indeed, are glorious works.   The storm proclaims God's glory.   But
the Church is God's glory in the highest.   All who are
thus called, with one loud voice, speak of the glories
of His grace, His love, His righteousness, His truth.
Oh, may the Lord be ever glorified in us !

10. " *The Lord sitteth upon the flood; yea, the Lord sitteth King for ever.*"

After the storm, torrents descend. The waters of Noah seem to drown the earth. As in the deluge, the Lord sat in calm majesty upon His throne in serenity surveying the scene; so now He reigns for ever King of kings and Lord of lords.

11. " *The Lord will give strength unto His people; the Lord will bless His people with peace.*"

Amid all storms of nature now, and troubles within, and in the final crash of worlds, God's people are undismayed. Strength for all trials is their portion. His blessing, which conveys all joy, is on them. Christ's legacy is peace. " Peace I leave with you: My peace I give unto you."

XL.

PSALM XXX.

SORROWS are transient. Joys are for evermore. May we so mourn, that we may be comforted!

---

1. *"I will extol Thee, O Lord; for Thou hast lifted me up, and hast not made my foes to rejoice over me."*

A train of mercies fills the Psalmist with thanksgivings. He had been brought low. His foes were ready to exult, but he was rescued. A saving arm had raised him. He who thus uplifts should be uplifted. Praise should magnify deliverance. In this praise there is the echo of the voice of Jesus. In His experience, too, His saints concur. They should sing as He sang.

2, 3. *" O Lord my God, I cried unto Thee, and Thou hast healed me. O Lord, Thou hast brought up my soul from the grave: Thou hast kept me alive, that I should not go down to the pit."*

These bodies are exposed to countless maladies. Our souls, too, suffer from disease and weakness. Prayer brings the Good Physician to our aid. He comes, and from His wings drop health and freshness. Sometimes the body totters over the grave. Sometimes spiritual life is almost extinct. But the Lord can grant revival. To all appearance the life of Jesus had expired. He was lain, as a dead man, in the grave; but He arose to live for evermore. In spirit

we here see the glorious resurrection. Let all the
members who revived in Him adopt these notes of
praise.

4, 5. " *Sing unto the Lord, O ye saints of His, and
give thanks at the remembrance of His holiness. For His
anger endureth but a moment; in His favour is life:
weeping may endure for a night, but joy cometh in the
morning.*"

The believer feels that an universal chorus should
rise as incense to the skies. Every heart should swell
the hymn. All share the mercies, all should return
thanksgivings. Memory suggests abundant themes.
In all His dealings God is a God of holiness and truth.
May we delight to sing, " Holy, holy, holy, Lord God
of hosts." There are times, when lovingkindness is
obscured by signs of displeasure. His seeming anger is
as the chill of death; but soon the cloud withdraws,
and favour, which is life, returns. The darkness
passes, fears vanish. The joyful morning dawns, and
all is bright. Here we see the resurrection-morn of
Christ. There had been darkness, but it soon vanished.
There is now the brightness of eternal day. We too
have now a night of trouble, but the trouble is light; it
lasts but for a moment. It works for us a far more
exceeding and eternal weight of glory. While we
weep still let us sing, " Joy cometh in the morning."

6, 7. "*And in my prosperity I said, I shall never be
moved. Lord, by Thy favour Thou hast made my
mountain to stand strong: Thou didst hide Thy face,
and I was troubled.*"

David was raised from deep troubles to great prosperity. Zion's stronghold seemed to be impregnable.

Sleeping in the lap of ease, he forgot his true support.
The Lord in mercy shook the pillow of carnal security,
and trouble brought him to a right mind.　　Seasons of
prosperity are full of peril.　　They induce forgetfulness of Him by whom alone we stand.　　But God
remembers us when we turn from Him.　　He looks
away.　　Troubles instantly rush in.　　The shining of
His face is the true joy.　　His look averted makes the
prospect dark.

8, 9, 10. "*I cried to Thee, O Lord; and unto the
Lord I made supplication.　　What profit is there in my
blood, when I go down to the pit?　　Shall the dust praise
Thee? shall it declare Thy truth?　　Hear, O Lord, and
have mercy upon me: Lord, be Thou my helper.*"

Trouble is sent in mercy.　　It subserves a blessed
end.　　It rouses the sleepy soul from dangerous lethargy.
It is a scourge which drives the careless to the mercy-
seat.　　Here, when God's smile ceases, importunate
petitions are in full activity.　　The gate of mercy
opens to the returning knock.　　Faith is an inventive
grace.　　From every trouble it can draw a plea.　　It
here reasons, My destruction brings no glory to the
courts of heaven: if my lips are silent in the grave,
no longer can my praise be heard; my grateful tribute
can no more set forth Thy truth.　　Then the prayer
renews its strength, and cries for audience, mercy,
help.　　Hence may our faith gather strong arguments
to supplicate for joyful resurrection.　　Let our deep
longings ever be to join the eternal hallelujahs, which
are God's glory in the highest.

11, 12. "*Thou hast turned for me my mourning
into dancing: Thou hast put off my sackcloth, and girded*

me with gladness; to the end that my glory may sing praise to Thee, and not be silent. O Lord my God, I will give thanks unto Thee for ever."

Images of exuberant joy conclude this ode. Mourning is gone. The sackcloth of woe is put aside. Every movement testifies exhilaration. The girdle of the loins is gladness. For what purpose is this glad exchange? The design is that God may be loudly praised by every utterance of the lips. This scene will soon be realized. The day of Christ draws near. Then will be fulness of joy. Then, O Lord our God, we will give thanks unto Thee for ever.

XLI.

PSALM XXXI. 1–14.

THE believer's security is in God in every trial, through life in death. May we be kept by His mighty power through faith unto eternal life!

---

1. "*In Thee, O Lord, do I put my trust; let me never be ashamed: deliver me in Thy righteousness.*"

The voice from the cross decides that we have here the thoughts and feelings of our blessed Lord. In the exercise of faith He leads the way. In prayer for favours He is our exemplar. It is good to tell our God how fully we rely on Him. We may be bold to ask deliverance on the plea of righteous covenant and holy promises.

2, 3. "*Bow down Thine ear to me; deliver me speedily: be Thou my strong rock, for an house of defence to save me. For Thou art my rock and my fortress: therefore, for Thy name's sake, lead me, and guide me.*"

The grace to be importunate in prayer is very precious, and should be sedulously cultivated. Faith deals familiarly, and supplicates that God would take the attitude of an earnest listener, and drink in every cry, and speedily arise to help. Faith rightfully expects that God would be true to the character which He has revealed. It argues, God's glorious perfections will be tarnished if the believer strays unguided.

4. " *Pull me out of the net that they have laid privily
for me; for Thou art my strength.*"

The blessed Jesus was exposed to many crafty
wiles, but never were His feet entangled. Snares
on all sides beset us. Conscious of inability to extricate ourselves, let us look to the strong to put forth a
mighty hand, most mightily to extricate us.

5. " *Into Thine hand I commit my spirit : Thou hast
redeemed me, O Lord God of truth.*"

Let us bless Jesus that His dying lips have given
special sanctity to these words. How many since
have thus breathed their last breath. May they be
our constant utterance, for we know not what word
may be our last. When we assuredly believe that God
has redeemed us by His Son's precious blood, and are
persuaded that His holy Word is truth, we may, without one fear, commit our spirits to His care. The
custody is safe. He must be more than God who
plucks our souls from His protecting hands.

6, 7, 8. " *I have hated them that regard lying
vanities: but I trust in the Lord. I will be glad and
rejoice in Thy mercy : for Thou hast considered my
trouble ; Thou hast known my soul in adversities ; and
hast not shut me up into the hand of the enemy: Thou
hast set my feet in a large room.*"

Many vain cheats are forward to beguile us. Riches,
honour, titles, reason, intellect, invite us to rely on their
aid. But they are empty bubbles. Their promises are
fraud. The believer flees with abhorrence from those
who walk in these deceits. He has a large volume of
experience. In trouble he has found that God's
thoughts were on him. All his adverse circumstances

have been lovingly regarded. In all his ways of sorrow God has been by his side. Deliverance and enlargement have been near. Great mercy has been shown; great gladness will acknowledge it.

9, 10. "*Have mercy upon me, O Lord, for I am in trouble: mine eye is consumed with grief, yea, my soul and my belly. For my life is spent with grief, and my years with sighing: my strength faileth because of mine iniquity, and my bones are consumed.*"

Our first thoughts here are thoughts of Jesus. He bore our sins; on Him our every iniquity was laid. He stood before God, laden with all our sins. By imputation He was a mass of guilt. This would be keen anguish to His soul. Grief would be His constant comrade. Sorrow would plough furrows on His brow. Declining strength would show the increased woe. He would often sigh, "Have mercy upon me, O Lord, for I am in trouble." Here, too, is the anguish of the conscience-stricken. When sin is once seen in all its hideous sinfulness, when guilt before God is once discovered, the misery would drive reason from its seat, unless the grief found vent in cries for mercy.

11, 12, 13. "*I was a reproach among all mine enemies, but especially among my neighbours, and a fear to mine acquaintance: they that did see me without fled from me. I am forgotten as a dead man out of mind; I am like a broken vessel. For I have heard the slander of many; fear was on every side: while they took counsel together against me, they devised to take away my life.*"

The Spirit vividly foreshows the sufferings of Jesus when He was despised and rejected of men. His chosen followers forsook Him and fled. He was carried as a dead man to the tomb. He was regarded as a broken potsherd worthless for further use. The Jews conspired to destroy Him. Nothing could allay their malice. Their cry was urgent, Let Him be crucified. Much of this cruel usage was experienced by the type. David fled as an outcast. Conspirators laid plots. Evil counsellors took evil counsel. The like enmity burns against every true disciple. Outward restraints may bind, but the inward hatred is the same:

14. *"But I trusted in thee, O Lord; I said, Thou art my God."*

God is the refuge of His people in all ages. To Him they fly. In Him they are secure.

XLII.

PSALM XXXI. 15–24.

15. "*My times are in Thy hand: deliver me from the hand of mine enemies, and from them that persecute me.*"

There is a flood of comfort in the thought that God's unfailing providence ordereth all our matters.   Each event is surely ordered.   If without Him no sparrow falls, surely without Him no ill prevails against us. His hand is over all.   He can deliver from each foe's malice, and each persecutor's rage.   Knowing this, let us direct our prayer to Him, the only source of help.

16, 17, 18. "*Make Thy face to shine upon Thy servant: save me for Thy mercies' sake.   Let me not be ashamed, O Lord; for I have called upon Thee: let the wicked be ashamed, and let them be silent in the grave.   Let the lying lips be put to silence; which speak grievous things proudly and contemptuously against the righteous.*"

The misery of the godly is the absence of the smile of heaven.   The soul cannot be still while such darkness and such chill continues.   It knows that the Lord can instantly cause brightness to return.   Hence the strong petition, Make Thy face to shine.   This light is full salvation.   Therefore faith adds, " Save me for Thy mercies' sake."   God's mercy is the only plea, but it is mighty and prevails.   Mercy implored is mercy won.   Grace ceases to be grace if it rejects the supplicant's cry.   Prayer will never hang down its head abashed. But a day of confusion quickly comes. Wicked lips spake with proud contempt against the blessed Jesus. Excuse will fail before the great white throne. Shame will then close their lips. When calumny assails us, let us reflect, How short is this day of evil! We shall sing loudly, while the lips of lies are only opened to bewail.

19. " *Oh how great is Thy goodness, which Thou hast laid up for them that fear Thee: which Thou hast wrought for them that trust in Thee before the sons of men!*"

Grateful experience cannot be silent. Exclamation will break forth. In the midst of trials comforts more than abound. God's treasure-house is full of joys. The believer finds that the store exceeds all thought, and baffles praise. He can only shout, How great is Thy goodness! Verily, it is great as God is great. To measure the infinitudes of grace is to measure God Himself. His precious dealings towards His favoured children is often so conspicuously displayed, that enmity itself cannot deny that God is with them of a truth.

20. " *Thou shalt hide them in the secret of Thy presence from the pride of man; Thou shalt keep them secretly in a pavilion from the strife of tongues.*"

When haughty man insults, and tongues send forth envenomed darts, the child of God has a sure hiding place. His God is present. He screens himself behind His sheltering wings. He enters the inmost curtains of a secreting tent. He is hid in light. It is a great mystery. None can explain but they who feel it.

21. *" Blessed be the Lord ; for He hath showed me His marvellous kindness in a strong city."*

Such, doubtless, would be David's feeling when he reigned in Zion; and, doubtless, such would be His praise. But this is especially the believer's song. He has a strong city. Salvation has God appointed for walls and bulwarks. He enters into Christ. He sits secure in an impregnable fort. No foe can pass the gates. No might can make impression on the walls. The foundations are exceeding strong. The towers over-top the skies. Serene in His fortress He learns many lessons, and feasts on precious truths. They all speak of mercy, grace, love; and all these sweet displays are wondrous. Wondrous indeed the kindness which looked on miserable rebels, and sent Jesus to seek and save! Wondrous the scheme! Wondrous the effects! Wonder of wonders that we should have interest in it! We can only cry, " Blessed God."

22. *" For I said in my haste, I am cut off from before Thine eyes : nevertheless Thou heardest the voice of my supplications when I cried unto Thee."*

The movements of the believer's mind are quite a paradox. Gleams of sunshine follow the cloudy gloom. He fears amid all confidence : he trusts amid all misgivings. He speaks in haste; but still his soul is tranquil steadfastness. He thinks that he is utterly rejected ; but still he prays. He believes that all hope is gone; but answers come to every cry.

23. *" O love the Lord, all ye His saints : for the Lord preserveth the faithful, and plentifully rewardeth the proud doer."*

Abundant motives call to the love of God: not least
His constant care of His true children, and His sure
vengeance on proud foes. Let us trust, and we are
safe. They who transgress shall surely be requited.

24. "*Be of good courage, and He shall strengthen
your heart, all ye that hope in the Lord.*"

Trust must rely only on our God. All other confidences are empty vanity. They who thus trust may
cast away all fear. Let them meet every trial bold
as the lion. Courage will become more courageous.
Strength from above will make the heart more strong.

XLIII.

PSALM XXXII.

WE are taught the blessedness of sin's pardon through the faith of Christ. O Lord, give us this blessing, and we shall be blessed!

1, 2. " *Blessed is he whose transgression is forgiven, whose sin is covered. Blessed is the man unto whom the Lord imputeth not iniquity, and in whose spirit there is no guile.*"

If he alone was blessed whom no sin had ever stained, this world would have a wretched doom! If he alone was blessed, whose feet had never strayed from godly ways, where could we hide our heads? But blessedness belongs to the transgressor pardoned— to the sinner, whose sins are no more seen by God— to the guilty, to whose account the guilt is no more reckoned. We are transgressors, we are sinners, we are deep-steeped in guilt. Is this blessedness vouchsafed to us? Yes, verily, if through grace we have received Christ. There is redemption through His blood, even the forgiveness of all our sins. His cross redeems from transgression, iniquity, and sin. His beauteous righteousness so hides all guilt, that God's omniscient eye no more discerns it. His blood wipes out all record of iniquity. For the believer's sins may be searched for, but they shall not be found. Such

blessedness is the fruit of faith. Oh, precious grace!
Blessed are they to whom it is freely given! From
faith's deep roots all virtuous blossoms spring. The
guileless mind, the truthful heart, the honest purpose,
are pre-eminently its fruits.

3, 4. *" When I kept silence, my bones waxed old,
through my roaring all the day long: for day and night
Thy hand was heavy upon me: my moisture is turned
into the drought of summer."*

Great is the anguish of the soul, when first the
Spirit reveals sin. Day brings no joy, and night supplies no ease. An intolerable burden oppresses the
mind. This is the Lord's hand. Thus He shakes
from security's delusive pillow. Thus He directs the
footsteps to the cross. But until Christ be seen, what
misery is undergone! Feverish heat dries up the pores.
The frame is parched, as plains beneath the sultry sun.
The body weakens; the bones are tottering as in extreme
old age; the howls of grief betray the tortured mind.

5. *" I acknowledge my sin unto Thee, and mine
iniquity have I not hid. I said, I will confess my
transgressions unto the Lord; and Thou forgavest the
iniquity of my sin."*

At length relief is found. God is revealed as pardoning all sin in Christ. The glories of the saving
cross are shown. The contrite sinner flies in haste.
He lies in deep humility. He pours out every secret
of his melted heart. He recounts the train of life-long
iniquity: He confesses, Thus and thus have I done.
The mass is mountain-high. The stain is deeper than
the scarlet-dye. The language of the cross is heard:
all is forgiven: all is blotted out.

6. "*For this shall every one that is godly pray unto Thee in a time when Thou mayest be found: surely in the floods of great waters they shall not come nigh unto him.*"

Because God is a God ready to forgive, His people throng the mercy-seat. If no mercy could be found, no prayers would plead. But no delays may check. Now God extends the sceptre of His grace. But the morrow may proclaim, Too late. Prayer brings security. Floods of trouble may rush in from all sides, but the godly are borne above all in a peaceful ark. A fiery deluge soon will drown the world: but the fierce billows will not reach the ransomed of the Lord.

7. "*Thou art my hiding-place; Thou shalt preserve me from trouble; Thou shalt compass me about with songs of deliverance.*"

No trouble can touch those who are securely hid in God. The preserved shall dwell amid incessant songs. And every song shall testify, Thou hast delivered us from the wrath to come.

8, 9. "*I will instruct thee, and teach thee in the way which thou shalt go: I will guide thee with Mine eye. Be ye not as the horse, or as the mule, which have no understanding; whose mouth must be held in with bit and bridle, lest they come near unto thee.*"

At each moment we lack wisdom. At each moment God waits to guide. We have large promises. Let us largely plead them. If our eyes are turned to Him, in His eye we shall read His will. Let us with all docility obey. The beasts give warning. Sharp discipline restrains the senseless and the stubborn.

10, 11. "*Many sorrows shall be to the wicked: but he*

that trusteth in the Lord, mercy shall compass him about. Be glad in the Lord, and rejoice, ye righteous: and shout for joy, all ye that are upright in heart."

Many sorrows now—many sorrows for ever, must be the sinner's doom. The mouth of the Lord has spoken it. Justice demands it.—In contrast view the faithful. Mercy precedes them. Mercy brings up their van. Mercy gleams on their right hand. Mercy smiles on their left. They dwell in mercy, and God's mercy is salvation. We cannot ponder too much the designation of God's people. They are righteous. They are sincere. As such they have a right to joy. But all their joy has Jesus as its source. Self only awakens grief and contempt. But they rejoice in the Lord, and in His finished work. May this delight be ever ours !

XLIV.

PSALM XXXIII.

ALL praise is due to God, for all He is—for all that
He has done.　May we begin the praise which shall
not end !

1, 2, 3.　"*Rejoice in the Lord, O ye righteous ; for
praise is comely for the upright.　Praise the Lord with
harp ; sing unto Him with the psaltery and an instru-
ment of ten strings.　Sing unto Him a new song, play
skilfully with a loud noise.*"

When we realize the blessings of salvation, we must
feel that every breath should praise the Lord ; and our
whole life should be thanksgiving.　We should awaken
every power, and enlist all art to magnify His name.
This service is God's due, and should be duly rendered.

4, 5.　"*For the word of the Lord is right ; and all
His works are done in truth.　He loveth righteousness and
judgment : the earth is full of the goodness of the Lord.*"

His Word, His works call loudly for this tribute.
They dazzle with the lustre of perfection.　It must be
so, for they spring from a fountain which is unmixed
holiness.　Survey the earth in all its marvellous
variety.　Each object, seen by faith's enlightened eye,
shows the impress of benevolence.

6, 7, 8, 9.　"*By the word of the Lord were the heavens
made ; and all the host of them by the breath of His*

mouth. He gathereth the waters of the sea together as an heap; He layeth up the depth in storehouses. Let all the earth fear the Lord : let all the inhabitants of the world stand in awe of Him : for He spake, and it was done ; He commanded, and it stood fast."

We adore the glory of the eternal Trinity. We adore the Word, co-eternal and co-efficient with the Father. By Him were all things made, and without Him was not anything made that was made. We adore the Spirit moving upon the face of the waters. We adore triune omnipotence. Without effort or tedious process the word is spoken, and all creation starts into life confirmed in perfect beauty. Who will not reverence such glorious power ? Throughout earth's length and breadth, man's posture should be reverence and awe.

10, 11. *" The Lord bringeth the counsel of the heathen to nought : He maketh the devices of the people of none effect. The counsel of the Lord standeth for ever, the thoughts of His heart to all generations."*

But man in proud madness plots against Almightiness. The result has ever been the same. God's glory shines more gloriously. Opponents perish in shame and merited confusion. So it must ever be. The glories of eternity, the hallelujahs of the ransomed, will proclaim that all His purposes have triumphed ; that all His plans have prospered ; that all His people are for ever saved ; that all His foes are brought to nought.

12. *" Blessed is the nation whose God is the Lord ; and the people whom He hath chosen for His own inheritance."*

Among the multitudes of earth happy are they who reject all idols and all vain confidence, and choose the Lord to be their God. They are blessed beyond what word can speak or thought conceive. They are the loved from eternity. They are the called of the Spirit. They choose Him because He first chose them. They fly to Him, because He bends their will, and gives them power.

13, 14, 15. "*The Lord looketh from heaven; He beholdeth all the sons of men. From the place of His habitation He looketh upon all the inhabitants of the earth. He fashioneth their hearts alike; He considereth all their works.*"

An eye from heaven pervades the world. It penetrates all space and looks internally into every breast. There is no heart which His hand framed not. And every step is patent to His omniscience.

16, 17. "*There is no king saved by the multitude of an host: a mighty man is not delivered by much strength. An horse is a vain thing for safety: neither shall he deliver any by his great strength.*"

Real strength is not in earthly things. They who seek help below the heavens seek it from a source too low. God only is real power. Much more will they find disappointment who trust to self in matters of salvation. Christ wrought it out. Christ only gives.

18, 19. "*Behold, the eye of the Lord is upon them that fear Him, upon them that hope in His mercy; to deliver their soul from death, and to keep them alive in famine.*"

God's children have most beautiful lineaments. They reverently fear; they confidently trust. They are well known in heaven. He who gave grace, discerns it. They may be brought into distress, but they come forth uninjured. At last they reach the haven of eternal life.

20, 21, 22. "*Our soul waiteth for the Lord : He is our help and our shield. For our heart shall rejoice in Him ; because we have trusted in His holy name. Let Thy mercy, O Lord, be upon us, according as we hope in Thee.*"

Faith is a happy grace : indeed no true joy lives except as springing from this root. Is it not joy to feel equipment against every foe ? What can injure those who have God for their shield ? What can resist those who have God for their help ? But in all joy faith is most humble. In its most lofty song, it bows the knee. In its most happy hope it cries for mercy. Let Thy mercy, O Lord, be upon us, according as we hope in Thee. Such is our prayer. Let speedy answers come !

XLV.

PSALM XXXIV.

GOD'S never-failing care demands unfailing praise. Sheltered beneath the covert of His wings, may we sing gratefully !

———————

1, 2. "*I will bless the Lord at all times: His praise shall continually be in my mouth. My soul shall make her boast in the Lord: the humble shall hear thereof and be glad.*"

We hear the voice of Jesus. On earth He dwelt in prayer and praise. Shall the Head thus speak, and shall not each member lengthen out the strain ? No moment comes which bears not blessings on its wings. Let each moment carry back thanksgivings. We should be ceaseless in telling out our mercies, that the lowly sons of God may be witnesses of our joys.

3, 4, 5, 6. "*O magnify the Lord with me, and let us exalt His name together. I sought the Lord, and He heard me, and delivered me from all my fears. They looked unto Him and were lightened; and their faces were not ashamed. This poor man cried, and the Lord heard him, and saved him out of all his troubles.*"

This precious record of experience is common to the whole family of faith. They have the common portion of fear and trouble ; but in all distress their course is the same. They seek the Lord. They turn their eyes to Him. To Him they raise the suppliant cry. They all are gladdened by the like result. They are all heard—relieved, delivered, saved. They never hang their heads depressed in shame. Oh! happy people! happy lot! One, too, is their grateful task. They call on all around to swell their praise.

7. *" The angel of the Lord encampeth round about them that fear Him, and delivereth them."*

If eyes were opened to behold surrounding scenes, what companies of heavenly guards would brightly shine around! Their ministering aid averts innumerable ills. They were sent in succour to our glorious Head. Unseen as truly their camp defends us.

8, 9, 10. *" O taste and see that the Lord is good : blessed is the man that trusteth in Him. O fear the Lord, ye His saints : for there is no want to them that fear Him. The young lions do lack and suffer hunger ; but they that seek the Lord shall not want any good thing."*

Heavenly counsels call us to know by glad experience the goodness of the Lord. The cup is brought to our very lips. We are invited to exhaust these waters of delight. The strongest in their strength may suffer famine ; but all abundance of real food is the rich table of the humble saint.

11. *" Come, ye children, hearken unto Me ; I will teach you the fear of the Lord."*

The heart of Jesus calls us children. He bids us to sit as children at His feet. Blessed are the lessons of His lips! The foremost is the fear of God. Oh, may we truly learn that fear!

12, 13, 14. *" What man is he that desireth life, and*

*loveth many days, that he may see good ? Keep thy tongue
from evil, and thy lips from speaking guile. Depart from
evil, and do good ; seek peace, and pursue it."*

The love of earthly life is natural to man ; but
life eternal is to see the goodness and the glory of the
Lord. This is the result of grace. Where grace is
freely given, the evidence is surely seen. It is no
barren tree. The lips are guarded. The tongue is
free from guile. The ways of the Lord are diligently
sought. The peaceable fruits of righteousness abound.

15, 16, 17, 18. *" The eyes of the Lord are upon the
righteous, and His ears are open unto their cry. The
face of the Lord is against them that do evil, to cut off
the remembrance of them from the earth. The righteous
cry, and the Lord heareth, and delivereth them out of all
their troubles. The Lord is nigh unto them that are of
a broken heart ; and saveth such as be of a contrite
spirit."*

Delight in prayer is evidence of grace. The
righteous cannot be silent. The watchful Lord hears
every movement of their humble spirits. He quickly
comes to bind up the mourning heart, and to deliver
from the grasp of sorrow. How sad is the reverse of
this sweet picture ! There is a multitude who throng
the paths of evil. The Lord's averted look to them is
misery and death.

19, 20. *" Many are the afflictions of the righteous :
but the Lord delivereth him out of them all. He keepeth
all His bones : not one of them is broken."*

Jesus at once appears. We learn from this particular,
to seek Him throughout these hymns. He never is
far distant from the eye of faith. When He was lifted

up upon the cross, the soldiers drew near to break His legs; but He was marvellously dead, and so they touched Him not. He drank to the dregs the cup of sorrow; but sorrow issued in eternal joy. Believers tread, too, the path of countless sorrows, but they lead to everlasting rest. No vital injury ensues. The Lord restrains the malice of the foe. There may be many wounds, but they are not to death.

21, 22. "*Evil shall slay the wicked; and they that hate the righteous shall be desolate. The Lord redeemeth the soul of His servants: and none of them that trust in Him shall be desolate.*"

The wicked embrace evil. It is a viper which will suck their blood. They greedily drink the cup, but it is deadly poison. Oh! seek the Lord. He gives His Son to be complete redemption. He gives the joy of His presence now. There is now no lonely day, and soon there will be union to the vast company of the countless saved. May we be there!

XLVI.

PSALM XXXV.

APPEAL is made to God for help. Many are our times of need. At all times we have access to our God.

———

1, 2, 3. "*Plead my cause, O Lord, with them that strive with me: fight against them that fight against me. Take hold of shield and buckler, and stand up for mine help. Draw out also the spear, and stop the way against them that persecute me: say unto my soul, I am thy salvation.*"

Jesus would thus ofttimes cry. None ever felt as He did the bitterness of man's malignity. He earnestly implored that God would maintain His cause. We thus are taught the way of help; and not of help only, but of perfect peace. For none can disturb the soul, to which God whispers, "I am thy salvation."

4, 5, 6, 7, 8. "*Let them be confounded and put to shame that seek after my soul: let them be turned back and brought to confusion that devise my hurt. Let them be as chaff before the wind: and let the angel of the Lord chase them. Let their way be dark and slippery: and let the angel of the Lord persecute them. For without cause have they hid for me their net in a pit, which without cause they have digged for my soul. Let destruction come upon him at unawares; and let his net that he hath*" *hid catch himself: into that very destruction let him fall."*

Thus Jesus prayed. In such prayer we have the clear prediction,—They who plot against Him plot against themselves. Into their own net they rush. Into their own pit they fall. The day draws near when this destruction will be witnessed. Perfect justice will endorse the doom.

9, 10. *" And my soul shall be joyful in the Lord : it shall rejoice in His salvation. All my bones shall say, Lord, who is like unto Thee, which deliverest the poor from him that is too strong for him, yea, the poor and the needy from him that spoileth him ?"*

Present deliverance awakens present praise ; but full joy waits for the future. Then joy will not so much regard the overthrow of foes, as the Lord's glory. The lips and every faculty shall sing to Him, who alone rescued from overpowering might. Without God we are weak to stand.

11, 12, 13, 14, 15, 16. *" False witnesses did rise up : they laid to my charge things that I knew not. They rewarded me evil for good, to the spoiling of my soul. But as for me, when they were sick, my clothing was sackcloth : I humbled my soul with fasting; and my prayer returned into mine own bosom. I behaved myself as though he had been my friend or brother: I bowed down heavily, as one that mourneth for his mother. But in mine adversity they rejoiced, and gathered themselves together : yea, the abjects gathered themselves together against me, and I knew it not; they did tear me, and ceased not. With hypocritical mockers in feasts, they gnashed upon me with their teeth."*

David's experience foreshadows Jesus. The judg-
ment-hall presents itself to view. We have another
proof that Jesus mainly speaks in these inspired
hymns. "The testimony of Jesus is the spirit of prophecy." Grace ever seeks to melt by kindness the obdurate heart, and to return all evil with abundant good.

17, 18. "*Lord, how long wilt Thou look on? rescue my
soul from their destructions, my darling from the lions.
I will give Thee thanks in the great congregation: I will
praise Thee among much people.*"

The cross again appears. We hear the earnest cry
of the uplifted Jesus; but faith still sees that rescue is
at hand. Promises are made that praise shall speak of
mercy. When congregations of the faithful meet, and
the Spirit works, there is fulfilment.

19, 20, 21. "*Let not them that are mine enemies
wrongfully rejoice over me; neither let them wink with
the eye that hate me without a cause. For they speak
not peace; but they devise deceitful matters against them
that are quiet in the land. Yea, they opened their mouth
wide against me, and said, Aha, Aha! our eye hath
seen it.*"

These plaintive sounds are from the cross. It was
deep aggravation that the sufferings came from them
whom He by dying sought to save. How sad that
the requital of such love should be such hate! If
such be the treatment of the holy Head, what must
the guilty members expect?

22, 23, 24, 25, 26. "*This Thou hast seen, O Lord:
keep not silence: O Lord, be not far from me. Stir up Thyself, and awake to my judgment, even unto my cause, my
God and my Lord. Judge me, O Lord my God, according*

*to Thy righteousness; and let them not rejoice over me.
Let them not say in their hearts, Ah, so would we have it:
let them not say, We have swallowed him up. Let them
be ashamed, and brought to confusion together, that rejoice
at mine hurt: let them be clothed with shame and dishonour that magnify themselves against me.*"

In these petitions we have assurance of the coming
judgment. Jesus is always heard. God will arise.
Confusion shall destroy them. Let us feel true compassion when the ungodly rage. Their gnashing of
teeth comes on apace.

*27, 28. " Let them shout for joy, and be glad, that
favour my righteous cause; yea, let them say continually,
Let the Lord be magnified, which hath pleasure in the
prosperity of His servant. And my tongue shall speak
of Thy righteousness, and of Thy praise, all the day
long.*"

Faith gathers joy and peace from pondering the
glorious issue. The conflict may be long and fierce,
but victory is near. The song of triumph soon will
be heard. Due glory will be given to God. His
righteousness shall be exalted. His praises shall be
very high. May our glad voices swell the Conqueror's
song !

M

XLVII.

PSALM XXXVI.

Two very diverse views appear. The wickedness of the wicked is very vile. The glory of God shines brightly. May our thoughts rise from earth and rest in heaven!

1. "*The transgression of the wicked saith within my heart, that there is no fear of God before his eyes.*"

There is obscurity in these words; but the truth they seem to teach is, that sin has a voice. It loudly speaks in the vile sinner's course, and the godly have intelligence to hear. Within their heart the echo sounds, that the transgressor fears not God. Awful is this state. The Lord of all power and might is ignored and is defied.

2, 3, 4. "*For he flattereth himself in his own eyes, until his iniquity be found to be hateful. The words of his mouth are iniquity and deceit: he hath left off to be wise, and to do good. He deviseth mischief upon his bed; he setteth himself in a way that is not good; he abhorreth not evil.*"

Dark colours are here laid. Conscience is steeped in deadness. The wicked clings to self-deception until discovery reveals his guilt. He shuns the path of holy wisdom. In secret hours he plots iniquity. He devises schemes of evil. No holy dread restrains him from commission. The evil thoughts bear fruits of evil life.

5. " *Thy mercy, O Lord, is in the heavens; and Thy faithfulness reacheth unto the clouds.*"

The eye of faith turns quickly from the hateful scene. It seeks relief in God. It looks above, and joys in sights of glory. Mercy is seen. It sits enthroned in heaven. It reigns supreme to bless God's happy children. By its side is God's unfailing truth. It pierces the clouds. It is co-inmate of the heaven of heavens. Let us delight to uplift our gaze, and see mercy and truth pouring down blessings on us!

6. " *Thy righteousness is like the great mountains; Thy judgments are a great deep: O Lord, Thou preservest man and beast.*"

Eternal rectitude rules all God's dealings. Ofttimes we are perplexed. We cannot read the purport. But nothing can cause God's righteousness to waver. It is fairly rooted as the everlasting hills. It is far easier to uproot their base than to subvert His equity. The orderings of His rule are far beyond our power to fathom. The lines of reason cannot descend into the deep abyss. But all is well. It is our wisdom to trust when we are weak to trace. We see a gracious hand preserves all living beings. The meanest of His creatures receive food. His care will not fail us.

7. " *How excellent is Thy loving-kindness, O God! therefore the children of men put their trust under the shadow of Thy wings.*"

No tongue can adequately praise God's loving mercies. They exceed all praise. They are inscribed on providential dealings. They are written in letters of gold throughout the Gospel-page. Who in the Spirit's light can see the Cross, and not exclaim, Our

God is Love! Attractive power goes forth, and allures
to Him for covert from every enemy; for comfort at
every moment. May our chosen home be shelter by
His side!

8. " *They shall be abundantly satisfied with the fatness of Thy house; and Thou shalt make them drink of
the river of Thy pleasures.*"

What precious joys await true faith! A feast is
spread, superabounding in spiritual delight. The
Word, the promises, the ordinances present enriching
food. A river never dry, ever full and ever flowing,
invites to constant draughts of pleasure. Let us
scorn the broken cistern of this world's vanity, and
dwell beside these heavenly streams until we reach the
land, in which the Lamb, which is in the midst of the
throne, shall feed us, and shall lead us unto living
fountains of water.

9. " *For with Thee is the fountain of life: in Thy
light shall we see light.*"

In the world is barren emptiness. It holds nothing; therefore, nothing can it yield. But God
in Christ is an unfathomable spring of life. Life
spiritual and eternal flow in deep streams from Him.
Oh! let us drink; let us drink freely and abundantly,
and thus live in joy, and live for ever.

10, 11, 12. " *O continue Thy loving-kindness unto
them that know Thee; and Thy righteousness to the
upright in heart. Let not the foot of pride come against
me, and let not the hand of the wicked remove me.
There are the workers of iniquity fallen: they are cast
down, and shall not be able to rise.*"

Assurance checks not, but rather quickens, prayer.

Continuance of love is sought while it is known that love can never fail. But let it never be forgotten that these prospects belong only to the happy seed, who receive God as reconciled in Christ; who know Him as their Father, and walk before Him in pure truth. While we pray constantly for deliverance from the assaults of wicked men, we may look onward to the time when all their evil shall have ended. They shall fall and never more rise. If we are made to differ, let us sing praises to God's free grace.

XLVIII.

PSALM XXXVII. 1–20.

THE temporal prosperity of wicked men soon vanishes.
True happiness is the portion of the godly. May such
be our lot!

1, 2. *" Fret not thyself because of evil-doers, neither be
thou envious against the workers of iniquity : For they
shall soon be cut down like the grass, and wither as the
green herb."*

Wisdom here speaks from the high throne. Prosperity may smile at the gay comrade of the wicked.
But let not our eyes view grudgingly. How long will
it continue? Their merry day is as the life of the
frail grass. Its greenness is for a little moment; it
soon dies.

3, 4, 5, 6. *" Trust in the Lord, and do good : so shalt
thou dwell in the land, and verily thou shalt be fed.
Delight thyself also in the Lord ; and He shall give thee
the desires of thine heart. Commit thy way unto the
Lord ; trust also in Him, and He shall bring it to pass.
And He shall bring forth thy righteousness as the light,
and thy judgment as the noon-day."*

We see the path in which true blessedness abounds.
It is here depicted as unwavering faith—the exercise of
every Christian grace, the choice of God as all delight,
and total surrender of our ways to Him. Then no

good thing will be withheld. Every holy desire will
be gratified. God will maintain our cause. No
clouds of calumny shall obscure our righteous dealings. Our integrity shall brightly shine as the sun at
midday.

7, 8. " *Rest in the Lord, and wait patiently for Him:
fret not thyself because of him who prospereth in his way,
because of the man who bringeth wicked devices to pass.
Cease from anger, and forsake wrath: fret not thyself in
anywise to do evil.*"

The happiest posture of the soul is calm repose in
God—a patient trust in His all-ruling hand. The
natural heart may feel the stir of irritation, when evil
plans obtain success. Let grace prevail to deaden
such motions, and to guide far from outbreaks of
vexation.

9, 10, 11. " *For evil-doers shall be cut off: but those
that wait upon the Lord, they shall inherit the earth.
For yet a little while, and the wicked shall not be: yea,
thou shalt diligently consider his place, and it shall not
be. But the meek shall inherit the earth; and shall
delight themselves in the abundance of peace.*"

Envy will die, if the true end of evil be remembered. Their transient joy leads to uttermost woe.
Their little flare subsides in blackness of darkness for
ever. But what sweet prospects shine before the
meek servants of the Lord! What precious promises
allure them! We look for the new heavens and the
new earth, wherein dwelleth righteousness. We know
that yet a little while and He that shall come will
come, and will not tarry. Then the kingdoms of this
world shall become the kingdoms of the Lord and of

His Christ, and we shall reign with Him for ever and ever.

12, 13, 14, 15. "*The wicked plotteth against the just, and gnasheth upon him with his teeth. The Lord shall laugh at him; for He seeth that his day is coming. The wicked have drawn out the sword, and have bent their bow, to cast down the poor and needy, and to slay such as be of upright conversation. Their sword shall enter into their own heart, and their bows shall be broken.*"

We are tempted to repine when all is bright around the wicked. We are more tempted to despond when their malignity is rampant. But how different will be our feeling when we discern that all their malice is their own injury! The Lord's hand so rules their violence that their blows fall on themselves; their swords are sheathed in their own hearts; they fight against themselves; they shall fall self-slain. When faith sees things in true light, it will be no more sad. No fears will trouble. Security will be realized.

16, 17. "*A little that a righteous man hath is better than the riches of many wicked. For the arms of the wicked shall be broken: but the Lord upholdeth the righteous.*"

The blessing of the Lord gives worth to riches, and dignifies the poorest lot. With the Lord's smile the humble board is rich; without it the tables of the wealthy contain no comfort. Soon the wicked will be crushed, while the righteous rise to glory.

18, 19, 20. "*The Lord knoweth the days of the upright; and their inheritance shall be for ever. They shall not be ashamed in the evil time; and in the days of famine they shall be satisfied. But the wicked shall perish, and the enemies of the Lord shall be as the fat of lambs: they shall consume; into smoke shall they consume away."*

All good is pledged to the sons of God in time and through eternity. The plenty granted to the wicked only fattens them for the day of slaughter. As curling smoke soon vanishes, so shall they disappear. May these warnings not be lost! May the Spirit bring the promises with power to our hearts!

XLIX.

PSALM XXXVII. 21–40.

21, 22. " *The wicked borroweth and payeth not again: but the righteous showeth mercy and giveth. For such as be blessed of Him shall inherit the earth; and they that be cursed of Him shall be cut off.*"

If abundance flows into the coffers of the wicked, it soon flows out : need comes in. Help from others must be sought; and dishonesty holds back repayment. The righteous, from his humble store, is able to be kind and generous. The blessing of the Lord is on them, and shall place them as heirs of that world where all things are new. But the curse devotes the wicked to eternal woe.

23, 24. " *The steps of a good man are ordered by the Lord; and He delighteth in His way. Though he fall, he shall not be utterly cast down: for the Lord upholdeth him with His hand.*"

What precious truths here offer comfort ! Our path seems sometimes to be dark; but let us seek the Spirit's guidance, and plead this promise, which ensures right direction, and God's smile upon our path. Our weak steps too often totter, and Satan seems ready to cast us down ; but help from heaven is near. We are not left to lie in mire of sin. We are not finally cast off. God's hand uplifts us, and gives sure support until life's journey ends.

25, 26. " *I have been young, and now am old ; yet have*

*I not seen the righteous forsaken, nor his seed begging
bread. He is ever merciful, and lendeth; and his seed is
blessed."*

The Psalmist states the experience of a long life.
Kindness and liberality are signs of grace. The good
man leaves a legacy of blessing to his children. The
smile of the Lord shines upon children's children.

27, 28, 29. *" Depart from evil, and do good; and dwell
for evermore. For the Lord loveth judgment, and for-
saketh not His saints; they are preserved for ever: but
the seed of the wicked shall be cut off. The righteous shall
inherit the land, and dwell therein for ever."*

The Spirit multiplies grand promises to enrich the
followers of Christ. What a cluster here sparkles ! The
love of God will always beam upon their path. No real
desertion shall ever leave them helpless. Security is
the realm in which they dwell. The full inheritance
of faith is theirs. Eternity is the measure of their
happiness. May the Spirit fix these truths upon our
hearts, and help us mightily to depart from evil, and
to do good ! May our holiness be sure evidence that
we have received grace !

30, 31. *" The mouth of the righteous speaketh wisdom,
and his tongue talketh of judgment. The law of his God
is in his heart; none of his steps shall slide."*

Here is the portrait of the blessed Jesus. Grace was
ever poured upon His lips. His words were perfect
wisdom. His heart was love without alloy. His feet
were ever steadfast in untainted holiness. Such is our
bright example. May our distinction ever be the
mouth of wisdom, the guileless tongue, the heart of
love, the upright walk !

32, 33. "*The wicked watcheth the righteous, and seeketh to slay him. The Lord will not leave him in his hand, nor condemn him when he is judged.*"

The words are primarily predictive of our ever-blessed Head. Spies marked His words and ways. The cry was, Crucify Him! Crucify Him! A mock trial preceded condemnation. But iniquity could not prevail. He rose the Conqueror of death. He mounted to the right hand of God. The servants must not expect to find more kindness. But let not the righteous fear persecutions. They strengthen faith; they ripen grace; they give occasion for faithful testimony. They prove reality of grace. They lead to sure deliverance and final glory.

34, 35, 36. "*Wait on the Lord, and keep His way, and He shall exalt thee to inherit the land: when the wicked are cut off, thou shalt see it. I have seen the wicked in great power, and spreading himself like a green bay-tree: yet he passed away, and, lo, he was not; yea, I sought him, but he could not be found.*"

Line upon line, precept upon precept, forbid impatience. They call to the patience of hope and the obedient course. The promise is again and again repeated that we shall dwell eternally blessed in a new scene. A vivid picture shows how short-lived is ungodly prosperity. We see a tree of verdant beauty. Deep are its roots. Widespreading are its branches. We admire it to-day. To-morrow we seek it, and it is gone. Thus while we gaze, the wicked pass away.

37, 38. "*Mark the perfect man, and behold the upright: for the end of that man is peace. But the transgressors shall be destroyed together; the end of the wicked shall be cut off.*"

Can we claim interest in these descriptions of God's children? if so, let us cast off all fear. Many may be our troubles on the stormy billows of time; but we shall in perfect peace enter the eternal haven. The ungodly have their voyage of restlessness, and their end is misery.

39, 40. *"But the salvation of the righteous is of the Lord; He is their strength in the time of trouble. And the Lord shall help them, and deliver them: He shall deliver them from the wicked, and save them, because they trust in Him."*

Salvation is a free-grace gift. God wills it. God achieves it. God bestows it. The gift is without repentance. It is never recalled. The saved are for ever saved. No enemy shall prevail. God, by His Spirit, works faith in their hearts. They trust in Him. He strengthens. He upholds. He calls to heaven: and heaven they attain.

L.

PSALM XXXVIII. I–I2.

THE Psalmist, in deep sense of sin, and writhing under just chastisement, spreads his sad condition before God.

---

1. "*O Lord, rebuke me not in Thy wrath: neither chasten me in Thy hot displeasure.*"

What anguish follows in the rear of sin! It is the fruitful source of every woe. It sows vile seed, and crops of suffering spring up. It is so in the case of God's own children. Through want of vigilance, through restraint of prayer, through deafness to the Spirit's voice, through stiflings of conscience, through yielding to the craving of the flesh, and neglect of the sacred Word, they often stumble and fall grievously. God sees. His displeasure is justly kindled. Indignation puts forth angry hand. The scourge is not withholden, and miserable is the offender's case. But he well knows that his afflictions spring not from the dust. He knows the hand which chides is the hand of paternal love. He feels that his sufferings call him to the mercy-seat. He cries not for entire removal of what is so fully merited, but for alleviation and relief. He pleads, Let not anger wholly crush me. Let not hot displeasure be too fierce a furnace. "O Lord, rebuke me not in Thy wrath: neither chasten me in Thy hot displeasure."

2, 3, 4, 5. "*For Thine arrows stick fast in me, and Thy*

hand presseth me sore. There is no soundness in my flesh because of Thine anger; neither is there any rest in my bones because of my sin. For mine iniquities are gone over mine head; as an heavy burden they are too heavy for me. My wounds stink, and are corrupt, because of my foolishness."

As piercing arrows inflict rankling pain, as heavy burdens overwhelm and crush, thus sense of sin and realized displeasure bring agony of soul, and lay it low in sorrow. A wounded and bruised spirit, who can bear ? There is close sympathy between the mind and body. The wasted flesh reflects the pining spirit, and the whole frame shows ravages of malady. Iniquities, which seemed at first but tiny drops, soon swell into the billows of the overwhelming deep, and threaten to engulf the struggling sufferer. When the sluices open, descending torrents come, as a drowning deluge. No images can exhaust the anguish. The putrid sores but faintly show the miseries of the sin-stricken soul.

6, 7, 8. *" I am troubled ; I am bowed down greatly ; I go mourning all the day long. For my loins are filled with a loathsome disease; and there is no soundness in my flesh. I am feeble and sore broken: I have roared by reason of the disquietness of my heart."*

The Spirit still draws back the veil and shows in fearful tints the deep afflictions of the awakened conscience. Trouble occupies the heart. The head hangs down. The stooping gait is evidence of failing strength. Let those who seek to find delight in sin ponder this portrait. Through the whole day, from rising to declining sun, mourning is the constant comrade. The falling tears, the sighing heart, proclaim that misery presents no respite. The ruined health adds woe to woe. Loud lamentations prove that deep disquietude prevails within. Who can contemplate these results, and not detest the cruel monster!

9. "*Lord, all my desire is before Thee; and my groaning is not hid from Thee.*"

Out of these fearful depths there is a ready access to the throne of grace. The afflicted soul looks upward and appeals to God. No direct application is expressed, but attention is humbly craved to the desires which have a language in the ears of God. "The Spirit itself maketh intercession for us with groanings which cannot be uttered; and He that searcheth the hearts knoweth what is the mind of the Spirit."

10, 11, 12. "*My heart panteth, my strength faileth me: as for the light of mine eyes, it also is gone from me. My lovers and my friends stand aloof from my sore, and my kinsmen stand afar off. They also that seek after my life lay snares for me; and they that seek my hurt speak mischievous things, and imagine deceits all the day long.*"

The Psalmist, in the bitterness of his sorrow, enlarges on the aggravations of his misery. When sorrows multiply, how sweet is the solace of sympathizing friends! The complaint is heard that not only such relief was denied, but that enemies endeavoured to ensnare him, and ceased not to propagate injurious deceits. Faith sees that a greater than David is here. The "Man of Sorrows" thus shows the writhings of His heart, when He appeared as by imputation the bearer of His people's sins. While in spirit we hear His moans, let us bless Him from our inmost souls for all His substitutional anguish. He was bruised for our iniquities: He was wounded for our sins.

LI.

PSALM XXXVIII. 13-22.

13, 14. *" But I, as a deaf man, heard not; and I was as a dumb man that openeth not his mouth. Thus I was as a man that heareth not, and in whose mouth are no reproofs."*

Affliction's school is not a joyous place. Lessons of mirth and merriment are not learned therein. Sorrow sits pensive on the pupil's brow; but it is a sorrow which leads to abiding fruits of peace. Tribulation worketh patience. Proud petulance receives a death-blow. Reproof upbraids not. Meek submission bows its humble head. Surely here the blessed Jesus is conspicuous. " He was led as a lamb to the slaughter; and as a sheep before its shearers is dumb, so He opened not His mouth." No cruel taunts drew from His lips an angry reply. Majestic silence was His rebuke to Pilate. To keep our mouths as it were with a bridle is divine art. This is the blessed fruit of discipline under sorrow's scourge.

15. *" For in Thee, O Lord, do I hope: Thou wilt hear, O Lord my God."*

The true believer looks not to himself for power of defence or triumph over foes. His hope is fixed on Heaven. He knows that succour is at hand, even the succour which God alone can give. His prayers will stir up God to help, even the God who pro-

N

mises to hear. Thus patience worketh experience, and experience hope.

16. "*For I said, Hear me, lest otherwise they should rejoice over me: when my foot slippeth, they magnify themselves against me.*"

Faith is permitted humbly to expostulate with God. Come, let us reason together. Audience is craved on the plea that if no answer come, and no upholding grace supported, ungodly triumph would rejoice, and God's great name would be blasphemed. God's children are always watched with spiteful malice. The slightest tottering in the upward path causes the foe to raise insulting head, and boast of his happy and superior lot.

17, 18. "*For I am ready to halt, and my sorrow is continually before me. For I will declare mine iniquity; I will be sorry for my sin.*"

The believer is always conscious that in himself no strength resides. Unless upholden, he will surely fall. He knows his weakness; and he deeply mourns. He knows how often he has sadly fallen. He tells out his iniquity into the ears of God, and spreads out his sorrowing case.

19, 20. "*But mine enemies are lively, and they are strong; and they that hate me wrongfully are multiplied. They also that render evil for good are mine adversaries; because I follow the thing that good is.*"

If outward circumstances proved internal state, the ungodly would often seem to have the favourite's lot. Lively mirth is noisy in their dwelling. Their bow remains in strength; their ranks expand in numbers.

The Psalmist witnessed this seeming prosperity. In every age the enemies of God are thus allowed to have their short-lived triumph. The godly are not thereby provoked either to distrust of God, or to retaliate on their foes. They know that their godliness is the cause of all their persecution, and that the path of righteousness leads through the land of hate and cruelty. But their constant effort is to overcome evil with good ; and to be meek followers of the patient Lamb of God, the . holy Jesus, who could testify, " Many good works have I showed you from My Father, for which of those works do ye stone Me ? "

21, 22. " *Forsake me not, O Lord: O my God, be not far from me. Make haste to help me, O Lord, my salvation.*"

Prayer is the believer's constant refuge. Blessed are the trials which impel to the mercy-seat. Here triple supplications call down the presence of the Lord. Forsake me not—be not far from me, or be very near me—make haste to help me. The prayer is intensified by the invocation, O Lord, O my God, O Lord, my salvation. It is a grand privilege to be permitted to use such wrestling earnestness. It will assuredly prevail. Answers will richly come ; and God will show Himself a very present help in time of trouble.

LII.

PSALM XXXIX.

THE Psalmist resolves to be guarded in his speech. He reflects on the brevity of human life, and the vanity of earthly show. He prays in prospect of his near departure.

1, 2, 3. "*I said, I will take heed to my ways, that I sin not with my tongue; I will keep my mouth with a bridle, while the wicked is before me. I was dumb with silence; I held my peace, even from good; and my sorrow was stirred. My heart was hot within me; while I was musing the fire burned: then spake I with my tongue.*"

A grievous picture meets our eyes. Sad it is, and sadly common. The children of God are encompassed by the children of the evil one. Provocations press them to utter strong reproof; but holy wisdom checks impatient utterance. The bridled tongue avails more than indignant remonstrance. But the inward agitation, like smouldering embers, will break forth in flames. Again we see the meek and lowly Jesus. Amid the frantic fury and cruel mockings of His unjust judges and the raging crowd, no railing word breaks from His holy lips.

4. "*Lord, make me to know mine end, and the*

measure of my days, what it is; that I may know how frail I am."

Troubles find mitigation in the thought that they are linked to fleeting time, and soon must reach their end. Sense of brief tenure and near dissolution check all outbreaks of disquietude. Hence it is good to pray, Lord, teach us our frailty.

5, 6. "*Behold, Thou hast made my days as an hand-breadth, and mine age is as nothing before Thee: verily every man at his best state is altogether vanity. Surely every man walketh in a vain show; surely they are disquieted in vain: he heapeth up riches and knoweth not who shall gather them.*"

The tiniest span is fit emblem of an earthly course. Its measure is as nothing when compared with things eternal. The things which are seen are temporal, the things which are not seen are eternal. Look at the state which worldlings prize as the pinnacle of bliss. Let riches abound, and honours crown the brow, and power raise to loftiest station; let health bloom brightly, and strength nerve the limbs, let no worldly wish be ungratified—the whole is but the shadow of a shade, an empty husk, an unsubstantial show: it is as the flower of the grass,—green in the morning, in the evening dry and withered. The riches piled with toil, anxiety, and ceaseless effort, must be left. To whom? Uncertainty conceals the heir. No mind can tell who shall succeed.

7. "*And now, Lord, what wait I for? my hope is in Thee.*"

The believer waits in full assurance that aid will come from heaven in God's good time. Let all trials

be welcomed which brighten the rays of godly
hope.

8, 9, 10, 11. " *Deliver me from all my transgressions;
make me not the reproach of the foolish. I was dumb, I
opened not my mouth: because thou didst it. Remove
Thy stroke away from me: I am consumed by the blow
of Thine hand. When Thou with rebukes dost correct
man for iniquity, Thou makest his beauty to consume
away like a moth: surely every man is vanity.*"

Consciousness of sin as the indwelling root of
suffering will always abide, and should always prompt
the prayer for deliverance by the mighty power of
grace; and this prayer should be quickened by the
fear lest the ungodly should gain advantage, and
impiously exult. The resolve should be renewed to
endure patiently from persuasion that the hand of
God thus chastens that the fruits of righteousness
should spring up. Reiterated prayer calls for with-
drawal of the heavy hand. The feeble and the
withered look soon shows the anguish of the afflicted
heart. Behold the moth-eaten garment, unsound and
rotten—it is the emblem of the countenance of the
sin-stricken.

12, 13. " *Hear my prayer, O Lord, and give ear
unto my cry: hold not Thy peace at my tears; for I
am a stranger with Thee, and a sojourner, as all my
fathers were. O spare me, that I may recover strength,
before I go hence and be no more.*"

When troubles increase, prayers should wax more
earnest. It is good to realize that this is not our rest.
Our abiding city is not upon earth. Where are our
fathers? Are we better than they? But they are gone;

and as they went, we follow. But it should be our
deep desire that our last days should be our best, and
that as life fades our faith should more exalt the
praises of our God. For this we need increase of grace.
May we be so strengthened that our departing steps
may show the upward path, and allure beholders to
follow our example !

LIII.

PSALM XL. I—IO.

MARVELLOUS deliverance follows continued patience. Others are thereby quickened to act faith. God's goodness is unspeakable. Christ is the end of the law. Earnest supplication is awakened by a sense of surrounding evil. Strong desire follows that confusion may overwhelm the cruel mockers, while gladness and praise cheer the godly.

I, 2, 3. "*I waited patiently for the Lord, and He inclined unto me, and heard my cry. He brought me up also out of an horrible pit, out of the miry clay, and set my feet upon a rock, and established my goings. And He hath put a new song in my mouth, even praise unto our God: many shall see it and fear, and shall trust in the Lord.*"

Patience is a precious grace. O Lord, increase it in us. Like love, it suffers long, and suffers not in vain. The tree shaken by winds, the vine well-pruned, becomes abundant in rich fruits. The Lord arises at the earnest cry, and brings a rescue. Tribulation is as a horrible pit, beset with terribleness, and presenting no escape. It is as the miry clay in which the shackled feet move heavily. How sweet the change when the Lord's rescuing hand brings help! Then a firm pave-

ment courts advance, and forbids all halting and backsliding. Unencumbered climbers nimbly tread the
upward path. The path, too, resounds with joy. The
song of praise which had been silent again breaks
forth: and the Lord's name is duly magnified. The
happy result is not confined to the emancipated pilgrim. Many observe not only the believer's fall, but
also the evidences of God's goodness towards him. They
see that God's blessing truly rests upon His people—
awe fills their minds, and they are led to make the
Lord their trust.

4. *"Blessed is that man that maketh the Lord his trust,
and respecteth not the proud, nor such as turn aside to
lies."*

The observers see where true blessedness resides.
It is discovered to be far from the haughty, whose confidence is in self, and whose devious wanderings are
amid falsehoods and deceits.

5. *"Many, O Lord my God, are Thy wonderful works
which Thou hast done, and Thy thoughts which are to
us-ward: they cannot be reckoned up in order unto Thee:
if I would declare and speak of them, they are more than
can be numbered."*

An obvious reflection cannot be restrained. God's
mercies in providence and grace exceed all powers
to number, all eloquence to unfold. His thoughts
are ever devising wondrous works in our behalf.
His mighty hand is ever outstretched to accomplish
His gracious plans. Where is a God like unto our
God: our praises cannot reach His goodness: but let
us love and adore Him more and more.

6, 7, 8. *"Sacrifice and offering Thou didst not desire;*

*mine ears hast Thou opened: burnt-offering and sin-offer-
ing hast Thou not required. Then said I, Lo, I come: in
the volume of the book it is written of Me, I delight to do
Thy will, O my God: yea, Thy law is within my heart."*

As illustration that God's gracious thoughts exceed
all limits, the work of redeeming love, the everlasting
covenant decreed in the councils of heaven, the coming
of the Son in the likeness of sinful flesh, His abroga-
tion of all typical shadows, are particularized. Christ,
by His Holy Spirit speaks: no doubt obscures this
truth. The Apostle to the Hebrews declares it. In
the sacrifices of the Jewish Church there was no
finality. They pointed to the Gospel - fulfilment.
Every dying victim bleeding on every altar pointed
to Jesus hanging on the accursed tree. The blood
streaming from each sacrifice foreshadowed the all-
cleansing blood of Calvary. But in the shadow there
was no satisfaction. By Christ alone is full atonement made and everlasting expiation rendered. To
accomplish this redeeming work, the Saviour must
assume our nature. A body must be prepared for
Him. As in the law, the willing servant testified by
boring of the ear his devotedness to his master's
service; so in the volume of eternal decrees, and in the
pages of Scripture, Christ's willing work is testified.
Redemption was the Father's will. To do this will
was Christ's intense delight. Father, we bless Thee
for Thy love, the cause of all salvation. Precious
Jesus, we bless Thee for Thy love which undertook
and finished the glorious work!

9, 10. "*I have preached righteousness in the great congregation: lo, I have not refrained my lips, O Lord, Thou*

knowest. *I have not hid Thy righteousness within my heart; I have declared Thy faithfulness and Thy salvation: I have not concealed Thy loving-kindness and Thy truth from the great congregation.*"

As Jesus fulfilled the priestly office by the sacrifice of Himself, so He fulfils His work as prophet. By His lips, by the announcement of His servants, taught and aided by His Spirit, the righteousness of God is proclaimed from age to age. No veil conceals the glorious mysteries of salvation. The whole scheme is traced to its grand source. The loving-kindness and truth of God is duly set forth. Happy they who are privileged to hear from faithful lips the words of life ! Happy they who gladly embrace them, and ascribe salvation to the free will and gracious purpose of the divine Jehovah !

LIV.

PSALM XL. 11–17.

11. " *Withhold not Thou Thy tender mercies from me,
O Lord: let Thy loving-kindness and Thy truth continually preserve me.*"

There is no sweeter encouragement in prayer than
the knowledge that the whole work of redemption has
been fully accomplished by our mystical Head; and
that all the mercies of the covenant of grace are a
purchased possession. The believer may draw near
with boldness and claim the guardian care, not only
of loving-kindness but also of truth. Believers are in
peril at every moment; but at every moment the
mercies for which Christ has paid the price of His
most precious death are near ; and loving-kindness and
truth are continually ready to uphold.

12. " *For innumerable evils have compassed me about ;
mine iniquities have taken hold upon me, so that I am
not able to look up : they are more than the hairs of mine
head ; therefore my heart faileth me.*"

To the eye of faith the blessed Jesus here conspicuously appears. "All we like sheep have gone astray ;
we have turned every one to his own way, but the Lord
hath laid on Him the iniquities of us all." " He was
made sin for us, who knew no sin, that we might be made
the righteousness of God in Him." Thus He stands
before God, by imputation as the greatest sinner ever

seen on earth. He denies not His sin-laden position.
He accepts all the iniquities of all His people, as verily
His own. He acknowledges their grievous weight.
They so depress Him that He cannot raise His eyes.
In numbers they exceed all power to count. In de-
vout consciousness of the immensity of relief, with
what fervour will the believer bless His burden-bearer
—His sin-sustainer—the Lamb of God, that taketh
away his sin !

1 3. *" Be pleased, O Lord, to deliver me : O Lord, make
haste to help me."*

Emboldened by the plea that all guilt is transferred to Christ, the believer urgently implores deliverance, and craves immediate succour from his God.
May the Lord increase our faith, that we may wrestle
in full assurance that all the provisions of the covenant
of grace are truly ours !

1 4, 1 5. *" Let them be ashamed and confounded together that seek after my soul to destroy it ; let them be
driven backward, and put to shame, that wish me evil.
Let them be desolate for a reward of their shame that
say unto me, Aha, aha ! "*

This petition is prophetic. It foresees the final
overthrow of Antichrist, and all the opposing hosts of
darkness. The seed of the woman shall surely bruise
the serpent's head. The Gospel has gone forth conquering and to conquer. Voices in heaven shall assuredly proclaim, " The kingdoms of this world are
become the kingdoms of our Lord, and of His Christ ;
and He shall reign for ever and ever." His enemies
shall lick the dust. The awful cry will be heard,
" Hide us from the face of Him that sitteth on the

throne, and from the wrath of the Lamb." Blessed
are they who have fled for refuge to the wounded side
of Jesus! They are delivered from the wrath to come.
When weeping, and wailing, and gnashing of teeth,
are the one sound of woe, they will commence the
everlasting hymn of praise.

1 6. " *Let all those that seek Thee rejoice and be glad
in Thee: let such as love Thy salvation say continually,
The Lord be magnified.*"

The character of the rejoicing company is distinctly
drawn. They seek the Lord: they love His salvation.
It is their grand desire to know more of Christ: they
forsake all to follow Him: they strive to grow in grace,
and in His knowledge; and their whole hearts delight
in the salvation which He so dearly purchased, and so
freely gives. Their joy is to exalt the Lord, and lift
high His praise.

1 7. " *But I am poor and needy; yet the Lord thinketh
upon me: Thou art my help and my deliverer; make no
tarrying, O my God.*"

Deep consciousness of poverty continually abides.
In us, that is in our flesh, there dwelleth no good thing.
Yet we are rich and have all things in the gracious
care of our God. His thoughts of love are ever on
His people. He is their help and their deliverer, and
their cry gives Him no rest, " Make no tarrying, O my
God."

LV.

PSALM XLI.

THE happy state of the compassionate is depicted. The vindictive malevolence of the ungodly is also shown. Prayer to God and profession of faith follow with warm ascription of praise.

1, 2, 3. " *Blessed is he that considereth the poor: the Lord will deliver him in time of trouble. The Lord will preserve him and keep him alive ; and he shall be blessed upon the earth: and Thou wilt not deliver him unto the will of His enemies. The Lord will strengthen him upon the bed of languishing: Thou wilt make all his bed in his sickness.*"

Tender compassion for the poor and suffering is the fruit of the Spirit in the minds of believers. It is a sweet feature in the family of faith. The Lord regards such with peculiar love. But they are not exempt from trouble. Their heavenward march is through much tribulation : sickness often assails their frames, languor depresses them, and weakness holds them to a bed of suffering. But they are not deserted—nay, they now are compassed with peculiar mercies. When heart and flesh appear to fail, the inner man is renewed with especial strength. Welcome all sickness which brings Jesus to the bedside !

4. " *I said, Lord, be merciful unto me: heal my soul ; for I have sinned against Thee.*"

The suffering saint draws nearer to his God. He cloaks not his sin: he sees in it the cause of soul-disease, and he supplicates for mercy to bring relief.

5, 6, 7, 8. "*Mine enemies speak evil of me; when shall he die, and his name perish? And if he come to see me, he speaketh vanity: his heart gathereth iniquity to itself; when he goeth abroad, he telleth it. All that hate me whisper together against me: against me do they devise my hurt. An evil disease, say they, cleaveth fast unto him: and now that he lieth, he shall rise up no more.*"

Sad is this picture of the treachery and deep malice of false friends. It is grief to them that the godly live. They long for the day when the grave shall cover them, and their fame no more be heard. This is the very treatment which assailed the holy Jesus. Grievous sins were laid to His charge. Watchful spies marked His words and steps; and base accusations were continually propagated, and when the grave received Him, vigilance guarded the tomb lest His predicted reappearance should be verified.

9. "*Yea, mine own familiar friend, in whom I trusted, which did eat of my bread, hath lifted up his heel against me.*"

Doubtless, in the first instance, Absalom is here portrayed. But in his heartless and unnatural rebellion he is the type of the vile traitor, whose wickedness can find no parallel in the history of crime. We see in him to what a depth of sin the graceless heart can sink. He walked the familiar friend of Jesus, he was constantly by His side, he witnessed His heavenly walk, and with all knowledge of His truth, he took a paltry bride to sell Him to His foes. We learn from this foreshadowing of the treason, that our blessed Lord approached redemption's work with full knowledge of the anguish and the sufferings before Him.   O blessed Jesus! we adore Thee that, foreknowing all, Thou didst endure all to raise us from sin and sin's deserts to the heights of heavenly glory!

10, 11. *" But Thou, O Lord, be merciful unto me, and raise me up, that I may requite them.   By this I know that Thou favourest me, because mine enemy doth not triumph over me."*

Predictions still speak.   From the dead Jesus was raised.   All power in heaven and earth was surrendered to Him.   All the enemies who fought against Him were crushed beneath the wheels of His car of triumph. Happy they who meekly bow before Him, and accept His blessed sway!

12, 13. *" And as for me, Thou upholdest me in mine integrity, and settest me before Thy face for ever.   Blessed be the Lord God of Israel from everlasting, and to everlasting.   Amen, and Amen."*

Jesus was upheld until He returned in triumph to the heaven of heavens, and took His seat as King of Glory on the right hand of the Majesty on High.   So each believer may plead with confidence the promise, " I will never leave thee nor forsake thee."   Constant smiles will gild the passage to the realms of everlasting light.   Let, then, the shout commence on earth, which shall continue through eternity's bright day, "Blessed be the Lord God of Israel, from everlasting and to everlasting.   Amen, and Amen!"

LVI.

PSALM XLII.

REJECTION is the pervading note of this hymn. The joys of the sanctuary are forbidden. Insulting foes augment distress. In conclusion, the soul is chided for yielding to despondency.

1, 2. "*As the hart panteth after the water-brooks, so panteth my soul after Thee, O God. My soul thirsteth for God, for the living God: when shall I come and appear before God?*"

A tender and expressive image meets us. The hart, exhausted by long flight beneath the scorching sun, or in the dusty plain, pants for the cooling stream in which to quench the pangs of thirst. How eagerly relief is sought! Here is the believer banished from the sweet refreshments of the sanctuary. It is not so much the outward form which is the object of desire, but the intimate communion with God, to which the services, when duly used, would surely raise. In true worship God's presence is sought and found, and thoroughly enjoyed.

3, 4. "*My tears have been my meat day and night, while they continually say unto me, Where is thy God? When I remember these things, I pour out my soul in me: for I had gone with the multitude, I went with*" *them to the house of God, with the voice of joy and praise, with a multitude that kept holy-day."*

Fast flowing tears testified the deep sorrows of the Redeemer's heart, when He heard the revilings of His foes. They taunted Him with the sneer, that surely His banishment from holy service was proof that God had forsaken Him. His mind reverted to the happy seasons when, in happy company, He sought the sanctuary, and joined His praises to those of the multitude of fellow-worshippers. It is the very ante-past of heaven, with one mind, and one mouth, to unite in public adoration.

5. *" Why art thou cast down, O my soul ? and why art thou disquieted in me ? hope thou in God ; for I shall yet praise Him for the help of His countenance."*

Too much depression is a sign of languid faith—dis-quietude should never occupy a godly heart. It is well to chide the soul, and rouse it from its down-cast state. Hope should go forth in lively exercise. In darkest days it should look to Jesus, and take courage. No-thing should weaken the assurance that the issue of the most grievous trials will be increased thanksgiving to our God.

6. *" O my God, my soul is cast down within me : therefore will I remember Thee from the land of Jordan, and of the Hermonites, from the hill Mizar."*

Its consolation is not easily eradicated. Like the noxious weed again and again it re-appears. But thoughts of God will still revive in the faithful breast. Though God may be apparently far distant, the eye of faith will turn towards Him. Though driven beyond

Jordan, the Psalmist still remembers Zion, and the tabernacles of his God.

7, 8. "*Deep calleth unto deep at the noise of Thy water-spouts: all Thy waves and Thy billows are gone over me. Yet the Lord will command His loving-kindness in the day-time, and in the night His song shall be with me, and my prayer unto the God of my life.*"

As wave upon wave, distress will sometimes follow distress. As descending rain swells the streams, and floods overwhelm the plains, so torrents of sorrow will oppress the heart. Yet the believer is sustained by undoubting trust. He knows that loving-kindness has received a mandate to visit him throughout the day, and to cheer him with songs in the night season, and to strengthen him to wrestle with God in prayer, as the God who maintains his life.

9, 10. "*I will say unto God my rock, Why hast Thou forgotten me? why go I mourning because of the oppression of the enemy? As with a sword in my bones, mine enemies reproach me; while they say daily unto me, Where is thy God?*"

When the believer can realize that God is his rock, he is bold to expostulate, and thinks it no presumption to implore attention to his suffering case. He states as the extremity of his anguish, that he is pierced to the quick by the impious insolence of cruel mockers, who reiterate the taunt, that God has forsaken him, and is indifferent to his woe. He appeals to God, Wherefore am I thus afflicted?

11. "*Why art thou cast down, O my soul? and why art thou disquieted within me? hope thou in God; for I shall yet praise Him, who is the health of my countenance, and my God.*"

Expostulation with the soul is repeated. Trials will return; and they must be met with renewal of spiritual reasoning. The covenant is for ever settled in heaven. Hope, therefore, should never fail. Deliverance will surely come. The voice of praise will again shout, "He is the health of my countenance, and my God."

LVII.

PSALM XLIII.

THE pensive note of the preceding hymn is here prolonged.   The circumstances are the same; the same,
too, are the exercises and the expressions of the mind.

---

1. "*Judge me, O God, and plead my cause against an
ungodly nation: O deliver me from the deceitful and unjust man.*"

Happy is the man who is conscious of his own
integrity.   He can lift up his eyes in holy confidence
to his God, and pray Him to vindicate his cause
against iniquitous oppression.   If God be for us, who
can be against us ?   There were many occasions in the
checkered life of David in which this cry would be
appropriate.   The aged monarch, the heart-broken
parent, would thus most fitly pray, when his own
child rose up to hurl him from his throne, and the
ungodly nation joined in the impious attempt.   Here
is the experience of many followers of Christ.   Because
they are not of the world, but Christ hath chosen
them out of the world, therefore the world hateth them.
In all these troubles they may appeal to God, and
never will they cry in vain.

2. "*For Thou art the God of my strength: why dost
Thou cast me off?   Why go I mourning because of the
oppression of the enemy ?*"

It is the province of faith to realize that in all seeming weakness there is really strength. But where is the treasure-house of strength? It is not in self. For man unaided is a broken reed,—light as the chaff before the wind—powerless as an infant in a giant's grasp. But his strength is firm as the everlasting hills. It is Jehovah in His might. While he trembles, he can still cry, Thou art the God of my strength. But still he is perplexed. Outward troubles seem to indicate desertion and rejection. The enemy oppresses; he cannot but mourn. Many thoughts arise, that these trials are to recall from devious paths, and are the chastenings of just displeasure. He draws near with bold familiarity, and supplicates revealing grace. It should be a frequent prayer, " Search me, O Lord, and know my heart : prove me, and know my ways : and see if there be any wicked way in me."

3. " *O send out Thy light and Thy truth : let them lead me, let them bring me unto Thy holy hill, and to Thy tabernacles.*"

Left to ourselves, we are in darkness, and we surely stray. Conscious of need and guidance, the disconsolate Psalmist prays for heavenly aid, and that light from above would clearly shine upon his path; and that all events in providence would be in accordance with the provisions of the everlasting covenant. They who truly follow the Lamb shall not walk in darkness but shall have the light of life. They know that the conditions of the covenant secure their everlasting weal, and they confidently plead that God would do unto them in accordance with its terms. He prays especially that he may be restored to the joys of holy worship. He thinks not so much of the comforts and splendour of his palace, of his costly board, and luxurious delights—his heart is fixed on the hill of Zion and the house of God. There he had sought spiritual communion—in comparison with this, he counted other things as less than dross.

4. " *Then will I go unto the altar of God, unto God my exceeding joy : yea, upon the harp will I praise Thee, O God, my God.*"

The essence of delight in public ordinances is the knowledge that sin is pardoned through atoning blood, and that there is free access to God through the expiating sacrifice of the dying Lamb. Then the heart swells with all the ecstasy of joy, happiness rolls in fullest tide, delight ascends to its highest pinnacle. God thus realized as reconciled, is exceeding bliss. The cup overflows. The bliss exceeds all bounds. Every faculty and every power is awakened to sing praise. Rapturous is the theme, when the soul intelligently sings, O God, Thou art my God!

5. " *Why art thou cast down, O my soul ? and why art thou disquieted within me ? Hope in God ; for I shall yet praise Him, who is the health of my countenance and my God.*"

To him who can call God his own God, no cause of disquietude remains. He can trample all fears and doubts beneath his feet. He can see clearly by the eye of hope the blissful prospect of deliverance.

LVIII.

PSALM XLIV. 1–14.

THE Church is here exhibited as in the depths of grievous trouble. But faith reviews the mercies of past days before it bewails present sufferings. Confidence in God is then professed, and prayer pleads with fervent zeal.

1, 2, 3. "*We have heard with our ears, O God, our fathers have told us, what work Thou didst in their days, in the times of old. How Thou didst drive out the heathen with Thy hand, and plantedst them; how Thou didst afflict the people, and cast them out. For they got not the land in possession by their own sword, neither did their own arm save them; but Thy right hand, and Thine arm, and the light of Thy countenance, because Thou hadst a favour unto them.*"

The study of God's dealings with His people sweetly quickens faith. What strength is gained by pondering the subjugation of the heathen tribes, the victorious march of Israel's hosts, and their grand triumphs over all foes! But, did this conquest arise from their own might? Their own sword was weak to conquer, their own arm was powerless to save. The might of Jehovah was their prowess, the favour of the Lord was their prevalence. The Lord fought for them, and they were invincible. Individual believers should constantly review their Ebenezers. A marvellous work has been transacted in their souls. Mighty foes have fought against them. Weak has been their own strength; yet they have prevailed. It is the Lord who has upheld and strengthened them, and caused their enemies to flee. Grace begins; grace carries on; grace will complete the work of deliverance and salvation.

4. " *Thou art my King, O God: command deliverances for Jacob.*"

The believer claims succour as a subject of the Lord of Hosts. Thou art my King: Thy sceptre is omnipotence. Thy word goes forth with absolute power. Resistance is vain. Speak, then, one word, and victory ensues.

5. " *Through Thee will we push down our enemies; through Thy name will we tread them under that rise up against us.*"

Who can resist when God comes forth to help. He is a horn of salvation. Creatures thus armed are terrible in fight: so the believer advances to sure conquest. Striding onward in the name of the Lord, he tramples down opposing hosts. Thus aided he will bruise Satan under his feet shortly.

6, 7, 8. " *For I will not trust in my bow, neither shall my sword save me. But Thou hast saved us from our enemies, and hast put them to shame that hated us. In God we boast all the day long, and praise Thy name for ever.*"

When the Holy Spirit reveals to us our own weakness, and nothingness, and sinfulness, all self-confidence is utterly destroyed; our best strength is feebleness. To trust in self is to lean on a rotten plank. But

still we are invincible, and utter confusion must overwhelm all adversaries. Let, then, every moment of
each day testify our unwavering confidence, and our
happy assurance that heavenly protection will never
fail. Let praise on earth begin, even the praise which
shall never end.

9, 10, 11, 12, 13, 14. " *But Thou hast cast off, and put
us to shame; and goest not forth with our armies. Thou
makest us to turn back from the enemy; and they which
hate us spoil for themselves. Thou hast given us like sheep
appointed for meat; and hast scattered us among the
heathen. Thou sellest Thy people for nought, and dost not
increase Thy wealth by their price. Thou makest us a
reproach to our neighbours, a scorn and a derision to them
that are round about us. Thou makest us a by-word
among the heathen, a shaking of the head among the
people.*"

In varied and most graphic terms the sufferings of
the godly are here depicted. Trouble is a needful
path. The discipline corrects many budding evils,
lops off the excrescences of pride, self-confidence, and
self-righteousness, leads to the healthy vale of humiliation, and meetens for the inheritance of the saints in
light. Hence we must, through much tribulation,
enter into the kingdom of heaven. In the furnace of
these trials the mourner is prone to write bitter things
against himself, and to draw fears of God's desertion.
But let patience have its perfect work: our fathers in
the faith have trodden this path before us. Mark the
great multitude, which no man can number, of all
nations, and kindreds, and people, and tongues, which
stand before the throne and before the Lamb, clothed

with white robes, and palms in their hands.   These are
they which came out of great tribulation, and have
washed their robes, and made them white in the blood
of the Lamb.   Good Lord, purge us, and we shall be
clean ; wash us. and we shall be whiter than snow.

LIX.

PSALM XLIV. 15-26.

15, 16. " *My confusion is continually before me, and the shame of my face hath covered me, for the voice of him that reproacheth and blasphemeth ; by reason of the enemy and avenger.*"

Enmity is placed between the diverse children of light and darkness. The ungodly vent their hate in torrents of reproach. These shafts inflict most grievous wounds. The downcast look, the heaving breast, bear testimony to the inward smart.

17, 18, 19. " *All this is come upon us ; yet have we not forgotten Thee, neither have we dealt falsely in Thy covenant. Our heart is not turned back, neither have our steps declined from Thy way ; though Thou hast sore broken us in the place of dragons, and covered us with the shadow of death.*"

Faith may be sorely tried, but still its constancy remains. The tree yet lives, though wintry blasts denude it. In all distress the mind adheres to God. The pledged allegiance is not broken ; and the vows of love and service are most diligently kept. The heart continues its covenanted affections, and the feet turn not from the narrow way of life. There is no faltering even in the extremity of misery. The seed of the old serpent will not relax in cruelty and venom, and death in many shapes may threaten, yet Christian principles will triumph. Prison-cells have sounded with the voice of trust, and martyrs at the stake have smiled amid their agonies.

20, 21. "*If we have forgotten the name of our God, or stretched out our hands to a strange god; shall not God search this out? for He knoweth the secrets of the heart.*"

The heart is kept steadfast, when persecution is most hot, by the reflection that God's eye watches each movement. "How shall I do this great wickedness and sin against God?" is a sure check when tempted to seek help from other than our God. "Thou God seest me" is a thought which braces the loins and brings needful strength.

22. "*Yea, for Thy sake are we killed all the day long; we are counted as sheep for the slaughter.*"

Persecution and oppression are the heritage of the Lord's followers in every age. They who hate the Lord will not have kindlier feelings towards His devoted flock. Since the day when righteous Abel fell by his brother's hand, the same spirit has not ceased its cruel work. Alas! what scenes of malignant enmity has this earth witnessed: what cries of misery have ascended from the tortured in gloomy dungeons and in open martyrdom! If like opportunities were given, like cruelties would be re-enacted. Paul, writing by the Spirit's guidance, warns that the portrait which this verse exhibits will represent the persecuted flock until the end of time. But encouragement is added. Vain the sword, the stake, the prison, and all the train of multitudinous barbarities. "In all these things we are more than conquerers through Him that loved us." The inward joy exceeds all outward pain. While the flesh quivers, the spirit sings, "None but Jesus." A car of agony conveys the happy sufferers to fulness of joy and pleasures at God's right hand for evermore.

23, 24, 25, 26. *"Awake, why sleepest Thou, O Lord? arise, cast us not off for ever. Wherefore hidest Thou Thy face, and forgettest our affliction and our oppression? For our soul is bowed down to the dust; our belly cleaveth unto the earth. Arise for our help, and redeem us, for Thy mercies' sake."*

The reality of the misery is not denied. Appearances seem to justify the apprehension that God's eye no longer rests on the oppressed. But still faith lives, and waxes bolder in wrestling importunity. It will not let God go. Its cries are redoubled for early succour. No merit is pleaded—nay, all unworthiness is allowed. Deliverance is implored, but only on the ground that God is rich in mercy. In the lowest depths faith looks up to God, as the Father of all mercies, as delighting in mercy, whose mercy endureth for ever, and the cry ascends, "Send help according to the multitude of Thy tender mercies." Happy they who boldly urge the prevailing plea, "Redeem us for Thy mercies' sake."

LX.

PSALM XLV. 1—9.

THIS hymn is fitly termed a song of loves. It is a prelude to the Song of songs. The spiritual Bridegroom is rapturously commended. The Spouse is shown in lovely features. The extension of Christ's kingdom, and due praise is promised.

1. "*My heart is inditing a good matter: I speak of the things which I have made touching the king; my tongue is the pen of a ready writer.*"

One object ever sits supreme in the believer's heart. Christ is the noble theme which claims his fervent commendation. Praises break forth as water bubbling from a heated caldron. They cannot be repressed. When Jesus is thus the subject in all the majesty and glory of His kingly office, the fluency cannot be checked. As a skilled writer quickly moves his pen, so the believer's tongue is prompt and ready to express due praise. Boundless is the subject, commensurate is the utterance.

2. "*Thou art fairer than the children of men; grace is poured into Thy lips: therefore God hath blessed thee for ever.*"

The Church, taught by the Spirit, warmly cries, "Behold thou art fair, my love; behold thou art fair." Christ is indeed the chiefest among ten thousand, the altogether lovely. What eloquence can show His beauty ? He is the brightness of His Father's glory, the express image of His person. Every charm which wins admiring gaze dwelt resplendently in Him. Wisdom in the highest flowed from His lips, and such power attended His words that the blessing of en-lightening grace and saving impression touched His hearers.

3, 4. "*Gird Thy sword upon Thy thigh, O most mighty, with Thy glory and Thy majesty. And in Thy majesty ride prosperously because of truth and meekness and righteousness; and Thy right hand shall teach Thee terrible things.*"

Faith in prophetic terms calls on the Lord to equip Himself for glorious triumphs, and to ascend the car of His majestic course. He is most mighty. Who can withstand Him ? His weapons secure prosperous result. His truth lays error low in the dust of shame. His meekness sweetly allures sinners to receive Him. His righteousness conceals all guilt, and is a glorious robe for all who own His sway. Who can con-template without awe the exploits of His matchless might ? Let our souls mark and tremble and adore.

5. "*Thine arrows are sharp in the heart of the king's enemies; whereby the people fall under Thee.*"

Sharp indeed are the arrows of conviction, when directed by the Spirit. The contrite sinner feels the grievous wound, and humbly mourns his miserable state. He who inflicts the wound alone can cure. The blood alone can ease the rankling smart.

6, 7. "*Thy throne, O God, is for ever and ever: the*

P

sceptre of Thy kingdom is a right sceptre. Thou lovest righteousness and hatest wickedness; therefore God, Thy God, hath anointed Thee with the oil of gladness above Thy fellows."

The glorious truth that Jesus is eternal God is here proclaimed. The Spirit speaks from heaven, and His voice addresses Him as God. His essential Deity is the foundation of salvation. This gives infinite efficacy to His atoning blood, indisputable perfection to His justifying righteousness, and enables Him to satisfy the claims of every attribute of Jehovah. Let the true believer constantly address Him, My Lord and My God. His throne is for ever established, and His sceptre ruleth over all on principles most just and equitable. Righteousness is the government of His subjects. Holiness is happiness. Hence happiness is the atmosphere of His happy kingdom. God gives the spirit of joy without measure unto the King, and His blessed subjects are joint-heirs with Him of all the gifts of righteousness and grace.

8, 9. *"All Thy garments smell of myrrh, and aloes, and cassia, out of the ivory palaces, whereby they have made Thee glad. Kings' daughters were among Thy honourable women: upon Thy right hand did stand the queen in gold of Ophir."*

The image of royal pre-eminence is still continued. The King is pictured as coming forth from his beauteous palace arrayed in all the splendour of regal attire. The perfumes of his robes spread fragrance around. Upon his right hand is the Queen, the type of His believing people, arrayed in the splendour of the purest gold, the figure of that glorious righteousness which He bestows. The allegoric picture adds a circle of attendants to complete the group. No special lesson is conveyed by this company. But ardent feeling cannot be restrained that we may have a place in this assemblage, and pay homage to the King in His beauty.

LXI.

PSALM XLV. 10-17.

10, 11. "*Hearken, O daughter, and consider, and incline thine ear; forget also thine own people, and thy father's house; so shall the King greatly desire thy beauty: for He is thy Lord; and worship thou Him.*"

The Holy Spirit, speaking from heaven, invites attention to His words. It is sad that such exhortation should be needed. It is more sad that it should ever issue forth in vain. Not only should the ears be open, but the heart should diligently ponder. Words from above should be a perpetual feast. The Spirit here exhorts the bride to cast away remembrance of her first estate, the home of her birth and her native companions. By nature we are born in sin—the children of wrath, the inheritors of corrupt affections, the companions of aliens and outcasts. When the Spirit reveals Jesus, all tenderness and love, a marvellous change ensues, all things are counted less than dross in comparison of Him. In His comeliness we become comely. Our cry is, Thou art our Lord—we love, we worship, and adore.

12. "*And the daughter of Tyre shall be there with a gift; even the rich among the people shall entreat thy favour.*"

It sometimes happens that they who receive honour from the Lord receive honour from men also. There is an inward recognition that respect is due to them and outward reverence is duly paid.

13. *" The King's daughter is all glorious within ; her clothing is of wrought gold."*

This is a lovely picture of the true believer. His inward state is glorious. He is adorned with every grace, and grace is the seed of glory. The Spirit, by His power, rules throughout the inward man, and implants faith, and hope, and love, and every holy principle, affection, and desire. All that is vile, corrupt, base, and earthly, is cast out; that which is sown is glory in the bud, and soon will be glory in full flower. But, though thus glorious, the believer cannot inherit glory, unless every sinful spot be hid. Christ works for His people a righteousness which He imputes. It is His perfect obedience with which He invests His every member. It is pure, and perfect, and without one stain of blemish. Wrought gold depicts it. Brightly they shine on whom it is bestowed.

14, 15. *" She shall be brought unto the King in raiment of needlework : the virgins her companions that follow her shall be brought unto Thee. With gladness and rejoicing shall they be brought : they shall enter into the King's palace."*

The bridal allegory is continued. The bride is seen in raiment beautified by art's elaborate skill. Attendant maidens swell the train. All sounds of joy give notice of the glad approach. The royal residence is reached, and gates are opened to give welcome. The happy emblems fitly picture the triumphant scene, when the marriage of the Lamb

shall be come, and His wife shall have made herself
ready. Let all who love the Lord, and have in faith
and truth devoted themselves to Him, rejoice with joy
unspeakable and full of glory. The day is coming
when they shall be publicly recognized, and, clad in
the perfect robe of righteousness, they shall enter
heaven with all manifestations of joy and pure delight.
With such bright prospects who will not sing, We
bless Thee, we praise Thee, we adore Thee, O Lord,
our God ?

16. " *Instead of thy fathers shall be thy children,
whom thou mayest make princes in all the earth.*"

Scripture is the exceeding joy of faith, because of
the enchanting pictures which in ever-varying form it
presents. We have seen the widespread family of the
redeemed. In every clime, in every age, they live and
flourish. High, too, is their dignity. Wherever they
appear they excel as princes. They rule over sin and
all the poor attractions of the world, while others
yield, and toil as slaves beneath the lash of Satan.

17. " *I will make Thy name to be remembered in all
generations: therefore shall the people praise Thee for
ever and ever.*"

It is the duty of the Church—it is, too, her most
happy work—to celebrate the praises of the Lord, and
to tell aloud of His love and goodness, of His majesty
and glory. Thus, from age to age, and in earth's
utmost range, the name of Jesus is magnified and
glorified. Bless the Lord, O my soul, and let all
saints prolong the song of thankful praise !

LXII.

PSALM XLVI.

GOD'S near protection is a stronghold against all fear.
The wonders of His mighty hand should excite terror
in His foes, and confidence in His people.

---

1. " *God is our refuge and strength, a very present help
in trouble.*"

Such is the boast of all the sons of faith. Their
path is through a land of trouble. Their bark is tossed
by raging billows. Their foes are many from within
and from without. They flee to God, and are secure :
to God who is for ever near. How safe are they who in
this refuge dwell ; how strong are they, whose strength
is God !

2, 3. " *Therefore will not we fear, though the earth be
removed, and though the mountains be carried into the
midst of the sea ; though the waters thereof roar and be
troubled, though the mountains shake with the swelling
thereof.*"

Tremendous images here show all nature in commotion. Ocean roars, and is agitated from its lowest
depths. Mountains tremble from the lashing of the
waves ; their heads submerged no longer show their
peaks. The scene is earth in the extremity of confusion. We are here taught to view the heart tossed
and disturbed by all the violence of troubles—they

break like mighty billows, threatening to destroy ; but no fears prevail. Amid convulsing elements there is the calmness of serene repose.

4. " *There is a river, the streams whereof shall make glad the city of God, the holy place of the tabernacles of the Most High.*"

As a river flowing through a city spreads gladness all around, as the refreshing streams bring plenty, and cause health to smile, so the presence of God is constant joy and peace to the believing heart. This heart is the abode of God—the place where He holds dwelling, and manifests His presence. So fears cannot approach, and gladness holds its constant reign.

5. " *God is in the midst of her ; she shall not be moved: God shall help her, and that right early.*"

How blessed is the state, when God will not withdraw. No trouble can give real alarm. No apprehensions agitate. God will give early help, and His help is perfect peace.

6, 7. " *The heathen raged, the kingdoms were moved: He uttered His voice, the earth melted. The Lord of hosts is with us ; the God of Jacob is our refuge.*"

What though mighty powers, with mighty rage, muster their hosts ; what though extensive kingdoms are in commotion, and all appearances threaten destruction—it gives the Lord no trouble to defeat the adversaries. He only speaks the word, and they sink low in ruin. His voice annihilates, and they disappear as snow when melted by the sun. The believer gives no place to fear. If hosts are all arrayed against him, the Lord of hosts is on his side. He who upheld the fathers of the Church still lives :

His covenant of old is verity and truth. He will perform the oath to Abraham, and the promise to Jacob. If we be Christ's, then are we Abraham's seed, and heirs according to the promise.

8, 9. " *Come, behold the works of the Lord, what desolations He hath made in the earth. He maketh wars to cease unto the end of the earth ; He breaketh the bow, and cutteth the spear in sunder ; he burneth the chariot in the fire.*"

Our minds are prone to disregard the mighty workings of the Lord. His hand is ever doing wonders, which we fail to notice. But it is our wisdom to observe how He manifests His interposing power to make desolate the regions of His foes. Whatever be the hostile preparations and the stores of ammunition, He can bring all to nought.

10, 11. " *Be still, and know that I am God : I will be exalted among the heathen, I will be exalted in the earth. The Lord of hosts is with us ; the God of Jacob is our refuge.*"

Let, then, all perturbing thoughts be banished. Let tranquil patience exert calm sway. God will be manifest as supreme sovereign, curbing the heathen's rage, and exercising unlimited control throughout the earth. Let all His people rejoice evermore, and loudly sing, from realizing hearts, "The Lord of hosts is with us : the God of Jacob is our refuge !"

LXIII.

PSALM XLVII.

A VIEW is presented of the kingdom of Christ most gloriously established, and universal praises are evoked.

1, 2. "*O clap your hands, all ye people; shout unto God with the voice of triumph.　For the Lord most High is terrible; He is a great King over all the earth.*"

A note of rapturous prediction pervades this hymn. The day of glory is anticipated, when angels' voices shall proclaim that the kingdoms of this world are become the kingdoms of our God, and of His Christ, and He shall reign for ever and ever.　The word is now verified, "In Thee shall all the families of the earth be blessed." The Jewish Church shall expand her arms to embrace the called of the Gentiles—and they are received as fellow-heirs, and of the same body, and partakers of His promise in Christ.　The Lord is magnified in all His power and majesty—the terribleness of His vengeance over all who yielded not obedience to His sway is awfully displayed—and on His head are crowns of supremacy over all the earth.　Oh! day of gladness, and unspeakable delight!　The happy subjects of these joyful realms are stirred up to show their ecstasy by every sign.　We, too, in prospect of such happiness, should shout our praises and proclaim our triumph.

3, 4. " *He shall subdue the people under us, and the nations under our feet. He shall choose our inheritance for us, the excellency of Jacob whom He loved.*"

Many and mighty were the enemies of Christ's kingdom—long and fierce was the conflict. At times the ungodly seemed to prevail, and the palm of victory seemed to be in their hands. But now Christ is gloriously triumphant. His foes all lick the dust : the feet of His people trample upon the subjugated hosts. The division of Canaan among the tribes was proof of His providential care. The same care still guards all temporal matters for us. As Jacob excelled Esau in his inherited blessings, so Christ's people inherit all good things — things present and things to come. Christ loves them with an everlasting love : He loves them and rejoices over them to do them good.

5, 6, 7. " *God is gone up with a shout, the Lord with the sound of a trumpet. Sing praises to God, sing praises ; sing praises unto our King, sing praises. For God is the King of all the earth ; sing ye praises with understanding.*"

Christ is now exhibited in another aspect of His glory, that thanksgiving may be more fervently awakened. He is presented to the eye of faith as ascending to the heaven of heavens, to take His seat on the right hand of the Majesty of high. Attending angels shout, and welcoming hosts re-echo the glad sound. Are conquerors thus welcomed when they return in triumph—and shall not all tokens of joy sound the praises of Jesus returning from His glorious victory ! Let us, for whom the victory is achieved, sing praises ; yea, sing praises with understanding. Let us thoroughly discern the causes of our joy. It is because Jesus has vanquished our every foe; has gloriously accomplished our full redemption—has finished the undertaken work, and has saved us with an everlasting salvation. Let us ponder the work until its length and breadth be fully grasped; and let every discovery stir us up to sing praises with understanding.

8, 9. " *God reigneth over the heathen: God sitteth upon the throne of His holiness. The princes of the people are gathered together, even the people of the God of Abraham; for the shields of the earth belong unto God: He is greatly exalted.*"

Joy would ever brighten in the dwellings of the righteous, if the truth were always before their eyes, that God sitteth supreme upon the throne of His holiness. The kings of the earth are mighty, but all their power is derived from Him. As shields they give protection, but His hand is over all. Greatly He is exalted. Let Him be greatly extolled. Let us sing praises, sing praises, with understanding.

LXIV.

PSALM XLVIII.

THE beauty of Jerusalem is a picture of the beauty of the Church. God's favour to it foreshadows His favour to His people in all ages.

1, 2, 3. *"Great is the Lord, and greatly to be praised in the city of our God, in the mountain of His holiness. Beautiful for situation, the joy of the whole earth, is Mount Zion, on the sides of the north, the city of the great King. God is known in her palaces for a refuge."*

Great indeed is the Lord. In His power, His love, His dealings, His every attribute, His greatness is unspeakable. In every faculty of mind and body, at every period of our time, His praise should be our glad employ. As Jerusalem stands pre-eminent above all the abodes of earth in charms of clime and loveliness of local beauty—as admiration proclaims Mount Zion to be the joy of the whole earth, so God's people surpass in every excellency. The Spirit, in a preceding hymn, had depicted the Church as all-glorious within, and as arrayed in raiment of wrought gold. Her inward beauty is the grace so plentifully bestowed by His hand. Her outward glory is the robe of righteousness with which she is invested by her Lord. Zion's royal residents dwelt in security. If any foe affrighted, they fled unto the Lord as a sure refuge, and were in safety.

4, 5, 6. *"For, lo, the kings were assembled, they passed by together. They saw it, and so they marvelled; they were troubled, and hasted away. Fear took hold upon them there, and pain, as of a woman in travail."*

Jerusalem was often threatened by mighty potentates, and with all their power; but vain were their assembled troops. They were compelled in shame and distress to seek security in flight. Thus, too, the legions of darkness have encamped around God's people. The arch-enemy, their malicious leader, has urged them forward. But the city of the righteous has been impregnable. Inglorious flight has dispersed all foes, and victory has signalized the Church.

7. *"Thou breakest the ships of Tarshish with an east wind."*

Another image here depicts the utter ruin of the Church's foes. How weak are ships to withstand the fury of the raging wind! It raises huge billows to overwhelm them. It dashes them resistless against the iron rocks. Thus weak are all adversaries against the might of God.

8. *"As we have heard, so have we seen in the city of the Lord of hosts, in the city of our God: God will establish it for ever."*

Many are the promises and predictions that God will uphold His people. Many realizations are before us to confirm our faith. We have every assurance that no destruction shall extinguish the true Church.

9, 10. *"We have thought of Thy loving-kindness, O God, in the midst of Thy temple. According to Thy name, O God, so is Thy praise unto the ends of the earth: Thy right hand is full of righteousness."*

Troubles should not detain from public ordinances. In the holy services we should be taught that our God is love. Not only are all His dealings full of loving-kindness, they are altogether righteous. To God's people His love is righteous, and His righteousness is love. Therefore no fear should harass or disturb.

11, 12, 13, 14. " *Let Mount Zion rejoice, let the daughters of Judah be glad because of Thy judgments. Walk about Zion, and go round about her: tell the towers thereof. Mark ye well her bulwarks, consider her palaces, that ye may tell it to the generation following. For this God is our God for ever and ever: He will be our guide, even unto death.*"

God's people have indeed cause for constant joy. On every occasion He appears on their behalf. It is wisdom fully to contemplate the Church. Behold her type, the city upon Zion's hill. Her fortifications render her impregnable. As her walls and towers protect her, so God defends His people with all His attributes and all His might. Let us realize, too, that we have covenant property in God. He is our own God, and never will cease to be so. While life lasts, He will lead in the way everlasting, and then receive us to be with Him for ever.

LXV.

PSALM XLIX. 1–9.

THE truths of the Bible call for universal heeding. The mysteries will repay all study. Natural men, in their best state, are immeasurably inferior to the people of God.

1, 2. " *Hear this, all ye people ; give ear, all ye inhabitants of the world : both low and high, rich and poor, together."*

The revelation of God alike concerns the whole family of man. Wherever man lives, he lives defiled by sin, and justly exposed to wrath. As the malady is one, so too is the remedy. All need it ; to all it is proclaimed in the Gospel. What madness can be greater than to close our ears to the precious tidings ! The low are raised by it ; the high are stripped of their lofty looks. The rich are ennobled by it with the true riches ; the poor obtain the true treasure.

3, 4. " *My mouth shall speak of wisdom ; and the meditation of my heart shall be of understanding. I will incline mine ear to a parable ; I will open my dark saying upon the harp."*

The treasures of true wisdom are folded up in God's Word. There He, who is the wise, the all wise, the only wise, declares His mind and will. The Bible-student will read, and will declare. His heart will meditate, but not concerning foolish trifles. Solid intelligence will be the food of his thoughts. He will diligently listen to the mysteries of redemption, shadowed out in great variety of images; and his melody will be concerning hidden wonders.

5. " *Wherefore should I fear in the days of evil, when the iniquity of my heels shall compass me about ?*"

Countless are the exhortations to the believer never to give place to fear. His constant response should be, I will trust and not be afraid. Days of evil will often overshadow him; reminiscences of past iniquity may leave impressions on the mind, deep as the prints of the heels upon a soft or sandy path. In this there may be ground of humiliation, but there is no cause for misapprehension. The covenant of peace stands sure, and never can be broken. The reconciliation is for ever made; the promise will be realized; goodness and mercy shall follow him all the days of his life, and he shall dwell in the house of the Lord for ever.

6, 7, 8, 9. " *They that trust in their wealth, and boast themselves in the multitude of their riches ; none of them can by any means redeem his brother, nor give to God a ransom for him ; (for the redemption of their soul is precious, and it ceaseth for ever ;) that he should still live for ever, and not see corruption.*"

The riches of this world are eagerly sought by natural men. They delight in the enjoyments which are thus purchased, and the homage and adulation which are thus won. It is their pleasure to vaunt themselves in their seeming distinction above their fellows. But what is their real value when viewed in

Q

spiritual light? They are light as chaff—they are worthless as the vilest dross. How can they deliver a sinner from the grasp of death? How can they prolong his days on earth, or raise from the corruption of the grave? Shall earthly riches be presented to God as an equivalent for the forfeited soul—shall they be proffered as a redeeming price? Is there satisfaction in them to the outraged attributes of God? Can they avail to mitigate merited wrath? The very thought is folly. Man in the utmost grandeur of outward possession is utterly without avail to redeem his brother.

A glorious parenthesis is here inserted. It casts a ray of joy over a saddening truth. It speaks of redemption, and tells us that it requires vast price. Here the blessed Gospel brightly shines. We bless our dying Jesus, our curse-removing Lord, our death-enduring Substitute, that He has accomplished redemption. It was bought by a precious price—even by the price of His own blood—which had infinite efficacy because of His essential deity. It out-valued all the silver and the gold which earth ever produced. It outweighed all treasures. By it every attribute of God is satisfied, and magnified, and glorified. Let us, too, be satisfied with it. This ransom has no need of gradual progress. By the one death of Jesus it is for ever secured. It needs no repetition. By His one offering once made, He has perfected for ever them that are sanctified.

LXVI.

PSALM XLIX. 10–20.

10. *" For He seeth that wise men die, likewise the fool and the brutish person perish, and leave their wealth to others."*

It is an obvious fact, compelling universal acquiescence, that mental faculties secure not length of days. Men of the shrewdest intellect move onward to the grave. By their side men lie who are least endowed. Alike they might have been enriched with large abundance of this world's wealth. But their feeble hands cannot retain the grasp. They cannot bear their treasure hence. Other inheritors must succeed and count the riches as their own.

11. *" Their inward thought is, that their houses shall continue for ever, and their dwelling-places to all generations ; they call their lands after their own names."*

They seem to dream of earthly immortality. They imagine perpetuity of their names. They inscribe their titles on their stately homes, or on their wide possessions.

12, 13. *" Nevertheless, man being in honour abideth not : he is like the beasts that perish. This their way is their folly ; yet their posterity approve their sayings."*

As riches are no protection from the grave, neither do honours bring deliverance. Titles may be grand, distinctions may be brilliant, yet the possessors soon lie low. Mortality is common to them, even as it is to all the herds of animal creation. Their forgetfulness of short-lived continuance is justly termed their folly. But it is marvellous, that their descendants tread the same senseless path. They are not instructed by the ignorance of their predecessors—they rather commend their seeming wisdom.

14. "*Like sheep they are laid in the grave; death shall feed on them; and the upright shall have dominion over them in the morning; and their beauty shall consume in the grave from their dwelling.*"

The titled and the wealthy worldlings have not stronger tenure of life than the flocks of the meadows. Death claims them as its prey, and feeds upon their lifeless bodies—from their stately halls they must be carried to mingle with corruption. The morning of the resurrection comes—then the poor believer, however scorned in his passage through life, shall shine in manifested superiority, and shall put on the beauteous robes of everlasting glory.

15. "*But God will redeem my soul from the power of the grave; for He shall receive me.*"

The believer knows his foundation of perpetual joy. It is true that his body must taste corruption, and lie for a little season in the grave; but he knows that God who has redeemed his soul, by the precious blood of His dearly-beloved Son, will also soon raise his body from the transient tenure of the grave. The redeemed soul shall again inhabit a redeemed body. The blessed consummation shall be complete. The glorified body and the glorified soul shall constitute the glorified man. Thus perfect he shall be upraised to the palace of the King of kings, and shall reign in those bright realms into which death shall never enter.

16, 17, 18, 19, 20. " *Be not thou afraid when one is made rich, when the glory of his house is increased ; for when he dieth, he shall carry nothing away; his glory shall not descend after him : though while he lived He blessed his soul; and men will praise thee when thou doest well to thyself. He shall go to the generation of his fathers ; they shall never see light. Man that is in honour, and understandeth not, is like the beasts that perish."*

Established truths are here repeated. The believer is exhorted to keep his faith from wavering, when he sees prosperity gilding the path of the worldling. The brevity of all mortal condition should check all temptation to be staggered by its prosperity. Worldlings may hold dazzling superabundance ; but how long can they call these things their own ? They must leave all behind; they can carry nothing hence. Their prosperity might excite adulation and the homage of fellow-mortals. But departure must take place—even to eternal wretchedness—even to blackness of darkness for ever. The cause of this misery is the want of saving knowledge. There is ignorance of self, of sin, of God, of Christ, of redemption, of salvation. O Lord, open Thou our eyes, give us intelligence to know Thee, the only true God, and Jesus Christ whom Thou hast sent.

LXVII.

PSALM L. 1–13.

WE have in this Psalm a revelation of glorious truth. The final judgment is announced in awful sublimity. Formalists are rebuked, and warned of the nullity of legal dependencies. In conclusion we have directions as to true worship.

1, 2. *" The mighty God, even the Lord, hath spoken, and called the earth, from the rising of the sun unto the going down thereof. Out of Zion, the perfection of beauty, God hath shined."*

May faith be granted that we may realize the scene. The great white throne is set. The mighty God is seated on His sovereign tribunal. Before Him all who have ever breathed the breath of life are summoned to appear. From all the regions of earth—from every quarter of the globe—the inhabitants are called. We are thus mercifully forewarned. We must take our station before the Judge of all mankind. Let us see to it that we are prepared to meet Him. To prepare us for the great day, God has revealed to us all Gospel truth. Out of Zion He hath shined. We have not been called to Mount Sinai, whence flowed the fiery law, amid all the terrors of lightning, and thunder, and appalling clang. We have been invited to listen to the silver notes of the sweet Gospel. God has erected on earth His Church, the perfection of

beauty. Here all grace and mercy shine. Here blood
is presented to cleanse from all sin; a righteousness to
cover all iniquity; and the plea is presented, Christ
died for pardon at the judgment-bar and full admission
to the glories of heaven. From this throne of Zion
let us draw near to meet the final judgment.

3, 4, 5, 6. *" Our God shall come, and shall not keep
silence: a fire shall devour before Him, and it shall be
very tempestuous round about Him. He shall call to
the heavens from above, and to the earth, that He may
judge His people. Gather My saints together unto Me;
those that have made a covenant with Me by sacrifice.
And the heavens shall declare His righteousness: for God
is judge Himself."*

We return to the judgment-seat. As when God
gave the law awful terrors surrounded Him, so when
He comes to execute judgment all majesty shall be
displayed. His irresistible voice shall ring through
universal nature. All elements shall send forth the
dead whom they contained. But now His professing
people are specially named. But all professors are not
real children. All who are of the Church are not the
Church. Have we become His through the blood of
the everlasting covenant? Have we made fellowship
with Him through the true Sacrifice, even the Victim
who died at Calvary? If so, let us joyfully exclaim,
He who shall come to institute judgment is our God,
and His right hand is full of righteousness.

7. *" Hear, O My people, and I will speak; O Israel,
and I will testify against thee: I am God, even thy
God."*

How tenderly this warning intervenes! God's

people are disposed to settle on their lees, to slumber on the pillow of self-confidence, to drink the noxious goblet of carnal security. Therefore God, in the plenitude of His mercy, would rouse them. He beseeches them to listen to His gracious expostulation. He will not hide from them their grievous faults, and He prefaces His reasonings with them by the loving assurance, that He who chides is God, even thy God. O Lord, give us the hearing ear.

8, 9, 10, 11, 12, 13. "*I will not reprove thee for thy sacrifices, or thy burnt-offerings, to have been continually before Me. I will take no bullock out of thy house, nor he-goats out of thy folds: for every beast of the forest is Mine, and the cattle upon a thousand hills. I know all the fowls of the mountains; and the wild beasts of the field are Mine. If I were hungry, I would not tell thee: for the world is Mine, and the fulness thereof. Will I eat the flesh of bulls, or drink the blood of goats?*"

How vain is all dependence on external service! As aids to faith all outward rites are valuable, but it is the vanity of vanities to dream that by such observance we make God our debtor. The universe and all which the universe contains is His created property. In all our offerings we only bring Him His own. Let us never fancy that there is merit in most costly rites. When we bring our best to Him we give no satisfaction to His justice, or make atonement to His outraged Law. In Christ—in Christ alone—satisfaction resides. Let us bring Him always in the arms of our faith, and plead for mercy only for His sake.

LXVIII.

PSALM L. 14–23.

14. " *Offer unto God thanksgiving ; and pay thy vows unto the Most High.*"

There is an offering in which God delights—the offering of the calves of our lips—the praises of devoted hearts. Let thanks, like incense, ever reach the courts of heaven. There is a grateful fragrance which He will never scorn. When we entered into covenant with God in Christ we vowed to present unto Him ourselves, our souls and bodies, to be a reasonable, holy, lively sacrifice. How happy is it to redeem this vow !

15. " *And call upon me in the day of trouble ; I will deliver thee, and thou shalt glorify Me.*"

Amid truths of awful grandeur this bright gem seems unexpectedly to shine. Its value is unspeakable. Its comfort to believers in all ages passes knowledge. Wondrous is the word, "Whosoever shall call upon the Name of the Lord shall be saved." The text before us gives special illustration. Many are the believer's troubles—they are needful, and the chastening is not withheld. But a remedy easy and ready is prescribed. His strength may so fail that he cannot stir. But he can always call, and never shall he call in vain. His call shall bring his God to his aid. His hand shall bring deliverance. Light shall spring up out of darkness. It shall be ever true, " This poor man cried, and the Lord heard him and delivered him out of all his trouble." God's glory shall be the issue; increasing praises shall break from the delivered heart.

16, 17. "*But unto the wicked God saith, What hast thou to do to declare My statutes, or that thou shouldest take My covenant in thy mouth? seeing thou hatest instruction, and castest My words behind thee.*"

The scene changes. Loving words are not now heard. The wicked, the gross transgressors, those whose steps are in the way of open offence, are addressed. God expostulates with such, if peradventure they will repent and turn in deep humility to Him. Such is the deceivableness of the unregenerate man that it will be secure in profession of covenant relationship to God, while the Lord of grace is really hated, and all its saving truths are contemptuously rejected.

18. "*When thou sawest a thief, then thou consentedst with him, and hast been partaker with adulterers.*"

An awful picture is exhibited of the extremity of iniquity into which carnal men will rush. They will practise the vilest dishonesty, and lie in the filth of the grossest uncleanness. Yet God in His mercy follows them with remonstrance,—" Turn ye, turn ye, why will ye die?"

19, 20, 21. "*Thou givest thy mouth to evil, and thy tongue frameth deceit. Thou sittest and speakest against thy brother; thou slanderest thine own mother's son. These things hast thou done, and I kept silence; thou thoughtest that I was altogether such an one as thyself: but I will reprove thee, and set them in order before thine eyes.*"

The tongue, which betrays the inmost working of

the heart, pours out torrents of evil and deceit. Even
natural affection expires, and calumnies assail the sons
who hang on the same mother's breast. God shows
abundance of patient longsuffering; but deluded
sinners misinterpret His gracious character. Because
wrath is restrained the impious thought is cherished,
that the evil which they love and practise is not
abomination in God's sight. But the day comes when
longsuffering can endure no more. Their wicked deeds,
in all their enormities, shall confront the evil—all
the circumstances shall stare them in their face; no
extenuation can cloak the guilt which must be confessed to uttermost confusion.

22. " *Now consider this, ye that forget God, lest I tear
you in pieces, and there be none to deliver.*"

Tender grace exhorts to deep thought. Let all who
have not God before them consider their awful state
before the day of vengeance bursts upon them. Then
the rejected Saviour saves no more. But now Jesus
stands ready to deliver from the wrath to come. To
Him let us cling steadfastly.

23. " *Whoso offereth praiseth glorifieth me: and to him
that ordereth his conversation aright will I show the
salvation of God.*"

Precious conclusion of this wondrous Psalm! What
condescension to accept our worthless praise! What
godlike condescension to assure us that these praises
augment His glory. Let our every breath be praise.
In the paths of holiness God will be met revealing all
the mercies of His Gospel. Christ will appear with
uttermost salvation in His hands; and glorying in
Him as full redemption, we shall boldly meet the
judgment-seat.

LXIX.

PSALM LI. 1–8.

Of all the Psalms, this is that, perhaps, which is most frequently interwoven in the believer's prayers and pondered in his meditations. It has been the outbreak of innumerable hearts, and has been, and still is, the wrestling cry at the mercy-seat. Repeated are the prayers for pardon of vile guilt: struggling are the cries for renewing and sanctifying grace. Professions are uttered of devotedness to God's service, and prayers are added for the Church.

1, 2. " *Have mercy upon me, O God, according to Thy loving-kindness; according unto the multitude of Thy tender mercies, blot out my transgressions. Wash me throughly from mine iniquity, and cleanse me from my sin.*"

In the deepest sense of guilt, prayer cries loudly for mercy. The measure of needed mercy is expressed. The measure is quite measureless. It is according to God's loving-kindness. But His love is everlasting love. It has no origin. It can have no end. It is, moreover, in accordance with the multitude of God's tender mercies. But who can count them ? Infinitude is their scope. Such mercy is indeed needed ; for nothing less than mercy thus limitless could reach the extent of the prayer for the remission of such transgressions, such iniquity, and such sin.

3. *" For I acknowledge my transgressions: and my sin is ever before me."*

The awakened sinner panted for relief ; for grievous was the burden which oppressed him. He did not cloak his awful guilt—he felt it, and he confessed it. He did not strive to escape the tormenting memory. There was an appalling object ever in his sight—his fearful deeds. He is not taught of God, who is not conscious of ever-present guilt.

4. *" Against Thee, Thee only, have I sinned, and done this evil in Thy sight ; that Thou mightest be justified when Thou speakest, and be clear when Thou judgest."*

The real character of sin is rebellion against God. This constitutes its essence, its magnitude, its malignity. Doubtless fellow-men may be most grievously injured and outraged and afflicted. Many may be wounded ; many tears may have been drawn forth, but the main evil assails God. The blow is aimed at God's supremacy. Hence God's truth and justice are exalted to their highest pinnacles. In every threat, in every denunciation, in every execution of vengeance, homage is rendered to these essential attributes. When sin is punished, holiness is vindicated.

5. *" Behold, I was shapen in iniquity ; and in sin did my mother conceive me."*

Sin is here traced to nature's original corruption. The tree is radically unsound. No sound fruit can hang from its branches. The spring is poisoned, the waters which flow from it are polluted. When Adam yielded to the tempter's wiles, the whole line of his descendants perished in him. Sad, indeed, is our case, except redeeming grace transplants us from the ruined stock, and grafts us into the heavenly vine.

6. " *Behold, Thou desirest truth in the inward parts ; and in the hidden part Thou shalt make me to know wisdom.*"

When sin is deeply felt and openly confessed, conscience feels that God requires true sincerity throughout the heart. The folly of mocking God with unmeaning tears or unreal prayers is felt; and there is most earnest supplication to God to implant wisdom in the heart and soul, and to guide in the way everlasting.

7. " *Purge me with hyssop, and I shall be clean ; wash me, and I shall be whiter than snow.*"

Obliteration of guilt is again implored in terms redolent of Gospel-sweetness. Faith clearly sees the purport of sacrificial rites. It knows that the blood streaming from the dying victim foreshowed the blood of the Lamb of God, which taketh away the sin of the world. It knows that this blood is expiation perfect, entire, and for evermore : that its sprinkling removes every stain of evil, and makes the contrite believer pure as purity can be in the sight of God.

8. " *Make me to hear joy and gladness ; that the bones which Thou hast broken may rejoice.*"

The anguish of the soul under sense of God's wrath is pictured by the keenest pains of body ; even by the agony of bones fractured and bruised. When healing comes, how great is the relief ! Such is the transport of delight which thrills through the soul when God restores His smile, and whispers peace to the conscience. Let each mourning penitent cease not the wrestling cry, " Make me to hear joy and gladness, that the bones which Thou hast broken may rejoice."

LXX.

PSALM LI. 9–19.

9. " *Hide Thy face from my sins, and blot out all mine iniquities.*"

Pardon is still the foremost thought in the contrite Psalmist's mind. He supplicates it under another image. He fears lest God should keep his sins in the light of His countenance. He therefore prays that an averted look should no more have them in view. Conscious of innumerable transgressions, and feeling need of entire pardon, he beseeches that not one single offence should remain unsprinkled by the obliterating blood.

10. 11 " *Create in me a clean heart, O God; and renew a right spirit within me. Cast me not away from Thy presence; and take not Thy Holy Spirit from me.*"

Desire of pardon is linked to earnest longing for renewing and sanctifying grace. The cleansing of the heart is the absolute work of God. It is a new creation. It is calling that into existence which no power of man could accomplish. Conscious of utter impotency, the cry struggles for creating and renewing grace. Supplication is added for continuance of God's life-giving presence, and the perpetual indwelling of the Holy Spirit.

12, 13. " *Restore unto me the joy of Thy salvation; and uphold me with Thy free Spirit: then will I teach transgressors Thy ways; and sinners shall be converted unto Thee."*

Who can express the joy of realized salvation! It is heaven begun. It is the commencement of the never-ending bliss. But it may be forfeited and interrupted for a while. Allowed sin is quick to extinguish. Let instantly recourse be made to prayer. Let God, who only gave and only can renew, be supplicated to restore. The effect of this reviving grace is earnest effort to call others to the ways of God, and faith in Christ. He who enjoys this gracious treasure burns with longing that others may partake.

14. *"Deliver me from blood-guiltiness, O God, Thou God of my salvation; and my tongue shall sing aloud of Thy righteousness."*

Remembrance of some special sin will ofttimes haunt the heart. A frightful spectre will stand before the eyes. It was so now with David. The awful thought was present, that his abominable sin had caused a fellow-creature's death. He saw that his hands were stained with murderous spots. He must be a stranger to all peace, until sure of deliverance from this heinous guilt. With his soul, therefore, he prays that such mercy might be vouchsafed unto him. The result would be sure; he would be loud in praise, proclaiming that God was a covenant-keeping God, and righteous in fulfilling His promises to forgive all sin through the atoning blood.

15, 16. *"O Lord, open Thou my lips; and my mouth shall show forth Thy praise. For Thou desirest not sacrifice, else would I give it; Thou delightest not in burnt-offering."*

When the grace of praise is freely poured into the heart, the power to give utterance must still be added. A channel must be opened for the stream to flow. An open lip must be desired in addition to a full heart. Faith sees that the outward rite of sacrificial homage is the real demand of God. Enjoined services may not be withheld; they testify obedience. But they should do much more. They should evince the soul's entire dependence on the hidden meaning—the true Lamb of God, the all-atoning blood, the death which satisfies every violated attribute. Christ is the end of the law for righteousness to every one that believeth.

17. *" The sacrifices of God are a broken spirit: a broken and a contrite heart, O God, Thou wilt not despise."*

God is a Spirit, and His eye is on a spiritual service. He turns not with indifference from a spirit broken and crushed, and ground to powder, by the weighty hand of the accusing law. He sees the buddings of real faith, and true apprehension of the appeasing victim. He is ever ready to bind up that which is thus broken. Happy they who thus mourn, for they shall be comforted!

18, 19. *" Do good in Thy good pleasure unto Zion: build Thou the walls of Jerusalem. Then shalt Thou be pleased with the sacrifices of righteousness, with burnt-offering, and whole burnt-offering: then shall they offer bullocks upon Thine altar."*

The penitent cannot conclude without embracing the whole Church in his fervent prayer; he supplicates mercy for his beloved Zion, and protection from all her foes. Safe in the loving-kindness of her God, her altars will blaze, the victims will die in countless numbers, the blood will flow in constant stream; but it will not be a mere superabundance of outward rites. In all Christ is seen.   Christ is magnified.   Christ is honoured.   Christ is All.

LXXI.

PSALM LII.

THE proud boasting and the malicious plots of the ungodly come to a fearful end. The case of the righteous greatly differs, and calls for praise.

---

1. " *Why boasteth thou thyself in mischief, O mighty man ? the goodness of God endureth continually.*"

Deep is the malignity of the heart which the Spirit has not softened. To plot mischief is most vile : but it rests not in devising evil; it delights in its sin, and vauntingly exults in its shame. How vain is this pride ! It checks not the operations of God's goodness. This attribute will ever live while God lives, and will ever be His people's shield. Child of God, believe this and fear not.

2, 3, 4. " *Thy tongue deviseth mischiefs ; like a sharp razor, working deceitfully. Thou lovest evil more than good, and lying rather than to speak righteousness. Thou lovest all-devouring words, O thou deceitful tongue.*"

Doeg instantly appears. In dark colours his hateful portrait is displayed. With crafty calumnies he maligned the servant of the Lord. With evil reports he stirred up the king's wrath. This malevolence was his delight. He found enjoyment in pouring forth devouring words.

5. " *God shall likewise destroy thee for ever : He shall*

*take thee away, and pluck thee out of thy dwelling-place,
and root thee out of the land of the living."*

They who thus propagate malicious lies against
God's servants little think that they are planning
their own ruin. They consider not that God's eye
watches their secret devices, and that His just wrath
will surely be aroused. They dig a pit for others,
and surely their own steps lead to it. Destruction is
planned, but it is destruction of themselves. No
wicked ways can prosper. The end of evil is sure
misery. They who would chase others from the earth,
will surely find that vengeance follows in their rear.
How often requital pursues them in this time-state!
How often in their sufferings do they read their sin!
How often does the crop of misery prove what seed
had been sown!

6. *" The righteous also shall see, and fear, and shall
laugh at him."*

The righteous diligently observe God's ways. It is
a book of wisdom full of precious lessons. They mark
the outgoings of requiting wrath : holy awe fills their
hearts. They tremble at the issue of sin's course. A
sneer can scarcely be repressed at the folly of the
insulting boaster.

7. *" Lo, this is the man that made not God his
strength ; but trusted in the abundance of his riches,
and strengthened himself in his wickedness."*

Pitiable indeed is the man who makes his own arm
his strength, and rejects the living God. Where is
there greater folly than to put confidence in a mass of
silver and gold. How quickly does it fade away, and
leave the proud possessor in the straits of penury!

But the height of madness is to regard wickedness as might, and to believe that the ways of wickedness lead to success and prosperity. The only man who is truly strong, and has enduring treasure, and will prevail, is the humble follower of the Lamb.

8. *" But I am like a green olive-tree in the house of God : I trust in the mercy of God for ever and ever."*

David discerned how different was his case, and he well knew who made him to differ. While Doeg and all of the same vile character was cast off as a withered branch, he was verdant and fruitful as an olive-tree in most luxuriant soil. He owed his position and his verdant boughs, and clusters of rich fruit, to God's abundant mercy, and in that mercy was all his trust for ever and ever. Stable is this foundation of our hopes. Let nothing move us from it.

9. *" I will praise Thee for ever, because Thou hast done it : and I will wait on Thy name ; for it is good before Thy saints."*

Such distinguishing mercy requires that every breath should be praise. But who can adequately praise God for what He has done, and is doing, and will do for His servants ? In humble patience let us wait on all the attributes which make up His name. Let all God's people see our grateful course.

LXXII.

PSALM LIII.

A REPETITION of an awful scene is again presented. Again the whole world is seen as lying in the wicked one. But the year of the redeemed again appears. May such sight of evil deeply appal us; while we joy in forethought of deliverance!

―――――

1. " *The fool hath said in his heart, There is no God. Corrupt are they, and have done abominable iniquity: there is none that doeth good.*"

The heart is the true mirror of the man. Its language speaks the real character. If we could hear the secret whispers of a graceless heart, the sound would be uniformly evil. The godless cherish the delusion that there is no being greater than themselves. Their conceit ignores divine supremacy, and scorns to yield to a superior yoke. Such men exist in fearful numbers. The faithful Word declares it, and truly adds that they are fools. They may pride themselves in imagined wisdom, but their real place is in the depths of ignorance. Their light is darkness: their boasted knowledge is extremest folly. It follows that atheism in heart is wickedness in life. The spring being impure what can flow from it but defilement? The tree is rotten at the core; the branches cannot be sound. Their works—the emblems of their hearts—can only be abomination. They only pollute the earth—hateful to God, injurious to man. Are there no exceptions ? Not one by nature. There is no good but what the Holy Spirit implants. Where He is absent only evil dwells, and He has no abode in unregenerate men.

2. *" God looked down from heaven upon the children of men, to see if there were any that did understand, that did seek God."*

We are now directed to Jehovah on His heavenly throne. His piercing eye surveys the universe. He reads the secret of every heart ; no thought escapes His omniscient view. What is the purport of His all-pervading search ? It is to ascertain whether all thoughts are turned to Him—whether His knowledge is the prime pursuit—whether prayer seeks the revelation of His will—whether His mind is explored in the pages of His Word—whether His works are studied as picturing His character. Thus to seek God is truest wisdom. Let no man boast of understanding whose mind delights not in this employ. God looks down in search of this. Let us now hear His verdict.

3. *" Every one of them is gone back ; they are alto-gether become filthy : there is none that doeth good, no, not one."*

Mark the case before the flood. We have the counterpart at present. Every imagination of the thoughts of the heart was only evil continually. Men wandered from all paths of righteousness and truth. Their feet were set in error's broad decline. Their garments were sin-soiled ; their words were only filth. Uncleanness in its foulest phase was their one element.

Let us pause for one moment to bless God that the blood of Jesus Christ can cleanse from all these stains, and make us whiter than the whitest snow.

4. " *Have the workers of iniquity no knowledge ? who eat up My people as they eat bread : they have not called upon God.*"

Jehovah sees this universal evil, and He speaks. His voice is strong expostulation. It traces sin to the true source—ignorance. If truth were sought, and seen, and loved, and followed, how different would be man's walk ! Men work iniquity because their minds are blinded. Next, evil breaks out in persecution. But who are the persecuted ? "My people," saith the Lord. We hear the tender voice, "Saul, Saul, why persecutest thou Me ?" The issue of such conduct is the restraint of prayer. "They call not upon the Lord." Thus we have in connected links four marks of unregenerate men—ignorance, iniquity, persecution, prayerlessness.

5. " *There were they in great fear, where no fear was : for God hath scattered the bones of him that encampeth against thee : thou hast put them to shame, because God hath despised them.*"

But to the wicked there is no calm peace. Great are their fears. Clear tokens show that God is mighty in His people's midst, and that His presence is their sure defence. They may well fear whose weapons are directed against God. The godly make the Lord their refuge. He is the high tower to which they always fly. Beneath the covert of His wings they find protection. Let persecutors sneer and ridicule such trust; but happy experience shows that none seek God in vain.

6. " *Oh that the salvation of Israel were come out of Zion !   When God bringeth back the captivity of His people, Jacob shall rejoice, and Israel shall be glad.*"

This darkness issues in a glorious dawn. Israel's long night shall cease. She shall arise and shine. Her light shall come. Her tedious years of cruel thraldom shall reach a blessed close. Her sons shall return from distant lands. Her many promises shall have exact fulfilment. From Jerusalem the blessed tidings of salvation shall resound. " If the casting away has been the reconciling of the world, what shall the receiving be but life from the dead ? "   Then, indeed, shall joy and gladness be the portion of Israel's sons. Then shall praise and thanksgiving ring throughout earth's length and breadth. Let us trust, and pray, and hope. Bright days are coming. Hasten the joy, O Lord, in Thine own time !

LXXIII.

PSALM LIV.

DEEP distress afflicts the Psalmist. He knows his
refuge, and flees to it. In confidence of gracious aid
he vows the sacrifice of praise. We, too, are born to
trouble. May we in faith use our ever-present help !

1, 2. " *Save me, O God, by Thy name, and judge me
by Thy strength. Hear my prayer, O God ; give ear to
the words of my mouth.*"

David is here encompassed by distress. Billows on
billows threatened his ruin. Traitors were ready to
surrender him to his cruel foe. Vain is all human
succour, and he betakes himself to God. He invokes
His aid by all the precious attributes which constitute
His name. In intensity of supplication he calls upon
God, and all that God is, to save him. He looks for
vindication to the omnipotence of God's might. In
wrestling earnestness he beseeches that heavenly ears
would listen to his cry, and that his words might
not be cast out at the mercy-seat. Let us, too, diligently ponder the revelation of God's character, and
summon every attribute to advocate our cause. Save
me by Thy name, is an all-prevailing plea.

3. " *For strangers are risen up against me, and op-
pressors seek after my soul : they have not set God before
them.*"

David uses not vague and general petition. He

clearly states his especial errand to the mercy-seat.
He points to the betrayers who were active to deliver
him to the infuriate king. He points to their ungodly
treachery. They were enemies to God, and therefore
enemies to God's servant. Prayers sometimes err in
being diffuse in generalities. We should distinctly
see our present need, and distinctly specify it. The
plea is strong when we can urge that our cause is
God's cause, and that they who hate us hate God also.

4, 5. " *Behold, God is mine helper: the Lord is with
them that uphold my soul. He shall reward evil unto
mine enemies: cut them off in thy truth.*"

Distresses rather brighten than extinguish faith.
They open the door for its expanded exercise, and in
its exercise it recruits its strength. Unless it be
brought to trial its existence might be doubted. We
often pray, O Lord, increase our faith. The answer
may be an accumulation of distress. Such is David's
case in this crisis of his life. The treachery of false
friends pierced him to the heart. But they led him
to feel that he had a friend who could never fail, and
amid his fears he firmly realizes, " God is mine helper."
This truth, when tightly grasped, raises us victorious
above desertion and betrayal. He knew that they
who would maintain his cause would surely prosper,
because omnipotence was on their side. Strong is the
little band of whom it may be truly said, The Lord is
with them. He foresaw, too, the total overthrow of
his enemies. He knew the many promises which predicted their final overthrow. All these he steadfastly
believed, and he humbly prays that God would fulfil
His word, redeem His pledges, and do as He has said.

6, 7. " *I will freely sacrifice unto Thee; I will praise Thy name, O Lord, for it is good.   For He hath delivered me out of all trouble; and mine eye hath seen his desire upon mine enemies.*"

Can faith thus brightly blaze, and joy not fill the heart ?   David foresees complete deliverance and free- dom for holy worship. He feels that he will soon be at liberty to bring his victims to the altar, and to en- compass the mercy-seat with incense of thanksgiving. He sees his enemies low in complete defeat, and his every desire most fully granted.   It is a happy exer- cise to give free scope to the expanded wings of faith, and to anticipate the blessed day when victory over every foe shall be assuredly attained, and Hallelujahs become the endless song.

LXXIV.

PSALM LV. 1–15.

In the eventful life of David trouble follows trouble as wave succeeds to wave. His intervals of rest were very few. Throughout his days darkness seems often to gather clouds. But he finds refuge in God; and deliverance was his happy experience. This God is our God for ever and ever. Let us trust. He will not fail us.

1, 2. "*Give ear unto my prayer, O God; and hide not thyself from my supplication. Attend unto me, and hear me: I mourn in my complaint, and make a noise.*"

It is a wondrous privilege that we may be importunate with God. It is no presumption to use holy boldness, and to give Him no rest in cries for audience. We are permitted to tell out our sorrows in mourning terms, and to pray that our sadness may attract attention. Strong crying and tears marked our Lord's hours of supplication. We cannot err in following Him.

3, 4, 5. "*Because of the voice of the enemy, because of the oppression of the wicked: for they cast iniquity upon me, and in wrath they hate me. My heart is sore pained within me; and the terrors of death are fallen upon me. Fearfulness and trembling are come upon me, and horror hath overwhelmed me.*"

It is good in prayer to specify the cause of our distress. What we deeply feel, we should distinctly state. David is cast down by the open reviling of his enemies, who scrupled not to impute all wicked ways unto him. Here we see the type of Him who suffered such malignant charges against His holy walk. The Psalmist states his agonized condition. Trust in God destroys not feelings of alarm, though they restrain them from overwhelming force. In this fearful description of his inward agony, can we fail to see the path which our great Redeemer trod? What was His state of mental misery when He felt the crushing burden of His people's sins, and was bowed to the earth by its overwhelming load? Sorrow was indeed the occupant of His heart when the exclamation was pressed out, " My God, my God, why hast Thou forsaken Me?" We may be terrified, but we must never yield to despair.

6, 7, 8. "*And I said, Oh that I had wings like a dove! for then would I fly away, and be at rest. Lo, then would I wander far off, and remain in the wilderness. I would hasten my escape from the windy storm and tempest.*"

It is a feeling common to the breast of man to flee disquietude and to desire rest. There is a charm in tranquil peace which sweetly attracts desire. Rest and peace are among the sweet promises from our great Lord's lips. "Come unto Me, all ye that labour and are heavy laden, and I will give you rest." "Peace I leave with you; My peace I give unto you." Sweet is the promise, "The Lord Himself shall give you peace always and by all means." Hence, as the timid dove with rapid wing flees to the lonely desert, and seeks shelter from tempestuous winds, so the soul longs for the tranquillity of repose. But in these desires there must be moderation. When called to combat we must not use the dastard's flight. When called to patient endurance we must not show impatience. If we would win the crown we must not shrink from the cross. We may find rest in trouble, when rest from trouble is wisely withheld.

9, 10, 11. " *Destroy, O Lord, and divide their tongues : for I have seen violence and strife in the city. Day and night they go about it upon the walls thereof: mischief also and sorrow are in the midst of it. Wickedness is in the midst thereof; deceit and guile depart not from her streets.*"

We have here an awful picture how sin will spread, and sinful men sow seeds of mischief. When this is evident, let the godly man appeal to heaven, and pray God's power to check the evil. We have encouragement in the case of the Babel-builders, and thus may ask for plotting tongues to be divided.

12, 13, 14, 15. " *For it was not an enemy that reproached me ; then I could have borne it : neither was it he that hated me that did magnify himself against me; then I would have hid myself from him : but it was thou, a man mine equal, my guide, and mine acquaintance. We took sweet counsel together, and walked unto the house of God in company. Let death seize upon them, and let them go down quick into hell : for wickedness is in their dwellings, and among them.*"

The bitterest pang is when hostility is found in one who was loved as a familiar friend, and trusted as a faithful guide, and sought as a confidential adviser, and walked with, as a fellow-worshipper. David drank this bitter cup ; so did our beloved Lord. Judas from walking by His side hastened to the blackest crime. But he went to " his own place." Awful is the thought. It is recorded for our warning.

LXXV.

PSALM LV. 16 23.

16, 17. " *As for me, I will call upon God : and the Lord shall save me. Evening, and morning, and at noon, will I pray, and cry aloud ; and He shall hear my voice.*"

Under the pressure of such a weight of woe David makes holy profession. Let the wicked rage—let foes prove treacherous—let malignity in every form assail, he will still look to God. The severest trials are only blessings in disguise when they quicken our speed to the mercy-seat. Then burdens become light, and darkness brightens, and songs of deliverance break forth. David resolves that he will not use his voice in lamentations or reproach, but will call upon God ; and he will do so not in formality, or in lifeless exercise, but in the full assurance of faith, that audience will be given. Happy are they who know that they have free access to the ears of God, and that their petitions, perfumed with the Redeemer's blood, will encircle the mercy-seat with fragrant incense. He resolves, too, that stated periods should be set apart by him for distinct worship. Doubtless, we should be always in a prayerful frame, and constant ejaculations should carry our desires on high. But still to prevent forgetfulness, it is the part of wisdom diligently to adhere to regulated times. Thrice in each day did David make distinct supplications.

18. " *He hath delivered my soul in peace from the battle that was against me ; for there were many with me.*"

Happy is the mind which is enriched with large experiences of felt mercies. No act of heavenly goodness should be forgotten. The catalogue is capable of almost daily enlargement, and it should be studied with devout thanksgiving. David had been a warrior from his youth. He had taken part in many battles. He had been preserved, not in safety only, but in peace. He had felt that God was on his side, and that in God's succour he was stronger than all the hosts of men. While others trembled he knew no fears.—Is not this God our God for ever and ever ? Leaning on His arm, should we not realize immovable support ? David felt that there were many with him. The eyes of Elijah's servant were opened to behold the surrounding mountains filled with horses of fire and chariots of fire. Is it not true that thus many are with us, and that the angel of the Lord encampeth round about them that fear Him and delivereth them ?

19. " *God shall hear, and afflict them, even He that abideth of old. Because they have no changes, therefore they fear not God.*"

David's faith grows stronger as his trials swell. Unwavering is his confidence that his prayers shall all be heard, and vengeance shall destroy his foes. He states the ground of his confidence, even his knowledge that God changes not, but is the same yesterday, and to-day, and for ever. With Him there is no variableness, neither shadow of turning. His mercy, which hath been from everlasting, endureth for ever. A reason is subjoined why the ungodly disregard the Lord. They have no changes—they are at ease. Soft is the nest in which they quietly repose. They have present comfort, and they fondly think that it will ever last. Whereas the children of the Lord, who are emptied from vessel to vessel, learn in each change to cling more closely to their God.

20, 21. " *He hath put forth his hands against such as be at peace with him; he hath broken his covenant. The words of his mouth were smoother than butter, but war was in his heart: his words were softer than oil, yet were they drawn swords.*"

A picture is reproduced of the falsehood of the ungodly. They treacherously assail the friends who trust them—their pledged promises are wantonly disregarded. With gentle language and with oily tongue they flatter and profess love, while the bitterest enmity is lurking in their hearts. This cruel trial burst with intensity on the head of Jesus. The traitor drew near with words of reverence and love, with perfidy in his heart.

22, 23. " *Cast thy burden upon the Lord, and He shall sustain thee: He shall never suffer the righteous to be moved. But Thou, O God, shalt bring them down into the pit of destruction: bloody and deceitful men shall not live out half their days; but I will trust in Thee.*"

A precious exhortation follows, supported by precious promises. It is granted that burdens may press heavily upon the child of God: but he is exhorted not to sink beneath them, but to cast them on Him who is ever at hand to receive them, even the Lord. Oh, for faith most fully to obey, and thus to obtain entire relief! Let us clasp to our hearts the promise, " He shall sustain thee." Amid most raging billows Peter did not sink. Mountains of adversity crushed not David. Two inferences follow. He had full assurance that his cruel and treacherous foes were only digging the pit of misery for themselves, while his deliverance would only deepen his unfailing confidence in God. Oh for more of this happy trust! It is worth more than ten thousand worlds.

LXXVI.

PSALM LVI.

SIMILARITY of circumstance leads to similarity of conduct. Continued troubles prompt continued prayer. Prayer may wrestle long, but it will never strive in vain. Answers will come—the answers will be deliverance. In reading this, may we gain holy comfort!

1, 2. *"Be merciful unto me, O God ; for man would swallow me up : he fighting daily oppresseth me. Mine enemies would daily swallow me up : for they be many that fight against me, O Thou most High."*

We are not left in doubt as to the occasion which prompted this hymn. David flees from the persecuting Saul. His steps guide him to a persecuting land. He would make Gath his hiding-place; but vain is his hope of refuge in man. There is no friendly succour for him there. The men of Gath would give him up to Saul. His eyes are open to his perilous condition. A multitude pursue him with inveterate hate. The wild beasts rushing with open mouths to devour their prey are the fit emblem of his pursuing foes. He clearly sees that in man there is no safety for him. He looks away. He looks above. He asks no pity from surrounding foes, but he asks pity from Him whose pitying ears are ever open to the cry of faith. He humbly prays, Be merciful unto me, O God! There is mighty power in the cry, " God be merciful to me, a sinner ! " It never will go forth in vain. It takes Him by storm whose delight is mercy, whose riches is His mercy, whose mercy is built up for ever.

3, 4. " *What time I am afraid, I will trust in Thee. In God I will praise His word ; in God I have put my trust : I will not fear what flesh can do unto me.*"

Natural feelings have deep root, and will continue to spring up in the most enlightened hearts. When David looked around he saw encompassing enemies. Saul threatened in the rear—the Philistines encamped in front. Thus when he looked to man timidities were prone to rise. Tremblings allowed that he knew fear, but happy confidence was not extinct. Many waters cannot drown love ; many troubles cannot slay faith. Out of the lowest depths he looked above, and saw bright light. His heart responded, I am afraid, but I will trust. God was his confidence. God's word was the strong foundation on which his heart was fixed. Realizing his oneness with his God, he felt that all God's promises were his unfailing heritage. His word was a panoply which shielded his breast ; it was the helmet which guarded his head ; it was the sword before which no foe could stand ; it was the light which dispelled all darkness ; it was the song which drowned the clattering of advancing foes. Blessed is the man who can similarly cry, In God I will praise His word. But what praise can do justice to its exceeding excellence !

5, 6, 7. " *Every day they wrest my words : all their thoughts are against me for evil. They gather themselves*

*together, they hide themselves, they mark my steps, when
they wait for my soul.   Shall they escape by iniquity ?
in thine anger cast down the people, O God."*

The constant effort of the godly to walk without
reproach in the sight of man fails to secure success.
Words uttered in loving spirit and in pious frame are
perverted by the lips of calumny.   The ungodly unite
in cruel plots, and watch, with base design, the most
blameless walk.   Instantly the case of our beloved
Lord appears.   False witnesses were suborned ; things
were laid to His charge from which he was entirely
apart.   If these things were done in the green tree,
what shall be done in the dry ?   Faith then puts the
crucial question, Shall they escape by iniquity ?   They
may escape the censure and condemnation of the world,
but there is a judgment coming, in which assuredly
they will be cast.

8. " *Thou tellest my wanderings : put Thou my tears
into Thy bottle : are they not in Thy book ? "*

" Thou God seest me," is the sweet solace of the true
believer. " He knoweth the way that I take," will make
that rugged way seem smooth.   If perils and distress
so shake the heart that plenteous tears give evidence
of suffering, these tears are marked on high, and tender
compassion will wipe them all away.   The day is not
yet come when there shall be no more tears.   But
the day is always present when they awaken sympathy
in the Redeemer's breast.   He who wept on earth will
soon wipe all tears away.

9, 10, 11. " *When I cry unto Thee, then shall mine
enemies turn back : this I know ; for God is for me.   In
God will I praise His word ; in the Lord will I praise*

His word. In God have I put my trust : I will not be afraid what man can do unto me."

Faith boasts of near and assured deliverance. It is confident of success. Its deep feeling is, This I know. But whence the knowledge ? There is assurance that God is a present help. Hence the fear of man vanishes as mist before the rising sun.

12, 13. *" Thy vows are upon me, O God : I will render praises unto Thee. For Thou hast delivered my soul from death : wilt Thou not deliver my feet from falling, that I may walk before God in the light of the living ? "*

In days of trouble vows are often made that merciful deliverance shall be duly praised. Let these vows be fully paid, and let the assurance brighten, that He who died to save the soul from eternal death, will never suffer that soul to perish in the upward path. The haven is sure ; the voyage shall be without a wreck.

LXXVII.

PSALM LVII.

TROUBLE, prayer, confidence, and praise are the pervading notes of this instructive hymn. Our faith will surely have its trials. May each trial cause it to wax stronger! The shaken tree takes firmer root.

1, 2. "*Be merciful unto me, O God, be merciful unto me; for my soul trusteth in Thee: yea, in the shadow of Thy wings will I make my refuge, until these calamities be overpast. I will cry unto God most High; unto God that performeth all things for me.*"

The help of mercy is here keenly felt. A reiterated cry calls down its aid. In prayer importunity can never be excessive. Sometimes answers are delayed that this sweet exercise may be prolonged. Abundant pleas enforce the soul's desires. Here confidence in God is urged. It is a prevailing utterance, Help me, for in Thee is all my trust. As when storms give sign of near approach, or the hawk hovers in the sky, the affrighted brood seek shelter beneath the parent's wings, so the believer hides himself in God, and will not quit his refuge while perils are still near. Faith knows well the Covenant, and cries in full assurance that no good thing will be withholden, and that God, who begins the work of grace, will carry it to its end in glory.

3, 4. " *He shall send from heaven, and save me from the reproach of him that would swallow me up. God shall send forth His mercy and His truth. My soul is among lions ; and I lie even among them that are set on fire, even the sons of men, whose teeth are spears and arrows, and their tongue a sharp sword.*"

Here faith looks not for mercy only, but for fulfilment of the pledged word. Happy are they who are well versed in the exceeding great and precious promises, and can confidently pray, Do as Thou hast said. It is this confidence which sustains God's children even when malignity most rages and cruelty is most fierce. Such was David's case when Saul and all his court pursued with every form of persecution. He knew their savage malice ; his eyes were open to their unsparing violence ; but he looked upwards, and fainted not.

5. " *Be Thou exalted, O God, above the heavens ; let Thy glory be above all the earth.*"

It is a precious thought, that when God appears to vindicate His people's cause there is accession to the glories of His name. The adversaries cannot but discern the favouring and protecting arm. They tremble, and their fear gives reverence to God. Therefore when we beseech God to stand by our side, we ask that honour and praise and glory may be more truly given.

6. " *They have prepared a net for my steps ; my soul is bowed down : they have digged a pit before me, into the midst whereof they are fallen themselves.*"

After this prayer David reverts to his foes ; he sees their plots, and is oppressed : he sees the pit prepared in his path, but he feels that his steps will not be

entrapped, but that the ruin so craftily designed will
be ruin to the contrivers.

7. "*My heart is fixed, O God, my heart is fixed; I
will sing and give praise.*"

In all his troubles his steadfast confidence in God
could not be moved. He stood as a rock amid assail-
ing billows: he realized his sure deliverance; his ready
harp was tuned for praise.

8, 9, 10, 11. "*Awake up, my glory; awake, psaltery
and harp: I myself will awake early. I will praise
Thee, O Lord, among the people; I will sing unto Thee
among the nations: for Thy mercy is great unto the
heavens, and thy truth unto the clouds. Be Thou exalted, O God, above the heavens: let Thy glory be above
all the earth.*"

Intense is the desire of faith to glorify God. The
believer chides his tongue for being dull and remiss
in this delightful duty. He resolves to redeem time
from unnecessary repose that the refreshed faculties
may consecrate their powers to God. He resolves that
all to whom his voice could extend should hear of the
great attributes of God. His delight shall be to tell
of mercy and truth. But how can their infinitudes be
reached? High are the heavens above the earth, but
higher far is mercy which overtops the skies, and truth
which soars above our powers to comprehend. The
chorus again sounds, "Be Thou exalted, O God, above
the heavens; let Thy glory be above all the earth."

LXXVIII.

PSALM LVIII.

PERSECUTION in another form here agitates the Psalmist's mind. A fearful picture of the persecutors' hate
is next exhibited. Confidence in their ruin is expressed.
God surely will maintain the righteous cause.

1, 2. "*Do ye indeed speak righteousness, O congregation? do ye judge uprightly, O ye sons of men? Yea,
in heart ye work wickedness; ye weigh the violence of
your hands in the earth.*"

If any seat should be pre-eminently conspicuous in
honest equity, it is the tribunal of justice. But when
the cause of God has called for righteous judgment,
how often has iniquity perverted the decree! David
found no acquittal from the courts of Saul. Mark, too,
the Sanhedrim and the unstable judge who adminis-
tered the Roman law! Spotless innocence did not
avert unrighteous condemnation. No guilt was found;
freedom from shadow of blame was allowed; but the
sentence was, Let him die. Crucifixion was decreed.
Happy they who look to Him whose right hand is full
of righteousness, and look to the tribunal where the
plea "Christ died" cannot be urged in vain, but ensures not acquittal only, but exaltation to the throne
of glory.

3, 4, 5. "*The wicked are estranged from the womb;*

they go astray as soon as they be born, speaking lies. Their poison is like the poison of a serpent: they are like the deaf adder that stoppeth her ear ; which will not hearken to the voice of charmers, charming never so wisely."

Injustice and cruelty are here traced to the first cause of original corruption. These noxious streams issue from an evil spring. These hateful berries hang on branches rotten to the core. Men are shaped in iniquity ; in sin do mothers conceive their offspring. If heavenly grace comes not mercifully to renew, convert, and sanctify, a corrupt offspring cannot fail to move in paths of corruption. Mark what issues from the nursery—proneness to depart far from God ; tendency to fabricate untruth, and to misrepresent, and to delight in lies. Their words contain all venom. The viper's poison is the emblem of their destroying tongues. To all instruction they are deaf. As the adder with closed ears is unmoved by sweetest melody, so they are touched not by the silver notes of God's enchanting word.

6, 7, 8, 9. *" Break their teeth, O God, in their mouth ; break out the great teeth of the young lions, O Lord. Let them melt away as waters which run continually : when he bendeth his bow to shoot his arrows, let them be as cut in pieces. As a snail which melteth, let every one of them pass away ; like the untimely birth of a woman, that they may not see the sun. Before your pots can feel the thorns, He shall take them away as with a whirlwind, both living and in His wrath."*

The Spirit here, to support and console afflicted saints, gives strong assurance of approaching vengeance. The weapons of their foes shall be broken. Their power of evil shall gradually be brought to nothing, as waters lessen when they flow away. They may bend the bow, and prepare the arrows, but these implements shall take no effect. Graphic images of weakness portray their utter impotency to prosecute their schemes. Wrath shall break suddenly upon them, and sweep them from the earth, as the fury of an unexpected whirlwind. Quickly will they perish, even more quickly than the blazing fuel can warm a caldron.

10. *" The righteous shall rejoice when he seeth the vengeance; he shall wash his feet in the blood of the wicked."*

When God's holy indignation is thus conspicuously displayed, the godly should thankfully recognize God's just displeasure. Pity for the miserable offenders they should feel, but joy in God's glory should prevail. The blood of the wicked should be as a fountain, in which their feet should wash, and as a warning to walk more warily.

11. *" So that a man shall say, Verily there is a reward for the righteous: verily He is a God that judgeth in the earth."*

The truth will brightly shine, and compel acknowledgment that the righteous shall at last inherit manifestations of favour, and God's unerring tribunal will righteously dispense justice. When the great white throne is set, may we receive the welcome, " Come, ye blessed children of my Father, inherit the kingdom prepared for you from the foundation of the world."

LXXIX.

PSALM LIX.

IMMINENT perils surround the Psalmist. Foes environ his path. Means of escape seem utterly to fail. But God can never fail. Prayer flies to His presence : and faith rejoices in immovable confidence.

1, 2, 3, 4. *" Deliver me from mine enemies, O my God ; defend me from them that rise up against me. Deliver me from the workers of iniquity, and save me from bloody men. For, lo, they lie in wait for my soul : the mighty are gathered against me ; not for my transgression, nor for my sin, O Lord. They run and prepare themselves without my fault : awake to help me, and behold."*

David was imprisoned in his own abode. The door was guarded, and, to appearance, means of extrication could not be found. Instant death extended an un-resisted hand. But he sinks not in despair. He forgets not that God is his God, and that the God of all power was near. Conscious of freedom from all fault, he boldly looks up and cries, " Deliver me, O my God, save me, O my Lord."

5, 6, 7, 8. *" Thou, therefore, O Lord God of Hosts, the God of Israel, awake to visit all the heathen : be not merciful to any wicked trangressors. They return at evening : they make a noise like a dog, and go round*

about the city. Behold, they belch out with their mouth:
swords are in their lips: for who, say they, doth hear?
But Thou, O Lord, shall laugh at them; Thou shalt have
all the heathen in derision."

Importunity gives God no rest. It cries as though
slumber diverted attention. But He that keepeth
Israel will neither slumber nor sleep. In earnest supplication, he names his foes as utterly ignorant of God,
and in mind and feeling on a level with the worshippers of stocks and stones. He compares them to the
hungry dogs who, when the shades of evening prevail,
seek their accustomed haunts around the city, and
howl in search of the cast-out refuse. Impiously
they conceive the thought that the omniscient God
has closed His ears to their malignant threats. But
faith adheres to true views of God, and knows the
precious truth: "He that sitteth in the heavens shall
laugh, the Lord shall have them in derision."

9, 10, 11, 12, 13, 14, 15. "*Because of his strength*
will I wait upon Thee: for God is my defence. The
God of my mercy shall prevent me: God shall let me see
my desire upon mine enemies. Slay them not, lest my
people forget: scatter them by thy power; and bring
them down, O Lord our shield. For the sin of their
mouth, and the words of their lips, let them even be taken
in their pride; and for cursing and lying which they
speak. Consume them in wrath, consume them, that
they may not be; and let them know that God ruleth in
Jacob unto the ends of the earth. And at evening let
them return; and let them make a noise like a dog, and
go round about the city. Let them wander up and down
for meat, and grudge if they be not satisfied."

Mighty may be the foes of God's people, and terrible their strength; but from this fact faith gains the
argument that greater far is the omnipotence of God,
and therefore fear should be repressed.   There is much
preciousness in the title, "The God of my mercy."
God's covenant secures mercy's outpouring: and the
believer knows that mercy shall precede and follow
him.   Prayer sometimes deprecates the immediate
destruction of the foe.   It knows that there is much
teaching in God's continued exhibition in His people's
cause.   It therefore supplicates, not that they should
be slain, but scattered and exhibited in low estate.
The image is again repeated, that as evening-dogs
wander around in search of prey, they should be
permitted to show their vile desires.

16, 17. *" But I will sing of Thy power; yea, I will
sing aloud of Thy mercy in the morning: for Thou hast
been my defence and refuge in the day of my trouble.
Unto Thee, O my strength, will I sing: for God is my
defence, and the God of my mercy."*

The joy of faith is a flame, which waters
cannot quench.   It has a life, which never can be
slain.   It has wings ever ready to soar on high.
Paul and Silas, in their dungeon, prayed and sang
praises.   David, in his abode, closely besieged, professes that songs shall be on his lips.   He announces
the subject of his thanksgivings; they are the power, the
strength, the mercy of his God.   The same attributes
are our property, our defence, our refuge, our shield.
In the darkest days, then, let us sing.   When hope
seems gone, let us rejoice in the God of our salvation.

LXXX.

PSALM LX.

In the bright day of prosperity the gloom of adversity is not forgotten. The contrast elevates the joy of success. Abundant victories are realized, and God is acknowledged as the author and giver of all good things.

1, 2, 3. *" O God, Thou hast cast us off, Thou hast scattered us, Thou hast been displeased; O turn Thyself to us again. Thou hast made the earth to tremble; Thou hast broken it: heal the breaches thereof; for it shaketh. Thou hast showed Thy people hard things: Thou hast made us to drink the wine of astonishment."*

The past miseries of the kingdom are vivid to the mind of David. He remembered the internal commotions, and the people like sheep scattered and imperilled on the mountain's brow. He traced this to the just displeasure of God. He well knew that sin produced this alienation of God's favour. The prayer goes forth that righteous displeasure might now cease, and that God would again visit His people with His favour. He realized the terrible effects of God being estranged. He compares it to the terrors which result when the earth quakes and trembles to its base. He acknowledges the hard sufferings of the people, and marks the astonishment which darkened every brow. O sin, O sin! what miseries thou hast brought upon a fallen earth!

T

4, 5. " *Thou hast given a banner to them that fear
Thee, that it may be displayed because of the truth.
That Thy beloved may be delivered, save with Thy right
hand, and hear me.*"

The retrospect increases the joy that God, who had
afflicted, had not cast off.   Signs of favour had re-
appeared.   When the enemy came in like a flood, God
had lifted up a standard against him.   Around this
banner David mustered his people.   He saw in it a
proof that God would not suffer His truth to fail, nor
His pledged word to be trampled beneath ungodly feet.
He knew that God had a beloved flock, and that for
their sakes deliverance would be granted.   The Lord
of hosts had left unto Himself a blessed remnant " in
the midst of His people, as a dew from the Lord, and
as the showers upon the grass."

6, 7, 8, 9, 10. "*God hath spoken in His holiness; I will
rejoice : I will divide Shechem, and mete out the valley of
Succoth.   Gilead is mine, and Manasseh is mine;
Ephraim also is the strength of mine head ; Judah is
my lawgiver ; Moab is my wash-pot ; over Edom will I
cast out my shoe : Philistia, triumph thou because of me.
Who will bring me into the strong city ? who will lead
me into Edom ?   Wilt not Thou, O God, which hadst
cast us off ? and Thou, O God, which didst not go out
with our armies ?*"

Bright prospects glitter before David's eyes.   He
sees not only the firm establishment of Israel's kingdom beneath his sway, but the extension also of his
dominion among tributary states.   The assurance of
this grand supremacy is founded on the Word of his
God.   God had spoken in His holiness.   What God

had promised in His holy Word He would assuredly perform. Therefore David's heart, full of this faith, overflowed with joy. He realized the pre-eminence of Judah's tribe. He knew that laws and decrees should issue from it, and that in God's good time the great Deliverer should be among its sons. He realized too that other tribes would await His royal decrees, and that neighbouring provinces would bow before him. Moab should be reduced to servile work; Edom would be trodden down beneath his conquering feet; Philistia's triumph should be annexation to his rule. The spiritual improvement is most obvious. Relying on God's holy Word, we should rejoice in the secure establishment of grace within our hearts, and we should long more and strive more for the rapid growth of the Spirit's empire within, and the subjugation of all lusts and godless passions. David views the almost impregnable strength of Edom's fortress; but he knew that it must quickly fall: for God had returned to give victory to His arms.

11, 12. "*Give us help from trouble: for vain is the help of man. Through God we shall do valiantly: for He it is that shall tread down our enemies.*"

He sees that all his armaments are weak except upheld by God. He prays for this help. He believes that it will surely come. He believes that, through his God, valiant exploits would be performed, and that through his God his feet would crush the necks of His foes. We believe that through Jesus we too shall do valiantly, and that yet a little while and Satan will be crushed beneath our feet.

LXXXI.

PSALM LXI.

ATTENTION to prayer in a season of great distress is supplicated in the experience of former mercies. Promises are remembered, and grateful service is vowed.

1, 2. "*Hear my cry, O God; attend unto my prayer. From the end of the earth will I cry unto Thee, when my heart is overwhelmed: lead me to the Rock that is higher than I.*"

Prayer, which is our precious privilege, and should be our continuous delight, should ever be from the very depths of the heart, and in the earnest wrestlings of the soul. Can there be coldness, can there be weakness, can there be formality when we draw near to the immediate presence of our God, and pour into His listening ear our every want and our every desire? Here David is all zeal and all intense effort. He doubles expression to awaken a gracious hearing. Doubtless His need now was very great. But that need is no small blessing which raises us direct from earth and places us before our God. He was an outcast—banished from his home, from his family, and his cherished friends. Strangers and aliens were around him. But on the outstretched wings of faith he soars to a Heavenly Father's house. He desires to be uplifted from his low estate, and his feet set on

elevated ground. We have a Rock; and when standing upon it, impregnable is our position and glorious
is our prospect. That Rock is Christ. May our
prayer be constant that we may be kept grounded and
settled on Him, and never moved away from the hope
of our Gospel!

3, 4. "*For Thou hast been a shelter for me, and a
strong tower from the enemy. I will abide in Thy tabernacle for ever; I will trust in the covert of Thy wings.*"

Experience here supplies a prevailing argument.
The Psalmist could look back on many perils, but out
of them all the Lord had delivered him. That arm
was not shortened; that mercy was warm as ever. It
had never failed; it will never fail. Therefore in his
exile he had persuasion that he would be restored to
the city of his God, and join again in the services
which he loved. He knew that the wings which had
sheltered him would shelter him to the end, and
therefore his trust abided firm.

5, 6. "*For Thou, O God, hast heard my vows: Thou
hast given me the heritage of those that fear Thy name.
Thou wilt prolong the king's life; and his years as many
generations.*"

They who watch for answers to their vows will have
abundant cause for joy. God's Word is pledged in
many forms that prayer shall not go forth in vain.
All these promises are yea and amen in Christ Jesus;
and heaven and earth shall pass away, and all the
universe be wrapped in ruin, before fulfilment can be
denied. The answers come, and they abound in comfort and encouragement. David realized that through
faith he was heir to an inheritance which paled all

earthly possessions—the heritage of those that feared God's name. Blessings indeed are linked to this ennobling grace. It belongs to all who have found forgiveness in Christ Jesus. They love the Lord with all intensity of rapture: they love His Word and will; and nothing could induce them willingly to offend. Hence mercy compasseth them about. High as the heaven is above the earth, so great is His mercy towards them that fear Him. O Lord! implant Thy fear in our longing hearts! It will enrich us now and ever. This David fully realized. He saw that His days were coequal with the ages of eternity, and that all those days would be happiness and glory.

7, 8. " *He shall abide before God for ever: O prepare mercy and truth which may preserve him. So will I sing praise unto Thy name for ever, that I may daily perform my vows.*"

He looked onward to the fulness of joy in the presence of God, and to the pleasures which are at His right hand for ever. With this bright prospect, who will not fear His name—who will not devote himself to God's service? But all our vows and all our efforts are utter weakness unless we are aided from on high. In deep knowledge of his own nothingness, he supplicates that mercy and truth may ever be at hand for his preservation; and then he resolves that fit praises shall be rendered. Thus prayer and trust lead to everlasting joys.

LXXXII.

PSALM LXII.

FIRM confidence in God is here avowed. He is commended as a high fortress of protection. The ruin of
the ungodly is foreshown; exhortations to trust in God
follow, with recognition of His precious attributes.
May we be enabled to adopt His language as the feeling of our souls!

1, 2. *" Truly my soul waiteth upon God: from Him
cometh my salvation. He only is my rock and my salvation; He is my defence; I shall not be greatly moved."*

Amid all tossing conflicts and disquieting alarms,
the Christian has a home of sweet repose. He can re-
cline on God, and feel that everlasting arms are under-
neath him. This, amid all the troubles of his troublous
life, was David's sweet experience. He looked not to
man; he conferred not with flesh and blood. He
knew that from God only sure protection came. With
overflowing joy he testifies, " He only is my rock and
my salvation. He is my defence." A rock high above
all foes, immovable against all assaults—salvation to
the very uttermost from all the menaces of man, from
all the miseries of sin, from all the accusations of conscience, from all the powers of Satan. Sheltered in
Him, he had no fears that he should be cast down;
he might tremble when hard pressed, but he well
knew that he should not be greatly moved.

3, 4. " *How long will ye imagine mischief against a man ? ye shall be slain all of you: as a bowing wall shall ye be, and as a tottering fence. They only consult to cast him down from his excellency; they delight in lies: they bless with their mouth, but they curse inwardly.*"

From his high munition he expostulates with his crafty foes. He foresees that their schemes will soon be overthrown—that all their boasted prowess shall be crushed in ruins, as the wall falls whose foundations are undermined, and as the weak fence which shakes beneath the slightest touch. He avows his knowledge of their inward character—their plot to subvert them whom God has exalted. Falsehood and curses are their constant means of mischief.

5, 6, 7. " *My soul, wait thou only upon God; for my expectation is from Him. He only is my rock and my salvation: He is my defence; I shall not be moved. In God is my salvation and my glory: the rock of my strength, and my refuge, is in God.*"

By easy transit he reverts to God, and realizes his own happy state. He calls upon his soul utterly to reject all other trust, and to make God its only resting-place. Faith glows in brighter blaze, and renews expressions to testify the firmness of such hope. He recently had stated that he had no fears of being "greatly moved;" but now he rejoices in the persuasion that he shall not be moved at all. What God was to David, the same is He yesterday, to-day, and for ever. Let us fan by all means this persuasion into the strength of full assurance. Then we shall lift high our heads above surrounding troubles.

8. "*Trust in Him at all times; ye people, pour out your heart before Him: God is a refuge for us.*"

Faith ever strives to win others to partake in its delights. Here others are exhorted at all times to repose their confidence in God. Let them restrain no feeling. Let them hide no distress. Let them pour forth all their woes. Let their inmost need be referred to Him. Let their whole hearts be opened to His view. He will not turn away. He will give audience. His arms will be a sure and ready refuge.

9, 10. "*Surely men of low degree are vanity, and men of high degree are a lie: to be laid in the balance, they are altogether lighter than vanity. Trust not in oppression, and become not vain in robbery: if riches increase, set not your heart upon them.*"

Disappointment is the lot of them who turn from God to man. No sure help can ever be derived from such source. Survey our total race from highest station to the lowest grade. Weigh them together in the balances of truth. How worthless is their accumulated weight! One inscription marks them all— "Vanity of vanities. All is vanity." If wealth be hoarded, and iniquitous means obtain it, let the heart scorn it. There is no real help in it.

11, 12. "*God hath spoken once; twice have I heard this, that power belongeth unto God. Also unto Thee, O Lord, belongeth mercy: for Thou renderest to every man according to his work.*"

Blessed be God, He has revealed Himself. Again and again His attributes are set before us. Let them be our constant study and our constant trust. They tell us of His power. It is omnipotent. Is it not then sure protection ?   They tell us of His mercy.   It has no bounds.   Will it not extend to us ?   They tell us, too, that soon the judgment will be set and the books opened, and we shall be judged out of those things which are written in the books, according to our works.

LXXXIII.

PSALM LXIII.

WARM expressions show the intense longing of the soul for God. The joy of public ordinances is set forth; confidence is added in the final triumph of the righteous, and final ruin of their foes. May we thus follow after God!

1, 2. " *O God, Thou art my God; early will I seek Thee: my soul thirsteth for Thee; my flesh longeth for Thee in a dry and thirsty land, where no water is; to see Thy power and Thy glory, so as I have seen Thee in the sanctuary.*"

They are seated on the highest throne of joy, and revel in the sweetest sunshine of delight, who know that God is their sure possession. They who hold Him as their own by the hand of faith have greater riches than earth can give, and surer property than this world can amass. And can it be that we may enjoy this treasure! By the faith of Jesus we have this privilege of glorious possession. We may thus say with David, " O God, Thou art my God;" and again, " This God is our God for ever and ever." We may pour out our hearts in the darkest hours of desertion, " My God, my God, why hast Thou forsaken me?" They who have thus found the pearl of great price will be always intent to realize their joy. With morning light they will be eager to joy in this joy. David adds, " Early will I seek Thee." May He who is the first have our first thoughts ! David was now an outcast in a dreary waste, and far from the Temple with its holy rites. The land was barren, unrefreshed by fertilizing streams of service. David had worshipped in the might of faith, and thus through outward means had drawn near to see Him who is invisible. He ardently longed for return of these blessings ; with all his powers he longed to be in near approach to God.

3, 4. " *Because Thy loving-kindness is better than life, my lips shall praise Thee. Thus will I bless Thee while I live ; I will lift up my hands in Thy name.*"

Life is a wondrous gift. It links us to eternity. But what is life without the favour of our God ? If we receive not grace we cannot inherit glory. We only tread a dreary passage to a world of woe. God's loving-kindness is the gift of gifts. In thought of this, the Psalmist vows that praise should ever be streaming from his lips, and that in adoring love he would upraise adoring hands.

5, 6, 7. " *My soul shall be satisfied as with marrow and fatness ; and my mouth shall praise Thee with joyful lips ; when I remember Thee upon my bed, and meditate on Thee in the night-watches. Because Thou hast been my help, therefore in the shadow of Thy wings will I rejoice.*"

Amid external desolations inward joy can be abundant. The wilderness and the solitary place shall be glad ; the desert shall rejoice and blossom as the rose. The Lord will make the wilderness a pool of water, and the dry land springs of water. He will plant in the wilderness the choicest of the evergreens. As the body craves the support of food, so too the soul has craving appetites. But they are all satisfied. The manna falls, and gives support and strength. The pilgrim sits down beneath the tree of life. Its laden branches present refreshing produce. The fruit is sweet to the taste. They who hunger and thirst after God assuredly shall be filled. The richest fruit is ever by their side. When evening shades prevail, the inward light does not expire. When the body needs repose, the active mind will hold communion with the Lord, and the night-watches be calmed with heavenly meditations. Experience recalls past help. The soul nestles beneath the shadow of God's wings, and is right glad.

8, 9, 10. *" My soul followeth hard after Thee : Thy right hand upholdeth me. But those that seek my soul, to destroy it, shall go into the lower parts of the earth. They shall fall by the sword ; they shall be a portion for foxes."*

Real desolation is distance from God. This anguish the righteous soul cannot endure. With every energy, with every power, it presses after its beloved object. It seeks uninterrupted fellowship. But, ah! how often is it weak to follow—how often do the tottering limbs need to be upheld ! This help is very near. God extends His right hand, and thus the fainting one pursues his course. Divine help enables to draw nigh to God, and to reach the presence which is heaven begun. While the believer thus strives and prospers, misery overwhelms the enemies who seek his life. God needs not instruments of destruction. They shall be overwhelmed, and perish as they whose carcasses are the food of beasts of prey.

11. "*But the king shall rejoice in God ; every one that sweareth by Him shall glory : but the mouth of them that speak lies shall be stopped.*"

A glorious prospect ends this hymn. It is unspeakably blessed ; it is full of glory. May the prospect encourage us to join ourselves to the Lord, and to vow vows in His most holy name !

LXXXIV.

PSALM LXIV.

THE voice of prayer again is heard amid the multitude of afflictions. But deliverance shows a smiling face. Foes will fall prostrate and the righteous shall rejoice.

1, 2. " *Hear my voice, O God, in my prayer: preserve my life from fear of the enemy. Hide me from the secret counsel of the wicked; from the insurrection of the workers of iniquity.*"

The Psalmist is here seen as a child of sorrows cradled in distress. His daily portion is affliction's bread. He holds a cup filled to the very brim with trouble. He cannot stir but amid snares and hostile threats. On every side the enemy shows a front of menace. But he has his refuge. It is near. It is secure. It is the mercy-seat to which prayer brings him nigh. Who will dread trouble when such remedies are at hand! Foes may have cruel malice in their hearts, but all their malice will prove blessings in disguise when they convey on wings of prayer to God's immediate presence. Thus cruel distress is often made the means of boundless good. So it was with David. In his worst straits he could look up and cry, Preserve my life, O God, from fear of the enemy. He knew that the wicked laid their secret plots, and that the workers of iniquity were planning to rise up against him. But no fears disturbed his peace when he could appeal to God to spread His sheltering wings around him, and to hide him in His pavilion from the machinations of insurgents.

3, 4, 5, 6. *" Who whet their tongue like a sword, and bend their bows to shoot their arrows, even bitter words ; that they may shoot in secret at the perfect : suddenly do they shoot at him, and fear not. They encourage themselves in an evil matter : they commune of laying snares privily ; they say, Who shall see them ? They search out iniquities ; they accomplish a diligent search : both the inward thought of every one of them, and the heart, is deep."*

In warfare the sword is a mighty weapon. It inflicts deadly wounds and drives back the attacking foe. So, too, arrows do destructive work. The Psalmist felt these weapons were arrayed against him in the malice of attacking words. Sharp as the sword were their tongues, piercing as the arrows were their words ; secret was the ambush, and suddenly they rushed out to fight. They hold malicious counsels. They flatter themselves that darkness would conceal their plots. In disregard of the all-seeing Eye they vainly question, Who shall see us ? They use, too, every endeavour to malign. They strive to discover some evil which they may bring to light, and use in calumny against the objects of their hate. Who can fathom the evil of their thoughts, the evil of their hearts ? Truly this evil is a deep well.

7, 8. *" But God shall shoot at them with an arrow ; suddenly shall they be wounded. So they shall make their own tongue to fall upon themselves : all that see them shall flee away."*

If our hope sprang only from this world, our hands might hang down in despair. If help came only from the sons of men, helpless indeed our state would be. How soon should we be trampled down by overwhelming hosts; how soon would Satan send forth his legions to sweep us into uttermost destruction. But God is our hope, our help, our strength, therefore unfailing victory must be on our side. He will bend His bow, and His arrows never fail to reach their mark, and to discomfit the insulting hosts. In a moment, when they least expect defeat, like Sennacherib's hosts, they shall lie as dead men. Like Pharaoh's army, they shall be overwhelmed and no more seen. God need not to call in new implements of ruin; their own tongues shall put forth destructive power. Self-wounded, self-ruined, self-destroyed, they shall exhibit a spectacle so fearful that affrighted spectators shall dread their very sight.

9, 10. *" And all men shall fear, and shall declare the work of God ; for they shall wisely consider of His doing. The righteous shall be glad in the Lord, and shall trust in Him ; and all the upright in heart shall glory."*

Awe shall be widely spread when such requital is beheld. The hand of the Lord shall be conspicuous, and shall be reverently acknowledged. Intelligence shall perceive that God's mind has been the directing cause, and God's power accomplished the overthrow. Happy thankfulness shall pervade the hearts of the righteous. They shall rejoice not so much in the misery of the wicked and at their total overthrow, as that God's work shall be thus manifestly seen, that praises should adore Him, and all glory be ascribed to Him.

LXXXV.

PSALM LXV.

INCESSANT praise is God's undoubted due. Countless are the motives which awaken it. May it be the exercise in which our souls unweariedly delight!

---

1. *" Praise waiteth for Thee, O God, in Zion: and unto Thee shall the vow be performed."*

Among God's people in the Zion of His dwelling, praise is ever ready to break forth. At every moment, in every circumstance, it strives to issue from adoring lips. How happy are God's people if praise is happiness; for their happiness flows as a river. They may have been in trouble—they may have known affliction's darkest hour—they may have felt desertion's misery. In these trials they sought deliverance, and vowed to pay the tribute of thanksgiving. Deliverance has come—their vows are duly paid. They call upon their souls and all that is within them to bless God's Holy name and to remember all His benefits.

2. *" O Thou that hearest prayer, unto Thee shall all flesh come."*

Many sweet titles tell of our Lord's abundant goodness. We read of Him as a God ready to forgive—as a God who receiveth sinners. Here He is proclaimed as a God that heareth prayer. Time would fail to recount all the promises which assure us of accepting favour. We are invited—we are importuned—to draw near to the mercy-seat by repeated promises that if we ask we shall receive. What is the saint's life but the recital of prayers heard and prayers fulfilled! This truth rolls as an unceasing flood throughout the pages of the Bible. Oh! for more faith to clasp these grand assurances to our hearts. It would make earth one intercourse with heaven—it would show heaven descending unto earth on wings of glad reply. Why are we so poor and needy, so scanty in grace, so downcast in spirit? It is because our prayers are faithless. How different would be our state if earnest prayer gave God no rest—if wrestling supplications took heaven by storm! Then praises would proclaim that God is true; and praying lips can never pray in vain. This truth put forth into action would make this world a house of prayer. "Unto Thee shall all flesh come."

3. "*Iniquities prevail against me: as for our transgressions, Thou shalt purge them away.*"

The believer is ever conscious of his sin-soiled state. He meekly cries, "My sin is ever before me." But still praise superabounds. He knows that Christ has by His one offering purged away all his sins. He knows that the blood of Jesus Christ, God's Son, cleanses from all sin. In sense of this pardon, what praises, what thanksgivings he pours forth!

4. "*Blessed is the man whom Thou choosest, and causest to approach unto Thee, that he may dwell in Thy courts: we shall be satisfied with the goodness of Thy house, even of Thy holy temple.*"

The Book of Life, written before the foundation of the world, is here. Blessed indeed are they whose names are therein inscribed! The cause of this blessedness is everlasting love—its source is far above, out of our sight. But the effects are manifest. The happy objects of this love are won and drawn by grace. They cannot rest but in the presence of their God; and this they seek in holy ordinances, and here their souls are satisfied with tokens of God's goodness.

5-13. "*By terrible things in righteousness wilt Thou answer us, O God of our salvation; who art the confidence of all the ends of the earth, and of them that are afar off upon the sea: which by His strength setteth fast the mountains; being girded with power: which stilleth the noise of the seas, the noise of their waves, and the tumult of the people. They also that dwell in the uttermost parts are afraid at Thy tokens: Thou makest the outgoings of the morning and evening to rejoice. Thou visitest the earth, and waterest it: Thou greatly enrichest it with the river of God, which is full of water: Thou preparest them corn, when Thou hast so provided for it. Thou waterest the ridges thereof abundantly; Thou settlest the furrows thereof; thou makest it soft with showers; Thou blessest the springing thereof: Thou crownest the year with Thy goodness; and Thy paths drop fatness. They drop upon the pastures of the wilderness; and the little hills rejoice on every side. The pastures are clothed with flocks; the valleys also are covered over with corn; they shout for joy, they also sing.*"

Prayer calls God to manifest His power—answers are not withheld. Terrible is the overthrow of all evil: faith is confirmed, and the glory of God is widely seen. His power shines brightly through the realms of nature. The operations of His hand declare it. The mighty mountains stand fast through His resolve. The raging waves repose at His word : morning sweetly smiles, and evening closes on a rejoicing world. Refreshing streams irrigate the thirsty soil ; abundance richly follows : the year displays God's goodness as its diadem : fertility follows where His feet are set. Pastures and valleys are luxuriant plenty. Praise, then, is His just due. Let all within us praise His name.

LXXXVI.

PSALM LXVI. 1–9.

PRAISE is the note which sounds throughout this hymn. Marvellous mercies are recounted, both temporal and spiritual. All demand devout thanksgiving. As recipients of mercy, may our hearts joyfully respond!

1, 2. *" Make a joyful noise unto God, all ye lands: sing forth the honour of His name; make His praise glorious."*

An exhortation sounds to all the dwellers upon earth. All lands, with all their inhabitants, are called to loud and joyful praise. What mighty motives urge to this work. How sweetly mercy beams upon the world. Behold creation in its every part. How suited to provide for happiness and comfort. In every part we see benevolent contrivance for man's good. There is no moment when blessings are not strewed around. There should be no moment when responding praises should not ascend. Away with meagre praise and scanty meed of blessing. The exhortation bids us to make His praise to be glorious. It should be our noblest exercise. It should call forth the grandest energies of our noblest powers. But if temporal blessings require these bursts of adoration, how much more do the blessings of the Gospel demand the overflowings of this grace!

3. *" Say unto God, How terrible art Thou in Thy*

*works! through the greatness of Thy power shall Thine
enemies submit themselves unto Thee."*

We are encouraged to recite unto God the manifestations of His awful power. Thus to enumerate them
is to deepen in us the sense of their greatness. It is
a sad fact that from creation's hour hostile powers
have armed themselves against God. In vile hatred
they have raised their puny arm against His majesty
and rule. They have vainly thought to subvert His
empire—to wrest the sceptre from His hands. But
how tremendous has been their overthrow! He that
sits in the heavens has laughed. The Lord has had
them in derision.

. 4. *"All the earth shall worship Thee, and shall sing
unto Thee; they shall sing to Thy name."*

Prediction here proclaims the glories of the coming
kingdom. "The kingdoms of this world shall become
the kingdoms of our God and of His Christ, and He
shall reign for ever and ever." Every lip shall praise
Him. Every heart shall swell with adoration—one
loud hallelujah shall pervade the world.

5, 6. *"Come and see the works of God: He is terrible
in His doing toward the children of men. He turned the
sea into dry land: they went through the flood on foot;
there did we rejoice in Him."*

We are here invited to draw instruction from the
study of God's works. How precious is the contemplation! It shows in large and wondrous page how
God has manifested Himself in olden times. It tells
of deliverances in extremest times and from extremest
perils. Great is the value of such study. For the
God of our fathers is the God of His present family,

and will be the God of His children to the latest day. He is the same yesterday, and to-day, and for ever in love and power. In His loving-kindness and in His truth there is no variableness, neither shadow of turning. Ponder these manifestations in the deliverance of Israel from Egyptian bondage. In the rear the king pursues with overwhelming hosts—on each side heights impassable forbid escape—in the front the sea presents the obstruction of impeding billows. Moses is commanded to wave his rod. The waters part. A dry pavement opens the passage of deliverance. The people march as on dry land. In safety they look back and see the returning billows rolling their foes to fearful death. Terrible was the work. The past deliverance bids us take courage. So, too, when Canaan's promised land was reached, the rolling Jordan did not impede entrance. The waters parted. The hosts marched onwards as on dry ground. Marvellous was the deliverance—a type that no opposing foes shall check our entrance to our promised home.

7, 8, 9. "*He ruleth by His power for ever; His eyes behold the nations: let not the rebellious exalt themselves. O bless our God, ye people, and make the voice of His praise to be heard; which holdeth our soul in life, and suffereth not our feet to be moved.*"

The same power still sits on the throne of universal sway. The same eye still looks down upon the fury of the nations. Let the rebels take heed. Their destruction cannot be escaped. But let God's people bless and praise Him. Their souls yet live far above the reach of injury. Their feet still stand immovable. Let us trust more and more. Let us praise more and more.

LXXXVII.

PSALM LXVI. 10–20.

10, 11, 12. "*For Thou, O God, hast proved us:
Thou hast tried us, as silver is tried. Thou broughtest
us into the net; Thou laidest affliction upon our loins.
Thou hast caused men to ride over our heads: we went
through fire and through water; but Thou broughtest us
out into a wealthy place.*"

The dealings of God are all mercy and truth unto
His chosen heritage, but these dealings often show a
dark and trying aspect. A scourge is used, and grievous
troubles multiply. But such discipline is needful.
Without it we should slumber in our nests, and in-
dolently indulge sloth. Our feet would go astray, and
we should not meeten for the heavenly home. The
vine will not be fruitful unless pruned: the silver
will not be purged from dross unless the furnace be
again and again employed. It is our wisdom thus to
see the hand of love in all our seasons of affliction.
The Psalmist recognises God's hand in bringing him
into his many difficulties. The afflictions which oppress are the burdens which the Lord imposes. They
arise not from the dust: they are all designed to
humble, to excite watchfulness, to purify, to sanctify,
to bless, to produce conformity to our Elder Brother's
image. For a season our adversaries are permitted to
trample on us with insulting feet. This is a grievous
passage in our pilgrimage; but it has its end, and
proves to be the entrance of enlarged prosperities.

1 3, 1 4, 1 5. " *I will go into Thy house with burnt-
offerings ; I will pay Thee my vows, which my lips have
uttered, and my mouth hath spoken, when I was in
trouble. I will offer unto Thee burnt-sacrifices of fat-
lings, with the incense of rams : I will offer bullocks with
goats.*"

Times of trouble strongly attract us to the mercy-
seat. Prayer becomes more fervent, and grateful
service is devoutly vowed. These pledges should be
all redeemed, and public acknowledgment should be
rendered. Gratitude forgets not the large mercies of
deliverance. It delights to pour forth streams upon
streams of pious adoration. The Psalmist brought his
appointed victims to the altar : he shed the prefiguring
blood : he presented the foreshadowing offerings. We
know that these types were emblems of our blessed
Lord, through whom alone we can draw near to God ;
and who, by the incense of His blood, gives perfume
to our every service. In the full faith of Christ may
we thus ever worship ; pleading His blood, may we
bring all our vows. Acceptance comes when in His
name we thus approach.

1 6, 1 7. " *Come and hear, all ye that fear God, and
I will declare what He hath done for my soul. I cried
unto Him with my mouth, and He was extolled with my
tongue.*"

The Psalmist invites the saints who are around him
to come and listen to his grateful tale. Right indeed it
is to encircle God's throne with praises ; but gratitude
should not be limited to such devotion. Our lips
should tell aloud to all around His gracious dealings.
They that fear the Lord speak often one to another.

This exercise is not disregarded on high. A book of remembrance is written. Of what did the Psalmist speak ? Of all that God had done for his soul. Oh ! the breadth and length, the depth and height, of this most marvellous declaration ! He visited his soul in darkness, and gave the light of life. He found it in the prison-house of the devil, and translated it into the kingdom of grace and glory. He saw it laden with all iniquities, and removed the total burden. He saw it filthy in all the mire of evil, and clothed it with the garments of righteousness and salvation. Such is the burden of the believer's story ; but heaven must be reached and eternity exhausted before the whole can be told. He adds the assurance that he was incessant in prayerful cries, and that his tongue was ever loud in raising high the praises of his God.

18, 19, 20. " *If I regard iniquity in my heart, the Lord will not hear me. But, verily, God hath heard me ; He hath attended to the voice of my prayer. Blessed be God, which hath not turned away my prayer, nor His mercy from me.*"

He adds the solemn warning, that if iniquity is fondled in the heart, vain will be the utterance of his lips. Prayer is a holy exercise ; the admixture of unholiness reduces it to nullity. But his prayer was the offspring of sincerity and truth ; the answers which came gave evidence that the petitions were sanctified by the Spirit and accepted of the Lord. With what happiness would he exclaim, " Blessed be God, which hath not turned away my prayer, nor His mercy from me."

LXXXVIII.

PSALM LXVII.

A HYMN here meets us earnest in prayer, bright in prospects, shining in prophecies, glorious in anticipations. Hope gazes with delight on the fulness of the Gentiles—on the consequent ingathering of the Jews, and all the glories of the second Advent. May we here find a subject for our supplications—a theme for rejoicing hope!

1, 2. *" God be merciful unto us, and bless us ; and cause His face to shine upon us. That Thy way may be known upon earth, Thy saving health among all nations."*

We rightly use the promises of God when we turn them into earnest prayer. We cannot doubt that we pursue a track which leads to all riches of fulfilment when our lips plead that God would do unto us according to His word. Often are we assured that God is rich in mercy unto His people, and that His blessing is their promised heritage. How earnestly, then, and joyfully may we put God in remembrance, and plead with Him to be merciful unto us, and to bless us, and to lift up upon us the light of His countenance, and to cause the shining of His smile to beam around us. But such prayer should not be limited to our own joys only. It should enfold in its embrace the whole family of man. Our supplications should beseech Him to look beyond our own need, and to make known throughout the world His purpose, His will, His grace, His love, His design in sending Jesus to assume our flesh, His covenant of everlasting peace in Him. But such prayer lacks the essence of sincerity if it evaporates in word only, and makes no effort to secure fulfilment. How vain to pray and not to labour in the missionary cause !

3, 4. " *Let the people praise Thee, O God ; let all the people praise Thee. O let the nations be glad, and sing for joy : for Thou shalt judge the people righteously, and govern the nations upon earth.*"

What a glorious prospect here rises to our view ! What joy and gladness animate the scene ! What sound prevails ? It is the praises of our God. Whence issue forth these precious notes ? Not from one heart only ; not from one family only, but from all who throng the earth. From every clime, from every nation, from all who breathe the breath of life, adoration is uplifted. " Let the people praise Thee, O God, let all the people praise Thee." How earnestly should we pray, Come, Lord Jesus, come quickly, and establish this reign of universal gladness. For then shall all nations sing for joy. How abundant will be the cause of this thanksgiving. The blessed Jesus shall sit upon the throne of His kingdom. His happy subjects shall adore Him as King of kings and Lord of lords. His rule shall be righteousness. The laws of His empire shall be perfect holiness. Sin, with all its miseries, shall be cast out. Its hideous features shall be no more seen. Nothing shall appear which shall mar the happiness of all the rejoicing subjects. The tabernacle of God shall be with them. The purposes of redeeming love shall be fully manifested. A righteous King shall govern righteous subjects. "Come, Lord Jesus, come quickly."

5, 6, 7. "*Let the people praise Thee, O God; let all the people praise Thee. Then shall the earth yield her increase; and God, even our own God, shall bless us. God shall bless us; and all the ends of the earth shall fear Him.*"

Again and again shall prayer ascend for the ingathering of the Gentiles into the fold of Christ. The blessing is promised, and no rest should be given until the happy consummation comes, and the fulness of these new subjects shall be as life from the dead to the expectant world. Then, as when renewed fertility crowns the surface of the earth with goodness, so every token of joy and blessedness shall be seen throughout the world's length and breadth. "God shall bless us, and all the ends of the earth shall fear Him." Who can conceive the blessings which Christ Jesus bestows on His ransomed heritage? How can we adequately love and bless and praise and adore Him! Let us go forth in faith, and ponder the coming wonders of His reign. Let our lips often cry, "Come, Lord Jesus, come quickly."

LXXXIX.

PSALM LXVIII. 1–12.

HAPPY was the occasion of this hymn. David was permitted to see the joyful day when the ark, the type of the blessed Jesus, was brought to its resting-place in Zion. It was a fit occasion for joy and gladness ; and joy and gladness were largely manifested. The hymn thus used looks back to the history, and looks onward to the time, when Jesus, having subdued all foes, ascends in triumph to the heaven of heavens. God's mercies are throughout abundantly proclaimed. May we realize these mercies, and call upon our every faculty to give praise !

1, 2, 3. "*Let God arise, let His enemies be scattered : let them also that hate Him flee before Him. As smoke is driven away, so drive them away: as wax melteth before the fire, so let the wicked perish at the presence of God. But let the righteous be glad : let them rejoice before God ; yea, let them exceedingly rejoice.*"

God's glory is most dear to all His people. It is their anguish when His name is blasphemed and His cause reviled. Hence their constant aspiration that God would arise and gird Himself with strength, and drive His foes into perdition. The prayer continually goes up that this ruin may be complete. Let smoke ascend in thick clouds and darken all the view. Let

now a breeze arise; the mass immediately dissolves,
and vanishes from sight. So let the enemies of God
be driven into nothingness. As the wax seems to be
a solid mass, but instantly dissolves and flows away
when heat is applied, so let these enemies melt and be
nowhere found; but let the righteous rejoice in God's
gladdening favour: let there be no bounds to their
exulting praise.

4, 5, 6. " *Sing unto God, sing praises to His name :
extol Him that rideth upon the heavens by His name
JAH, and rejoice before Him. A father of the fatherless, and a judge of the widows, is God in His holy
habitation. God setteth the solitary in families: He
bringeth out those which are bound with chains; but the
rebellious dwell in a dry land.*"

How abundant are the topics of our praise! Who
can reach the heights — who can fathom the depths
—who can measure the infinitudes of the incommuni-
cable name, Jehovah! This tells His glory as the
cause of His own being, as the giver of life to all who
live. Above the heaven of heavens He sits, thus surpassing all thoughts of glory. We cannot praise Him
according to His greatness, but let us praise Him according to our powers. But though He is thus in-
finitely great, He condescends to look in pity on the
feeblest and weakest of our race: He supplies parental
succour to poor orphans: He suffers not the widow to
be oppressed: He causes the inmates of the house to
rejoice in happy fellowship, and mutually to supply
each other's need: He delivers from captivity those
who have been bound with fetters, and leads forth His
people from Egyptian bondage.

7, 8. *" O God, when Thou wentest forth before Thy people, when Thou didst march through the wilderness; the earth shook, the heavens also dropped at the presence of God: even Sinai itself was moved at the presence of God, the God of Israel."*

It is faith's happy exercise to fly back and ponder all God's gracious dealings from the birth of time. On all there is inscribed the evidence of His gracious care. All His attributes are manifested planning and executing mercies for His people. In the work past we have assurance of His present care and of His never-failing providence. He who loved the fathers of our family still loves with the same love, and will love for ever. The Psalmist reverts to God's wondrous goodness as He preceded His people through the wilderness. The redemption from Egypt's thraldom is a pledge of our redemption from the captivity of sin and Satan. The awful marvels displayed on Sinai, when the Mount trembled, and terror shook all hearts, teach us to this day to regard with awe the majesty of our God.

9, 10. *" Thou, O God, didst send a plentiful rain, whereby Thou didst confirm Thine inheritance, when it was weary. Thy congregation hath dwelt therein: Thou, O God, hast prepared of Thy goodness for the poor."*

Did God supply the need of the camp? Did manna never cease to fall and the stream to trickle? So to the present hour His bounty sustains and replenishes His people. They may be poor and needy, but the Lord thinketh on them, and makes preparation for them.

11, 12. *" The Lord gave the word; great was the com-*

pany of those that published it.   Kings of armies did flee
apace ; and she that tarried at home divided the spoil."

It is not the Lord's will that His goodness should
be disregarded or unacknowledged. Therefore in every
age He has raised up faithful men to bear record of
His grace and love. How earnestly should we pray
that He would supply a band of faithful ministers,
and give them the tidings that they should proclaim.
Then all enemies will flee, and the weakest will be
enriched with spoil.

XC.

PSALM LXVIII. 13–23.

1 3, 1 4. "*Though ye have lien among the pots, yet shall ye be as the wings of a dove covered with silver, and her feathers with yellow gold. When the Almighty scattered kings in it, it was white as snow in Salmon.*"

The Lord's people sometimes lie in depths of degradation, and their hands are soiled by servile work. In Egypt the children of Israel were debased to the drudgery of the lowest slaves; but the time of vile service passed away, and they shone brightly as the honoured and admired upon earth. They changed their garbs of degradation for the splendour of magnificent estate. When in Canaan, God appeared in their behalf, and the affrighted kings in vain fled for concealment; then they shone forth arrayed in panoply of royal state: the snow-capped mountain glittering beneath the sun's rays was an emblem of their high supremacy. Believers now may be poorly clad in raiment of corruption; but yet a little while, and their corruptible shall put on incorruption, and they shall shine arrayed in glory far brighter than the sun in his strength.

1 5, 1 6. "*The hill of God is as the hill of Bashan; an high hill, as the hill of Bashan. Why leap ye, ye high hills? this is the hill which God desireth to dwell in; yea, the Lord will dwell in it for ever.*"

Zion is here presented to admiration as far surpassing in beauty all surrounding heights. This Zion is a type of the Church of Christ. Where shall we find words to commend its all-surpassing beauty? It is beautified with the glories of salvation, and shines as the chosen, the beloved, the honoured of the Lord. How utterly vain is the self-exaltation of other institutions! how contemptible their puny efforts to aggrandize themselves! They are of the earth and earthy, and with the earth shall be laid low. The Church is of heaven and heavenly. It is the chosen abode of God. God is in the midst of her, therefore she shall not be moved. He dwells for ever in her as His favoured abode. Never will He leave her or desert her. Salvation is her walls and bulwarks. Heaven and earth shall pass away, but God will rest for ever in His loved abode.

17, 18. *" The chariots of God are twenty thousand, even thousands of angels: the Lord is among them, as in Sinai, in the holy place. Thou hast ascended on high, Thou hast led captivity captive: Thou hast received gifts for men ; yea, for the rebellious also, that the Lord God might dwell among them."*

The terrors of Sinai are an instructive study. God is represented as moving in majestic procession, attended by countless hosts of angels. Let us clasp to our hearts the precious knowledge that He sends forth these spirits to be our constant guardians and to minister to our protection. The ark ascending Zion's hill has a prophetic voice. It foreshadows our Jesus returning to take His seat at God's right hand, the mighty Conqueror over sin and death and hell, and all the legion who had fought against Him. The cruel enemy who had subjugated man is dragged as a captive fast bound to our Lord's victorious car. The Conqueror receives for His people the gifts and graces which He had so gloriously won : He pours down sanctifying graces into His people's hearts, that so their hearts may be a meet abode for the indwelling God.

19, 20, 21, 22, 23. "*Blessed be the Lord, who daily loadeth us with benefits, even the God of our salvation. He that is our God is the God of salvation ; and unto God the Lord belong the issues from death. But God shall wound the head of His enemies, and the hairy scalp of such an one as goeth on still in his trespasses. The Lord said, I will bring again from Bashan: I will bring my people again from the depths of the sea : that thy foot may be dipped in the blood of thine enemies, and the tongue of thy dogs in the same.*"

The goodness of our God each day heaps blessings on us so vast that we can scarcely bear the load ; for each, responsive thanks should swell to heaven. His crowning blessing is eternal salvation and deliverance from the grasp of death. Let us study the title— "God of our salvation." Let us study the blessing— Escape from "the issues of death." But while His people thus live and are thus saved, what mercies overwhelm the wretched multitudes who reject His offers of pardon and of life ! What awful images predict their doom !

XCI.

PSALM LXVIII. 24–35.

24, 25. " *They have seen Thy goings, O God; even the goings of my God, my King, in the sanctuary. The singers went before, the players on instruments followed after; among them were the damsels playing with timbrels.*"

The grand design of public ordinances is here commended. The ways and works of God are openly proclaimed. His character is displayed. True worship should exhibit God in the wonders of His grace and love, His power and glory. We should attend the service of the sanctuary with hearts intent to learn saving lessons of redemption's design and work. Happy the worshipper who retires bearing testimony, I have seen the goings of my God, my King. Every faculty and every arrangement should be devoted to render due praise. In the infancy of the Church external rites were diligently used to teach the truth that devotion should engage all our powers. Now that the true light shines and symbols have passed away, the essence of true devotion should wax stronger.

26, 27. " *Bless ye God in the congregations, even the Lord, from the fountain of Israel. There is little Benjamin with their ruler, the princes of Judah and their council, the princes of Zebulun, and the princes of Naphtali.*"

Happy is the congregation from which true praise ascends to heaven! It is the very antepast of heaven,

when united voices swell the chorus, and harmony
with one consent is raised by delighted crowds. All
who spring from the common lineage of Israel are
here invited to this blessed work. But the call applies to us; for if we be Christ's, then are we Abraham's
seed, and heirs according to the promise. Let us
obey, and bless the Lord in the assemblies of His
people. In this happy service all the families of man
should join. The tribes were all assembled to convey
the ark with all rejoicing to the hill of Zion. So all
ranks, all stations, all degrees should gladly join in
publicly ascribing honour to our God.

28. "*Thy God hath commanded thy strength: strengthen,
O God, that which Thou hast wrought for us.*"

The covenant of grace contains all things needful
for the Church's weal. The command is therein
registered, that strength for all service and all work
should surely abound. It is our privilege to convert
these provisions into prayer. Acceptance surely awaits
the petitions which wrestle with God for the performance of His pledged design, and for perfecting the
work commenced in His servants.

29, 30, 31. "*Because of Thy temple at Jerusalem shall
kings bring presents unto Thee. Rebuke the company of
spearmen, the multitude of the bulls, with the calves of the
people, till every one submit himself with pieces of silver:
scatter Thou the people that delight in war. Princes shall
come out of Egypt: Ethiopia shall soon stretch out her
hands unto God.*"

The public acknowledgment of God in the services
of the temple shall attract extensive attention and
awaken general homage. God's power shall subdue

all adversaries. The rebels, senseless as creatures of
the lowest grade, shall bring tokens of submission.
The cruel, who take pleasure in the miseries and car-
nage of war, shall be dispersed. Potentates from afar
shall recognize the supremacy of God, and shall flock
to do homage, and to lay their treasures at His feet.
Wise indeed are the rulers who reverence the King of
kings and Lord of lords, and who rejoice to be His
devoted subjects.

32, 33, 34, 35. "*Sing unto God, ye kingdoms of the
earth; O sing praises unto the Lord. To Him that
rideth upon the heavens of heavens, which were of old; lo,
He doth send out His voice, and that a mighty voice.
Ascribe ye strength unto God; His excellency is over
Israel, and His strength is in the clouds. O God, Thou
art terrible out of Thy holy places: the God of Israel is
He that giveth strength and power unto His people.
Blessed be God.*"

It is the wisdom as also the duty of the kingdoms
of the earth to give glory unto God. The exhortation
is predictive, and tells of the coming day, when the
kingdoms of this world shall become the kingdoms of
God and of His Christ, and He shall reign for ever
and ever. All worship of idols, of stocks and stones,
shall be cast to the bats, and God shall be adored
enthroned in the heaven of heavens, and spreading
awe throughout the world by the voice of His thunder.
Let all might and power be ascribed to God. Let
Him be adored as the giver of all strength to His
people. Worthy indeed is He that every voice of
every inhabitant of earth should shout from the inmost
soul: "Blessed be God!"

XCII.

PSALM LXIX. 1–12.

THE Psalmist is involved in intensity of misery. The severest troubles in every form assail him. The downfall of his enemies is foreshadowed, and the conclusion of the hymn is praise.

1, 2. *"Save me, O God ; for the waters are come in unto my soul. I sink in deep mire, where there is no standing ; I am come into deep waters where the floods overflow me."*

The picture is exhibited of a drowning man. He sinks in overwhelming waters. There is no standing for his feet. There is no rescue for him from immediate ruin and a watery grave. In this scene of misery we see the man over whom the waves of affliction pitilessly break. But the picture mainly represents the blessed Jesus. What sorrow ever was like unto His sorrow when He trod earth's path in human guise ! Satan assailed Him with his utmost fury. No rest, no respite was permitted. This arch foe, too, stirred up ungodly men to wound Him with all the darts of malice and of rage. Jesus well knew that earth could bring no help. He looked above, and prayed : " Save me, O God."

3. *" I am weary of my crying ; my throat is dried : mine eyes fail while I wait for my God."*

Incessant supplications tested His powers of utterance. He ceased not to pour forth cries. He looked above for succour. He watched for replies until His failing eyes were dim.

4, 5. " *They that hate me without a cause are more than the hairs of mine head: they that would destroy me, being mine enemies wrongfully, are mighty; then I restored that which I took not away. O God, Thou knowest my foolishness; and my sins are not hid from Thee.*"

Jesus appeals to God that all this enmity, proceeding from such a host of mighty foes, was utterly without a cause. The persecution was wrongful malice. He did no wrong. His work was to render good for evil. He here allows that, though guiltless in Himself, He stood before God as laden with all the follies and all the sins of His people. He received the burden transferred by God to Him, and acknowledged His imputed guilt.

6, 7, 8. " *Let not them that wait on Thee, O Lord God of hosts, be ashamed for my sake; let not those that seek Thee be confounded for my sake, O God of Israel. Because for Thy sake I have borne reproach; shame hath covered my face. I am become a stranger unto my brethren, and an alien unto my mother's children.*"

A new petition is preferred. Its intensity is seen by the strong expressions in which God is invoked: as the Lord God of hosts, clothed with universal power; as the God of Israel, loving His people with everlasting love. The petition is, that the righteous who wait on God and seek His face should never be disheartened or cast down by sight of the troubles which were so multiplied. He deeply felt that reproaches were heaped upon Him; but feeling that they arose from

His faithfulness to God, He drew encouragement from them in His approaches to the mercy-seat. Reproaches for the cause of God are highest honour. God's smile will more than compensate for all the sneers of man. But it is a grievous trial when they who are brought up in the same home, and are most closely joined by ties of blood, stand apart and evidence their alienation. Jesus knew this trial. His own brethren believed not on Him. The children brought up in His reputed father's house did not uphold Him.

9, 10, 11, 12. "*For the zeal of thine house hath eaten me up; and the reproaches of them that reproached Thee have fallen upon me. When I wept, and chastened my soul with fasting, that was to my reproach. I made sackcloth also my garment; and I became a proverb to them. They that sit in the gate speak against me; and I was the song of the drunkards.*"

Intensity of zeal for true religion often occasions the derision of the wicked. The disciples remembered this word when they witnessed Christ's indignation in the polluted Temple. How keenly, too, were Christ's feelings moved when He heard His Father's name blasphemed. No pious conduct could check the impious sneer. Every kind of insult met Him. Even they who sat in the seats of justice refrained not their lips from calumny, and the very drunkards made Him the jest of their insulting songs. How keen must have been the sufferings of the Lamb of God. Let us forget not that they were all endured for us.

XCIII.

PSALM LXIX. 12–24.

13. "*But as for me, my prayer is unto Thee, O Lord, in an acceptable time: O God, in the multitude of Thy mercy hear me, in the truth of Thy salvation.*"

We draw sweet profit from affliction's cup when prayer is quickened by it, and trouble has no depths from which the face of God may not be seen. Hence prayer is plied in the assurance that acceptance will not be denied. The time is always acceptable. Answers are always ready when supplications plead the name of Jesus. "He ever liveth to make intercession for us." God's mercy, too, and His covenant engagements, are prevailing pleas. Mercy ceases to be mercy, truth fails, if faithful prayer should not be heard.

14, 15. "*Deliver me out of the mire, and let me not sink: let me be delivered from them that hate me, and out of the deep waters. Let not the water-flood overflow me, neither let the deep swallow me up, and let not the pit shut her mouth upon me.*"

Troubles are again compared to deep and overwhelming water-floods, but God's helping hand is able to extricate from all the mire and all the depths; and prayer wrestles that this hand would help.

16. "*Hear me, O Lord; for Thy loving-kindness is good: turn unto me according to the multitude of Thy tender mercies.*"

Love is here seen as the source and origin of all God's gracious dealings. He loves, therefore He withholds nothing that is good; He loves, therefore He crowns us with loving-kindness. He has revealed His name as Love. On that name we may rest all our supplications. His name, too, is Merciful. He is rich in mercy. His mercy reacheth unto the heavens. His mercy endureth for ever. His mercies exceed all number; and as is their number, so is their tenderness. They will never fail, who pray to be dealt with according to the multitude of God's tender mercies.

17, 18. *" And hide not Thy face from Thy servant ; for I am in trouble : hear me speedily. Draw nigh unto my soul, and redeem it : deliver me, because of mine enemies."*

When troubles darken around, it is faith's province to seek the light of God's countenance. If clouds should veil God's smile, trouble would indeed oppress. Faith knows this well, and is earnest for speedy help. If answers have long delay, then affliction is affliction indeed. But faith will follow God with cries, that He would in mercy draw nigh. It pleads : The enemy is near ; come quickly to my help. Such pleading will prevail. For sure is the promise, " Draw nigh unto God, and He will draw nigh unto you."

19. *" Thou hast known my reproach, and my shame, and my dishonour : mine adversaries are all before Thee."*

The believer's heart is comforted by the knowledge that his God is ever by his side. A voice is ever ringing in his ear, " Fear thou not, for I am with thee." God's eye surveys his path. His ear receives his every breathing. He marks his every circumstance. All the malevolence of adversaries is clearly known. Hence help in every hour of need may surely be expected.

20, 21. *" Reproach hath broken my heart, and I am*

*full of heaviness : and I looked for some to take pity, but
there was none ; and for comforters, but I found none.
They gave Me also gall for My meat; and in My thirst
they gave Me vinegar to drink."*

But still reproaches inflict painful wounds.　Jesus
drank this cup.　His holy nature would peculiarly
feel the painful touch of hellish malice.　In our
afflictions, too, the sympathy of friends gives sweet
relief.　This was denied to Jesus.　In His deepest
woe no human arm was stretched to help Him.　The
Spirit here takes us distinctly to the Cross.　We see
the fulfilment of this cruel mockery when to the
parched lips of Jesus they extended a sponge filled
with vinegar, and put it to His mouth.　What misery
was ever like unto His misery !　But His sufferings
were vicarious, and by His stripes we are healed.

　22, 23, 24. *" Let their table become a snare before them :
and that which should have been for their welfare, let it
become a trap.　Let their eyes be darkened, that they see
not ; and make their loins continually to shake.　Pour
out Thine indignation upon them, and let Thy wrathful
anger take hold of them."*

The Spirit proceeds to predict the terrible vengeance
which must fall upon Christ's foes.　The believer reads
the terrible decree, and meekly bows his head.　He
humbly acquiesces in the Lord's predicted wrath.　He
knows that God is love, and that in love He will do all
things well.　Let us turn from the appalling picture,
blessing from our hearts our gracious Lord, who saves His
people from all the penalties of sin ; and, waiting for His
return from heaven, " whom God raised from the dead,
even Jesus, who delivered us from the wrath to come."

XCIV.

PSALM LXIX. 24-36.

25. "*Let their habitation be desolate, and let none dwell in their tents.*"

Judas stands an awful monument of the fulfilment of this word. In his miserable case we learn how surely the predicted wrath will come. There may be respite, but respite is not a full pardon. What God has righteously announced He will most righteously perform. What Truth has uttered shall be truly done. Let the ungodly take warning. The unrighteous shall go away into everlasting punishment, but the righteous into life eternal. Indignation and wrath, tribulation and anguish, are the sinner's inevitable doom.

26. "*For they persecute Him whom Thou hast smitten; and they talk to the grief of those whom Thou hast wounded.*"

The main feature of their sin is effort to destroy the cause of Christ. It pleased the Lord to bruise Him. He was smitten by the hand of justice for our iniquities; He was wounded for our transgressions; but the malice and hostility of man added great burdens to His crushed spirit. The persecution of Jesus extends to the persecution of all His members. The arresting voice checks Paul in his infuriate career: "Saul, Saul, why persecutest thou Me?"

27, 28. "*Add iniquity unto their iniquity; and let them not come into Thy righteousness. Let them be*

*blotted out of the book of the living, and not be written
with the righteous."*

It is their miserable case that they are permitted to
go on from sin to sin, and thus to fill up the measure
of their iniquity. The decree has gone forth, "They
are joined to idols; let them alone." No melting word
softens their obdurate hearts; no converting grace turns
them from the downward path. They never reach the
happy land, in which all are clad in the beauties of
God's righteousness, and have righteousness as the
girdle of their reins. Their names cannot be found
in the book of the living or in the catalogue of the
righteous.

29, 30. *"But I am poor and sorrowful: let Thy
salvation, O God, set me up on high. I will praise the
name of God with a song, and will magnify Him with
thanksgiving."*

Jesus confesses that He stands among men despised
and rejected—a very worm, and no man; but He well
knew that He would be delivered from the oppressive
burden of vicarious suffering, and raised to salvation's highest throne. He looked onward from the
day, when His lips uttered humble and mournful
prayer, to the day of triumphant gladness, when
thanksgiving will be the endless song.

31, 32, 33. *"This also shall please the Lord better
than an ox or bullock that hath horns and hoofs. The
humble shall see this, and be glad: and your heart shall
live that seek God. For the Lord heareth the poor, and
despiseth not His prisoners."*

How condescending is the heart of God! The
praises of His people are His chosen abode. While

formal service without sincerity and warmth finds no
acceptance, the voice of thanksgiving fills heaven with
grateful fragrance. The humble followers of the Lamb
mark such acceptance, and profit by such experience.
They see how Jesus was upheld; they see how favour
smiles upon His grateful followers; and they rejoice
in the joy of their fathers in the faith. Happy
are they who seek God, who make His word and
will their constant study, and who in their every step
follow hard after Him! They shall not be disap-
pointed. Spiritual life shall now uplift them; eternal
life shall soon be their glorious crown. For this earnestly have they prayed even in the prison-house of
this poor flesh. Their prayer has not been in vain.
The Lord has heard them. Their desires have obtained success.

34, 35, 36. " *Let the heaven and earth praise Him,
the seas, and every thing that moveth therein: for God
will save Zion, and will build the cities of Judah; that
they may dwell there, and have it in possession. The
seed also of His servants shall inherit it; and they that
love His name shall dwell therein.*"

In prospect of God's saving mercies to His people,
all the universe and every creature that has life is
exhorted to abound in praise. But what praise can
reach the glories of the prospect ? Prosperity shall be
granted to the earthly Zion; but such security was
but a dim outline of the glories of the New Jerusalem.
There the chosen seed shall dwell for ever. There
they that love His name shall have unending bliss.
Their praises shall be vast as eternity, for every
moment will give fresh cause for praise.

Y

XCV.

PSALM LXX.

RESPITE from trouble is not of long continuance. The tide flows back with unabated strength. Earnest prayer is the ready refuge: the confusion of foes is confidently expected, and faith looks with undimmed eye for sure deliverance.

---

1. *"Make haste, O God, to deliver me; make haste to help me, O Lord."*

When perils are urgent, destruction seems at hand. If they are not instantly removed all strength must fail. Unless the storm abates the little bark must soon be a wreck. Unless the devouring wolves are stayed the little lamb cannot escape. Unless returning light should dawn the footsteps will stumble in the darksome course. This sense of imminent destruction urges the Psalmist to be importunate in prayer. Boldness in supplication waxes very strong. He prays the Lord to awaken from appearance of indifference— instantly to put forth His strength—without delay to hasten to his rescue. Blessed be God, such importunity is not forbidden—nay, rather, it is earnestly encouraged.

2, 3. *" Let them be ashamed and confounded that seek after my soul: let them be turned backward, and put to*

*confusion, that desire my hurt. Let them be turned back
for a reward of their shame that say, Aha, aha !"*

The Psalmist clearly saw the wicked malice of his.
foes. Nothing would content them but to stain their
hands in his blood—to take away his life was their
one object. He as clearly saw how God could defeat
their schemes and lay them low in disappointment and
in shame. He spreads out this before his God, " Let
them be ashamed and confounded." They were rushing forward in all the fury of malignity, reckoning
that success would soon be theirs. The Psalmist's
hope was bright, and he appealed to God to turn them
backward, and overwhelm them in confusion. He
heard their mocking and derision. Their insulting
cries were anguish to his heart ; but he felt that
their noisy sneers and wicked merriment would soon
be exchanged for bitterness of woe. The deliverance
of the godly is just as sure as the deliverance of our
great Head from the cruel taunts of those, who mocked
Him in His extremest anguish. They shall shine
brightly as the sun in his strength, while the wicked
shall cry in vain for rocks and mountains to conceal
them.

4. *" Let all those that seek Thee rejoice and be glad in
Thee : and let such as love Thy salvation say continually,
Let God be magnified."*

In the extremity of anguish the saint will look
beyond his own sad case. The Psalmist prays not for
his own deliverance only, but for the joy and gladness
of the whole family of faith. This prayer should often
swell, too, in our hearts. It will not go forth in vain :
for peace and happiness are secured for us in the

covenant of grace. The desire is added, that one note should be pregnant on the lips of those who delight to realize salvation's blessedness. That note should be, Let God be magnified! How can He be praised enough, who has wrought such wonders for us, and who never ceases to bless us and to do us good?

5. " *But I am poor and needy; make haste unto me, O God: thou art my help and my deliverer; O Lord, make no tarrying.*"

The sense of need returns, and again the prayer is urged, that God would speedily put forth His mighty arm to save. Confidence is added that God would arise when thus importuned; and the Psalmist avows that he has no other hope of rescue. " Thou art my help and my deliverer." Surely the God of our salvation will show Himself to be a God ready to extend all needful aid.

XCVI.

PSALM LXXI. 1–9.

WEIGHED down under the burden of his many years, harassed by ingratitude and cruelty, David warmly expresses his unwavering confidence in God. Increasing afflictions seem to fan trust into a brighter blaze. Faith pursues its wonted flight to the high throne of grace. May we thus trust, thus pray, and thus be comforted!

1, 2, 3. "*In Thee, O Lord, do I put my trust; let me never be put to confusion. Deliver me in Thy righteousness, and cause me to escape: incline Thine ear unto me, and save me. Be Thou my strong habitation, whereunto I may continually resort: Thou hast given commandment to save me; for Thou art my rock and my fortress.*"

We trust in those of whose love we have undoubted assurance, and of whose gracious dealings we have had much experience. We believe that what has been will be, and that help in time past will continue help unto the end. With what power do these motives awaken trust in God! He has loved us with an everlasting love—a love so mighty and so true, that He gave Jesus to every suffering and every shame, that He might save us and bring us home to Him. Let past days speak. Let the volume of our lives be read. They are all records that His goodness and His mercy, and His providential care, and His sustaining power have never ceased to follow us. These motives urge us to put full trust in Him. Harder than the nether millstone would be our hearts if this trust faltered or decayed. When we avow this trust in Him, we may firmly clasp the assurance that we shall never sink in shame. Enemies indeed may never cease their vile attacks, but we may appeal to God's faithfulness and truth that He will raise us high above their malice; that He will incline His ear unto us and save us. Faith well knows that it has a high fortress of deliverance in God—an immovable Rock, on which it may take its stand, an abiding dwelling, to which it may always resort. It knows that such refuge is provided in the covenant of grace, that the Father stipulated for full deliverance, and that the Son undertook fully to accomplish the whole work. It draws near, therefore, with the sustaining cry, " Thou hast given commandment to save me."

4, 5, 6. " *Deliver me, O my God, out of the hand of the wicked ; out of the hand of the unrighteous and cruel man. For Thou art my hope, O Lord God : Thou art my trust from my youth. By Thee have I been holden up from the womb : Thou art He that took me out of my mother's bowels : My praise shall be continually of Thee.*"

In his petition he opens out his grievous trials. He was assailed by wicked and unrighteous and cruel men. They raised the hand of violence against him. They held back no efforts to destroy him. But he was far from hopeless. He knew that God had holpen him in former extremities. His opening years had been years of trial and of persecution. In his earliest

afflictions he had put all his trust in God, and he had
found God to be an all-sufficient help. He looked back
to days of infancy, and his earliest memories abounded
in tokens of God's goodness. In his present trial, then,
praise hastened to his lips, and all despondency vanished
in thanksgiving.

7, 8, 9. "*I am as a wonder unto many : but Thou art
my strong refuge. Let my mouth be filled with Thy praise
and with Thy honour all the day. Cast me not off in the
time of old age ; forsake me not when my strength faileth.*"

The trials and many afflictions of God's servants
will often appear strange to the observer. It is a
natural conclusion, that if God really befriended, He
would drive troubles far away—that if He really loved,
the bright shining of His smile would cause all to be
bright and joyous around. Such taunt assailed our
blessed Lord when He was uplifted on the accursed
tree. But the believer knows that such dealings are
not inconsistent with eternal love, nor in opposition to
the terms of the everlasting covenant. Therefore, in
his weakest moments he can appeal to God, " Thou art
my strong refuge." He would give praise to God and
ascribe honour to His name at every moment of his
time, with every breath of his mouth. But he especially desired that old age might not find desertion.
When strength fails and decrepitudes bring low, and
energies can no more strive, and strength can no more
show the brawny arm, false friends may turn aside
with unconcern. Such are not the ways of God.
Man's inability is His opportunity to display His
power and His love. While God is God, let no
believer fear.

XCVII.

PSALM LXXI. 10–24.

10, 11, 12, 13. "*For mine enemies speak against me ; and they that lay wait for my soul take counsel together, saying, God hath forsaken him: persecute and take him ; for there is none to deliver him. O God, be not far from me: O my God, make haste for my help. Let them be confounded and consumed that are adversaries to my soul ; let them be covered with reproach and dishonour that seek my hurt.*"

Afflictions come in gloomy guise: they cast dark mantles over the downcast sufferers. The wicked see this, and they vainly think that this depression is desertion. They plot together, and in their ignorance exult that God has forsaken them, that their fortress is laid low, that protection utterly has failed, and that the afflicted are now exposed an easy prey to persecuting rage. But how different is the sufferer's estimate of his condition. He knows that the cup of anguish is mixed and presented by a Father's hand ; his prayer becomes more urgent for speedy deliverance, and that confusion may overwhelm the adversaries. It is no presumption: it is abounding faith to cry, " Be not far from me: O my God, make haste for my help."

14, 15, 16, 17, 18. "*But I will hope continually, and will yet praise Thee more and more. My mouth shall show forth Thy righteousness and Thy salvation all the*

*day ; for I know not the numbers thereof. I will go in
the strength of the Lord God : I will make mention of
Thy righteousness, even of Thine only. O God, Thou
hast taught me from my youth : and hitherto have I
declared Thy wondrous works. Now also, when I am
old and grey-headed, O God, forsake me not, until I have
showed Thy strength unto this generation, and Thy power
to every one that is to come."*

Afflictions fan the flame of hope ; they bring more
fuel that the fire may burn more brightly ; they add
more oil that the flame may not expire. If trials came
not there would be no expectation of relief ; if relief
were not vouchsafed the voice of praise would not so
loudly sing. The Psalmist knew that righteousness
and salvation were laid up for him in the covenant of
grace, and he resolves that his lips should never cease
to give due praise. The mercies of his God exceeded
his powers to comprehend, therefore the praises should
exceed all powers to calculate. He utterly excluded
the thought of power in himself. His every step
should be in realizing apprehensions that Omnipotence
upheld him. Therefore God's righteousness should be
his only confidence and his only song. He could look
back on many days, in all of which God's gracious
dealings had been his instruction. His constant testimony had been that He whose name was Wonderful
had done wonders in his behalf. In this persuasion
he implored that God would still be with him in the
decrepitudes of age, and help him still to testify that
God's power and strength could never fail.

19, 20, 21. " *Thy righteousness also, O God, is very
high, who hast done great things : O God, who is like*

unto Thee ? Thou, which hast showed me great and sore troubles, shalt quicken me again, and shalt bring me up again from the depths of the earth. Thou shalt increase my greatness, and comfort me on every side."

Who can reach the summit of God's faithful dealings! In height they tower above the heaven of heavens. We mark, and can only humbly adore. O God, who is like unto Thee! Lips become mute when they presume to institute comparison. The joy of faith instantly superabounds. Assurance comes that He who brings His people into great and sore troubles, and lays them in the lowest depths, shall quicken them again. Such resurrection often occurs in the experience of the afflicted, and is an emblem of the glorious change which shall be seen in the great day of the Lord, when death shall be swallowed up in victory.

22, 23, 24. *" I will also praise Thee with the psaltery, even Thy truth, O my God : unto Thee will I sing with the harp, O Thou Holy One of Israel. My lips shall greatly rejoice when I sing unto Thee ; and my soul, which Thou hast redeemed. My tongue also shall talk of Thy righteousness all the day long : for they are confounded, for they are brought unto shame, that seek my hurt."*

Resolves to give God thanks become more fervent. All the powers of lip and soul, all the energies of mind and body, all the instruments which art can furnish shall here find delighted exercise. The day will be too short to proclaim the mercies of entire deliverance. Ah! how sad the contrast! While believers thus sing, the adversaries are confounded and brought unto shame.

XCVIII.

PSALM LXXII. 1–9.

THIS Psalm presents especial grandeur and magnificence. In the first instance we have a description of the glorious reign of Solomon. But this reign soon fades before the sublimities of the reign of Jesus, the glowing words portraying it in a diversity of aspects. An appropriate ascription of glory concludes.

---

1. " *Give the king Thy judgments, O God, and Thy righteousness unto the king's son.*"

The aged monarch looks with fervid interest on his successor. Well did he know that prosperity must be the gift of God, that no talents or possessions could prevail unless God upheld him. It is a blessed thing to know that every good and perfect gift is from above. David especially supplicates that justice and equity might be the rule of the young monarch's reign, and that all his doings might be ordered by desire to execute God's will.

2, 3. " *He shall judge Thy people with righteousness, and Thy poor with judgment. The mountains shall bring peace to the people, and the little hills, by righteousness.*"

The prayer is scarcely uttered before fulfilment is realized. The people are represented as prospering under righteous government—all orders of subordinate

officers are represented as conducing to the peace and
happiness of the subjects. But a far greater than
Solomon is here. We see our blessed Jesus seated on
the throne of David, and wielding the sceptre of His
righteousness. His sceptre indeed is a right sceptre.
All events regulated by Him bring peace and comfort
to those who receive Him as their Lord and King.
He will so govern that they who hold office in this
world shall own His sway, and shall be guided according to His good pleasure to subserve the interests of
His cause.

4, 5. " *He shall judge the poor of the people, He shall
save the children of the needy, and shall break in pieces
the oppressor. They shall fear Thee as long as the sun
and moon endure, throughout all generations.*"

The poor and needy seem to be Christ's especial
care. They may have little of the things of earth, but
Christ's smile and blessing marks them heirs of all
things. Men may oppress them. But this mighty
King will break the oppressor's rod. This prediction
finds its grand fulfilment when Jesus triumphs on the
cross, and rises from the grave the mighty Conqueror of
sin and Satan. The perfecting of His kingdom is next
declared. He shall never want subjects who, while
they love Him, still serve with filial reverence. While
the world lasts, His kingdom shall abide, and when
the world passes away His kingdom shall shine forth
in everlasting brightness.

6, 7. " *He shall come down like rain upon the mown
grass; as showers that water the earth. In His days
shall the righteous flourish; and abundance of peace so
long as the moon endureth.*"

A sweet and graphic emblem shows the fertilizing refreshment which His people shall receive. Let the eye look upon the pastures over which the scythe has passed. They seem brought low, they show no sign of fertility. But when the gentle rain descends and genial showers fall, how quickly will vitality spring up, and plenty flourish around. So our great King will visit the depressed hearts of people by His presence, by His Spirit, by His Word. Then sweet revivals shall occur, and grace uplift a joyous head. The beauties of His kingdom are exceeding great. His people are all righteous, and all the fruits of righteousness abound in them, especially the fruits of peace. "Peace I leave with you, My peace I give unto you." The world may be in terrible commotion, but peace sweetly sings in the believer's heart—a peace which passeth all understanding, a peace which this world can neither give nor take away. The King of Israel is " the Prince of Peace."

8, 9. "*He shall have dominion also from sea to sea, and from the river unto the ends of the earth. They that dwell in the wilderness shall bow before Him ; and His enemies shall lick the dust.*"

Omnipotence is the property of our great King. His dominion extends precisely as His will directs. Sometimes we seem to fear that His subjects are a little flock. But He has His hidden ones, and He shall see of the travail of His soul and be satisfied. The wildest nations shall be subdued when He is pleased to send His truth into their hearts : and they who oppose His sway shall lie low in shame. Come, Lord Jesus, reign Thou in the midst of Thine enemies !

XCIX.

PSALM LXXII. 10–19.

10, 11. "*The kings of Tarshish and of the isles shall bring presents: the kings of Sheba and Seba shall offer gifts. Yea, all kings shall fall down before Him; all nations shall serve Him.*"

These words receive a striking confirmation in the historian's page. The ships of Tarshish and of the neighbouring isles come laden with their treasures to enrich King Solomon. Superabundance has poured in to give supplies to render the Temple the glory of the world. The Queen of Sheba comes in person to render her homage, and her train is splendid with presents from her land. Thus, too, when Jesus lies a new-born babe at Bethlehem, Magi from the East are guided to His lowly dwelling, and spread their offerings at His feet. In after days Isaiah prolongs this prophecy that kings shall be Thy nursing fathers and their queens Thy nursing mothers. Does the historian relate that in fulfilment of these words, all the kings of the earth sought the presence of Solomon to hear his wisdom: and that he reigned over all kings from the river even unto the land of the Philistines, and to the border of Egypt: and shall we doubt that universal sway shall be our Lord's dominion, and that the crown of all shall be assigned to Him?

12, 13, 14. "*For He shall deliver the needy when he crieth; the poor also, and him that hath no helper. He shall spare the poor and needy, and shall save the souls of the needy. He shall redeem their soul from deceit and violence: and precious shall their blood be in His sight."*

We have here a sweet picture of the peaceful reign of Solomon; benevolent care protected all his subjects; their petitions found him ever ready to give audience; cruelty and oppression were checked, and all injury to them was regarded as the highest crime. How sweetly do we see Jesus here! His subjects may be low in earthly state, their abode may be in the midst of penury and need, but no earthly degradation lowers them in His esteem. They all have instant access to Him: and when their cry proclaims their need, His melting heart brings full deliverance. They may be permitted to suffer from deceit and violence, but their souls are safe in His redeeming arms. They may expire amid the martyr's pains, but injury to them is injury to Himself. He keeps them as the apple of His eye.

15, 16, 17. *"And He shall live, and to Him shall be given of the gold of Sheba: prayer also shall be made for Him continually; and daily shall He be praised. There shall be an handful of corn in the earth upon the top of the mountains; the fruit thereof shall shake like Lebanon: and they of the city shall flourish like grass of the earth. His name shall endure for ever: His name shall be continued as long as the sun; and men shall be blessed in Him: all nations shall call Him blessed."*

Other kings wax old: their strength declines, they go down to the grave. David, when he had served his generation, fell on sleep. Not so our glorious

King. Immortality is His property—eternal days are the duration of His reign. It is the joy of His willing subjects to present their offerings to Him, and prayer continually encircles His high throne. His subjects, too, shall marvellously increase. The seed of His truth sown in places unlikely to yield fruit shall bring forth abundantly, as corn cast on the top of barren tops of mountains shall sometimes gladden with signs of fertility. The crowded city, too, shall be thronged with converts—they shall spring up as among the grass, as willows by the watercourses. Ages shall run their course; but while the sun hangs out its glorious light, the name of Jesus shall be magnified, and nations blessed by His favour, upheld by His power, and magnified in His might shall honour Him as the one source of blessedness, and shall adore Him for ever as the blessed.

18, 19. *" Blessed be the Lord God, the God of Israel, who only doeth wondrous things. And blessed be His glorious name for ever : and let the whole earth be filled with His glory. Amen, and Amen."*

This glorious hymn can have but one conclusion. Doxology must be its end! But how can we praise Him enough to whom alone the wonders of redemption appertain? For ever and for ever let blessings magnify His glorious name. Throughout the length and breadth of earth may His glory be resplendent! May our grateful hearts respond, " Amen and Amen ! "

C.

PSALM LXXIII. 1—14.

THE mind is often sorely tried by seeing the wicked in such great prosperity. Doubts are disposed to rise in reference to God's righteous government. But these doubts soon vanish when His purpose and will are scripturally weighed. An increase of confidence is the happy result.

---

1. " *Truly God is good to Israel, even to such as are of a clean heart.*"

It is sweet happiness to have clear knowledge of the goodness of our God. It should be a frequent prayer that He would make all His goodness pass before us, and that He would proclaim in our hearts His glorious name, especially in the wonders of re-demption. We should, too, mark well our character to see if it be that of the family of His love. They are described as clean of heart. Not only are they clean from all outward stains of evil by the cleansing application of the expiating blood, but they are clean, too, by the mighty indwelling of the Spirit working through the wonders of the Word. " Now are ye clean through the word which I have spoken unto you."

2, 3. " *But as for me, my feet were almost gone ; my steps had well-nigh slipped. For I was envious at the foolish, when I saw the prosperity of the wicked.*"

From the contemplation of God's goodness the Psalmist turns to confession of his own weakness. His steps had been tottering—not firmly set in the narrow way of life—not boldly climbing Zion's upward hill. He had wavered, he had stumbled, he had almost found a grievous fall. But whence the occasion of such inconstancy? He saw the ungodly. Prosperity smiled on their path—their cup of happiness seemed to overflow. The Psalmist was staggered. Such dealings seemed inconsistent with God's discriminating government.

4, 5. *" For there are no bands in their death ; but their strength is firm. They are not in trouble as other men ; neither are they plagued like other men."*

Instances are given of their untroubled course. To many the bed of sickness is a bed of deep distress. Pains and weakness bring sufferings to the declining frame. From such anguish the wicked are sometimes free. They have lived in ease, in ease they now depart. The common lot of trouble has not been theirs. While other men were emptied from vessel to vessel of affliction, they have reposed on the soft down of comfort and of peace.

6, 7. *" Therefore pride compasseth them about as a chain ; violence covereth them as a garment. Their eyes stand out with fatness : they have more than heart could wish."*

But is such prosperity in itself a blessing? Unsanctified by the grace of God, it really has the character of curse. Elated by their seeming superabundance, they regard themselves as high above their fellow-men. Pride seems to be the girdle of their

loins: violence is the robe in which they strut. Their
very appearance indicates luxurious self-indulgence;
and their possessions surpass their utmost desires.
Such is the state to which prosperity will sink a graceless heart.

8, 9, 10. "*They are corrupt, and speak wickedly
concerning oppression: they speak loftily. They set their
mouth against the heavens; and their tongue walketh
through the earth. Therefore His people return hither;
and waters of a full cup are wrung out to them.*"

There is no check to the workings of their deep-
seated corruption. This is evidenced by the proud
blasphemy of their words. They openly profess oppression. There are no limits on earth to the outgoings of their presumptuous language. They scale the
very heaven of heavens, and madly insult God upon
His throne.

11, 12. "*And they say, How doth God know? and
is there knowledge in the Most High? Behold, these are
the ungodly, who prosper in the world; they increase in
riches.*"

The Psalmist confesses the evil conclusion which in
his weakness he was prone to make. It seemed an
easy inference that if God abhorred evil He would not
distinguish the wicked by seeming tokens of approval.
The increase of their wealth seems an evidence of their
being in favour. But a word is added which unmasks
the cheat. They have prosperity indeed, but it is
prosperity only in this world. But the world is a
vain show. It passes away and the lusts thereof.
They in their lifetime " receive their good things."

13, 14. " *Verily I have cleansed my heart in vain,*

*and washed my hands in innocency.   For all the day
long have I been plagued, and chastened every morning."*

We have awful warning here that Satan will often
urge God's children to form erroneous conclusions.   If
they listen to his vile suggestions, how erroneously will
they view themselves, and God's dealings with the
wicked.   Aware of the malice and the power of this
tempter, let us pray more and more for the enlightening
power of the Holy Spirit, and deliverance from the
tempter's arts.   Without God's light we stumble in
dark paths.

CI.

PSALM LXXIII. 15-28.

15. " *If I say, I will speak thus ; behold, I should offend against the generation of Thy children.*"

The faculties of observation and deduction correct erroneous impressions of God's dealings. The Psalmist feels this, and pauses in his wrong conclusions. He feels that to give utterance to such thoughts would be to impinge against all which God's children in their experience had found.

16, 17. " *When I thought to know this, it was too painful for me. Until I went into the sanctuary of God ; then understood I their end.*"

But still he found that providential orderings were a mystery with which unaided reason could not grapple. Reason had no torch to illumine the dark passage, but full knowledge was provided. Let God's people study His ordinances and His revealed Word. In them all knowledge is plainly written. They who are deeply versed in the declarations of the great Book are the wisest among the children of men. In Christ are hid all the treasures of wisdom and knowledge. To know Him is to know all things. Thus the Psalmist learned the true end of all this seeming prosperity. The path might be strewed with flowers and charms of beauty, but fearful indeed was the abyss to which it led.

18, 19, 20. " *Surely Thou didst set them in slippery places : Thou castedst them down into destruction. How are they brought into desolation, as in a moment ! they are utterly consumed with terrors. As a dream when*

one awaketh; so, O Lord, when Thou awakest, Thou
shalt despise their image."

Their path seemed free from peril, and obviously to
lead to joy and gladness. But the ground was slippery—there was no sure safety for the feet. We read,
"Their feet shall slide in due time." Then what prop
will sustain them—what arm will hold them up?
No deliverance is near. Downward—downward they
descend, like rolling stones from mountain-heights,
until they plunge into destruction's gulf. No time is
granted to amend their ways. Terror utterly consumes
them; and their sad beginning reaches an inevitable end.
The state of the ungodly is at best but a vain dream.
So when God comes forth in just displeasure, He shakes
them from their vain imaginations, and shows how contemptible were the images of their sleeping hours.

21, 22. "*Thus my heart was grieved, and I was*
pricked in my reins. So foolish was I, and ignorant:
I was as a beast before Thee."

The Psalmist, fully alive to the folly of his erroneous conclusions, feels bitter grief. We should indeed
be pained when we indulge in thoughts not enlightened
by the Word. We should open our eyes widely to
our folly, and grant that the very brute creation teach
us higher wisdom.

23, 24. "*Nevertheless I am continually with Thee;*
Thou hast holden me by my right hand. Thou shalt guide
me with Thy counsel, and afterward receive me to glory."

But comfort is not gone. Such folly has not drawn
down the chastisement of desertion. The believer
still adheres to God, and it is his joy to find that God's
right hand is extended to hold him up. He is glad-

dened by the sweet assurance that grace would be his
constant guide; that he would hear the voice, "This
is the way," when he would turn to the right hand or
to the left; and he knew that when the perils of the
way were passed, he would have abundant entrance
into the kingdom of heaven. His guide on earth would
give him welcome at heaven's gate.

25. "*Whom have I in heaven but Thee? And there
is none upon earth that I desire beside Thee!*"

The believer has Jesus for his portion. Can heaven
give him more? He rejoices in his superabundant
possessions, and counts all things but loss for this inheritance. He who has Christ indeed has all things. He
desires no more; for nothing could enlarge his treasure.

26, 27. "*My flesh and my heart faileth: but God is
the strength of my heart, and my portion for ever. For
lo, they that are far from Thee shall perish: Thou hast
destroyed all them that go a whoring from Thee.*"

Flesh and heart fail in hours of strong temptation:
flesh and heart oft fail when death draws near. But
the failure is not real. God's strength upholds; and
eternal bliss is the sure issue. But then the ungodly
lie down in woe.

28. "*But it is good for me to draw near to God: I
have put my trust in the Lord God, that I may declare
all Thy works.*"

It is the highest wisdom to draw nigh to God.
The promise is sure, "Draw nigh unto God, and He
will draw nigh unto you." Let us put all our trust in
our Heavenly Father's love, and devote all our time
and our powers to show forth the wonders of His
gracious works!

CII.

PSALM LXXIV. I–II.

HOSTILE invasion had brought ruin into the city. Grim desolation frowns where once the Temple magnificently stood. The outrage of the enemy is plaintively described. Importunity calls upon God to interfere, and confidence is expected that light would arise in darkness.

1, 2. "*O God, why hast Thou cast us off for ever? why doth Thine anger smoke against the sheep of Thy pasture? Remember Thy congregation, which Thou hast purchased of old; the rod of Thine inheritance, which Thou hast redeemed; this Mount Zion, wherein Thou hast dwelt.*"

The Psalmist thus writes with mournful eye fixed on the ruined city, and especially on the desolations of the Temple. In bitterness of heart he cries aloud to God. He seems to expostulate, Can it be that these miseries import our final desertion! The believer thus flies to the mercy-seat when adverse oppression casts him into the depths of grief. Let it be noted in what terms the aid of God is supplicated. His people are depicted as the sheep of His pasture. God is thus reminded of His tender office as the good and great Shepherd, who will never fail to tend His flock, and to protect them from all foes. They are described, too, as the congregation which He had purchased. Can Jesus ever forget the company for whom He shed His precious blood, and whom He bought at such high price out of the hands of their enslaving foes ? They are described, moreover, as the portion assigned by the measuring-rod to be His inheritance—the possession which will be His pride and His glory. They are called, moreover, the Mount of His abode. Never will He withdraw His presence. He will always abide in them, and they in Him. Safe indeed must they be who thus can claim an interest in God.

3, 4. "*Lift up Thy feet unto the perpetual desolations, even all that the enemy hath done wickedly in the sanctuary. Thine enemies roar in the midst of Thy congregations ; they set up their ensigns for signs.*"

The cry is earnest that God would no longer tarry, but advance to view the Temple's sad state. With noisy tumult the insulting foe had burst upon the assembled worshippers, and hostile ensigns had been erected in most holy places. This wretchedness is spread before the Lord. The feeling is deep that such iniquity would not be permitted to prevail.

5, 6, 7, 8. "*A man was famous according as he had lifted up axes upon the thick trees. But now they break down the carved work thereof at once with axes and hammers. They have cast fire into Thy sanctuary ; they have defiled by casting down the dwelling-place of Thy name to the ground. They said in their hearts, Let us destroy them together : they have burned up all the synagogues of God in the land.*"

It is high privilege in any way to be permitted to promote the interests of true religion. Fame rested on those who felled the trees of Lebanon to aid the erection of the Temple. Substance and tools are never better expended than in raising the sanctuary in which

God will be worshipped and His name proclaimed. No honour will be theirs whose parsimony expends on luxury and self-indulgence the means which might erect or beautify sanctuaries for holy worship. The Psalmist witnessed the destruction of what piety had raised, and the noble works of former zeal a prey for the devouring flames. But neglect may gradually accomplish what violence may rapidly effect. May such neglect be ever absent from us!

9. " *We see not our signs: there is no more any prophet: neither is there among us any that knoweth how long.*"

The eyes of the disconsolate in Jerusalem no longer rested on tokens that God was in their midst. The symbols of His presence had disappeared in smouldering heaps. The voices of accredited ministers no longer spoke in the Lord's name. No cheering predictions gave hope that this misery would soon brighten into former joys. Grievous indeed was such trial. No greater misery can oppress any people than to be deprived of godly teachers.

10, 11. " *O God, how long shall the adversary reproach? Shall the enemy blaspheme Thy name for ever? Why withdrawest Thou Thy hand, even Thy right hand? pluck it out of Thy bosom.*"

In such extremity of anguish prayer presents a ready refuge. All other help seems utterly to fail. But though the Temple be in ruins, God lives and loves, and is very near. He can repair the ruin; He can revive the services. To Him let approach be made. However hopeless the case may seem, let prayer be made, and all will be well.

CIII.

PSALM LXXIV. 12–23

12. "*For God is my King of old, working salvation in the midst of the earth.*"

When all is desolate faith brightly sparkles. It sings amid surrounding ruins. It looks above all to God, overruling all things for His glory and His people's good. It is assured that through all the earth, in all events, His people will be safely guarded.

13, 14, 15. "*Thou didst divide the sea by Thy strength : Thou brakest the heads of the dragons in the waters. Thou brakest the heads of leviathan in pieces, and gavest him to be meat to the people inhabiting the wilderness. Thou didst cleave the fountain and the flood : Thou driedst up mighty rivers.*"

God's wonders of old are the joy and comfort and support of His people in all ages. They read in them His constant love and His unfailing strength. The perils of the Church of old seemed to exclude all hope. But out of the furnace of Egypt He led forth His oppressed people. The sea parted and opened a safe passage for their feet. The monsters of the deep could do no hurt. They perished as the host advanced. The carcases of mangled foes were cast along the shore. Did waters fail ? Did the vast multitude look in vain for means to relieve their thirst ? Did the parched wilderness afford no ray of hope ? God graciously appeared. He gave the word. The smitten rock opened, and gushing streams flowed forth. He who wrought these wonders in old time is still the same in tender love, in watchful care, in all-controlling power. He has raised His people from extreme desolation. He still will be their Saviour.

16, 17. *" The day is Thine, the night also is Thine : Thou hast prepared the light and the sun. Thou hast set all the borders of the earth : Thou hast made summer and winter."*

The works of creation teach as clearly as the works of providence and grace. In the realm of nature how wondrous are the changes which occur. The day brightly shines, but shadow soon overcasts the scene, and night in thick darkness hides all things from view. Again the morning dawns, the night and shadows flee away, and joy and gladness smile on the face of the awakened world. The wealth and rich luxuriance of summer robes earth with beauty—makes it as Eden's garden of delights, and fills it with the melody of heaven. But bright days shorten—winter comes, and strips the fields and groves and gardens of their gay attire, and binds the babbling streams in fetters of ungenial ice. All these changes are the work of God. We are thus taught that changes, too, will mark the course of grace. It may not always be a summer-day. But faith knows that receding summer will return, and winter has its limits. Earth, too, has varying climes. God sets all the borders of the earth. Happy is it to mark His overruling hand, and to know well that He has done and will do all things well.

18. *" Remember this, that the enemy hath reproached, O Lord, and that the foolish people have blasphemed Thy name."*

Faith will remind God that the persecution of the godly is war against His kingdom. It will stir up God to bear in mind that His people are His chosen heritage. To touch them is to touch the apple of His eye.

19, 20, 21, 22, 23. "*O deliver not the soul of Thy turtle-dove unto the multitude of the wicked: forget not the congregation of Thy poor for ever. Have respect unto the covenant: for the dark places of the earth are full of the habitations of cruelty. O let not the oppressed return ashamed: let the poor and needy praise Thy name. Arise, O God, plead Thine own cause: remember how the foolish man reproacheth Thee daily. Forget not the voice of Thine enemies: the tumult of those that rise up against Thee increaseth continually.*"

The Church is here set before God under the tender image of a turtle-dove—timid and meek amid scenes of desolation. The gentle bird seems to enlist all sympathies. So God is moved to pity His disconsolate people. The Psalmist concludes with earnest cries for God to arise, to maintain His own cause, to extinguish all the cruelty and oppression of the wicked. Let the conclusion in our hearts be deep assurance that, though distress may be very great, God is still near, and will in due time manifest Himself for their comfort and deliverance.

CIV.

PSALM LXXV.

NOTES of thanksgiving introduce this hymn. Resolution is professed to minister right government. Promises of renewed praise are added.

---

1. " *Unto Thee, O God, do we give thanks, unto Thee do we give thanks: for that Thy name is near Thy wondrous works declare.*"

It is a joyful exercise to render thanks unto the Lord. Why is not this our main employ ? We rob our souls of much delight when lips are silent and not indulging in this happy work. What cause have we for never-ceasing adoration ? God's wondrous works in providence and grace are always loudly speaking. Every moment brings new tokens of His loving-kindness—they tell us that He is always near in manifestation of His name, which is the united display of His wisdom, power, and love. Let us draw near to Him in praise. He will draw near to us and cause His presence to be felt.

2. " *When I shall receive the congregation I will judge uprightly.*"

These words can leave no doubt that they proceed from one invested with supreme authority. A throne was his seat, a sceptre was in his hands. David is thus before us, rescued from his many perils, and raised to be the King of Israel. No exaltation is evinced. His one desire is to execute the rule of righteousness. We see, too, our Jesus. The sceptre of His kingdom is a right sceptre. Righteousness is His rule, both in and for His people.

3, 4, 5, 6. " *The earth and all the inhabitants thereof are dissolved : I bear up the pillars of it. I said unto the fools, Deal not foolishly ; and to the wicked, Lift not up the horn. Lift not up your horn on high : speak not with a stiff neck. For promotion cometh neither from the east, nor from the west, nor from the south.*"

David had seen the kingdom in weakness and confusion, without stability and strength, under the evil sway of Saul. That which should have a sure foundation was shifting and unstable as the sand. He profited by this sad misrule, and he resolved to regulate the empire, so as to sustain it in righteous ways. When will men learn that all wickedness is folly ! None are truly wise, but they who seek wisdom in the Word of God, and strive to embody its holy precepts in their daily walk. David exhorted his subjects to depart from evil's ways, and thus to become truly wise. He saw, too, that pride was at the root of all their wrong judgments and wrong conduct. He called on them to walk humbly with their God, and to see clearly that all true honour comes from Him. Let us receive and treasure the sure word, " Them that honour Me I will honour."

7, 8. " *But God is the judge : He putteth down one, and setteth up another. For in the hand of the Lord there is a cup, and the wine is red ; it is full of mixture ; and He poureth out of the same ; but the dregs thereof all the wicked of the earth shall wring them out, and drink them.*"

God's mode of dealing is often wrapt in mystery. We fail to understand why one is elevated to the highest rank, while others seem to waste their days in penury, obscurity, and low estate. But no misgivings should arise. It should be firmly fixed in our persuasions that in all these matters God's hand prevails. Thus, too, afflictions, sorrows, trials are all appointed by the same unerring wisdom. His hand holds a cup which is mixed in accordance with His righteous will. According to His good pleasure He causes the sons of men to drink thereof. But what will be the portion of the wicked ? Let them tremble. They are forewarned that they must wring out the dregs—indignation and wrath, tribulation and anguish for ever.

9, 10. *" But I will declare for ever ; I will sing praises to the God of Jacob. All the horns of the wicked also will I cut off ; but the horns of the righteous shall be exalted."*

In conclusion, we have the bright resolve of faith to uplift the voice of praise, to discountenance all evil, to proclaim the misery of God's adversaries, and the blessedness of His people. May this be our resolve, this our holy employ, till faith shall end in sight and hope in full reality ! Grant it, O our God, for the sake of our beloved Saviour, Jesus Christ !

END OF VOL. I.